CW00953825

AVANT-GARDE POST—

Avant-Garde Post—

RADICAL POETICS AFTER THE SOVIET UNION

Marijeta Bozovic

HARVARD UNIVERSITY PRESS

Cambridge, Massachusetts & London, England

2023

Publication of this book has been supported through the generous provisions of the
Maurice and Lula Bradley Smith Memorial Fund.

First printing

Library of Congress Cataloging-in-Publication Data

Names: Bozovic, Marijeta, author.
Title: Avant-garde post— : radical poetics after the Soviet Union / Marijeta Bozovic.
Description: Cambridge, Massachusetts ; London, England : Harvard University Press,
    2023. | English; extracts of poems in Russian with English translation.
Identifiers: LCCN 2023003205 | ISBN 9780674290624 (cloth)
Subjects: LCSH: Russian poetry—21st century—History and criticism. | Experimental
    poetry, Russian—21st century—History and criticism. | Avant-garde (Aesthetics)—
    Russia (Federation)—History—21st century. | Politics and literature—Russia
    (Federation)—History—21st century. | Poetics.
Classification: LCC PG3057 .B69 2023 | DDC 891.71/509—dc23/eng/20230515
LC record available at https://lccn.loc.gov/2023003205

To my children, Res and Sasha,
and to the future that they represent

CONTENTS

Preface   ix

Introduction: Return of the Russian Avant-Garde   1

1. The Poetics of Refusal: Kirill Medvedev   30

2. The Avant-Garde Journal 2.0: Pavel Arseniev and *[Translit]*   63

3. Language Poetry Is Leftist: The Long Durée of Aleksandr Skidan   98

4. Dmitry Golynko: Writing Poetry for Zombies   140

5. Poetry in the Age of Digital Reproduction: Roman Osminkin   173

6. Art Must Be Communist: The Voices of Keti Chukhrov   205

    Coda: The Passion of Galina Rymbu   231

    Notes   251

    Acknowledgments   289

    Index   293

PREFACE

*I*N 2012, DURING WHAT has been called retrospectively Russia's summer of idealism, I arrived in Moscow for research on contemporary art and poetry. Within a few days, my academic plans were eclipsed by the political protests taking place in the city. Something extraordinary and thrilling was afoot: a hum of vibrant activity; conversations on every corner; a vital if heterogeneous and centerless protest culture. At theater-of-witness performances (such as the experimental Teatr.doc) and in vigils in front of the courtroom alike, everyone was talking about Pussy Riot. Working in real time with colleagues in the Cement translation collective, I translated the closing statements of that trial for the American journal *n+1*. On the literary front, meanwhile, I was swept away by the poetry and political engagement of Kirill Medvedev, Pavel Arseniev, Roman Osminkin, and a new generation of poets associated with the St. Petersburg journal *[Translit]*, as well as by the theory and art practice of Chto Delat (What Is to Be Done?), one of the first leftist art collectives in post–Soviet Russia.

What was palpable—and shocking—was the sense of hope. The years 2011–2013 brought a global resurgence in public political action from the Arab Spring and Occupy Wall Street to Russia's new Decembrists, as the press dubbed the first protesters who took to the streets of Moscow in the winter of 2011. Against a cultural backdrop that had unlearned how to dream, these surges of energy were all the more remarkable. One particular moment is engraved in my memory: at a poetry festival in St. Petersburg, after sets by Medvedev's protest rock group Arkady Kots and Osminkin's Technopoetry, a young man (since identified as poet and activist Daniil Poltoratsky) began singing the 1908 Italian labor anthem "Bandiera Rossa," in Italian and then in Russian translation. The charm, the youth, the shock and vulnerability of his performance—on the post–Soviet Russian stage, of all places—felt like a visceral challenge, exposing a defeatism that had crept in after the bloody breakup of Yugoslavia and the NATO bombing of Belgrade (from where I emigrated as a child). Was it possible to rethink our histories from a future-oriented position, moving beyond nostalgia and protective cynicism alike? What does the cultural correlative of Alain Badiou's communist hypothesis look like, especially to the shell-shocked former Second World?[1]

Such moments and questions reshaped the direction of my research as a scholar of literature and culture. I planned a series of conferences, exhibits, courses, and research initiatives with colleagues in the United States, Russia, Poland, and countries of the former Yugoslavia, around what seemed to us all the central point of inquiry: What does leftist, politically transformative art look like, after state socialism? For whom, and more crucially, to whom does it try to speak? How might a new Russian left rewrite the histories of the twentieth century? In societies of spectacle and appropriation, of pessimism and traumatic traces, who dares to dream of radical social transformation today? Or have we really accepted, in words borrowed from Medvedev's poetry, that "no radical art actions are going to help here" ever again? Somewhere along the way since 2012, the lightly ironizing scare quotes around my identifications as a socialist feminist fell away.

The global political situation has changed grimly since those years and the start of my field research. One blow followed another: the passing of increasingly restrictive laws in Russia (not least the banning of so-called homosexual propaganda) in 2013; the annexation of Crimea in 2014; renewed tensions between Russia and the United States following the 2016 elections, leading right into the pandemic years after 2020; and in February 2022, the ongoing, once unimaginable, war. The Russian artists and activists that spoke up in the first decade of the twenty-first century have proven terribly right—and are now witnessing cultural repressions unheard of since Soviet times. Kirill Medvedev is arrested periodically, such as in 2020 at a solidarity protest in front of the Belarus embassy in Moscow. Unlike most of the protagonists of these chapters, he has chosen to stay in the country despite evident personal danger due to his documented dissident status and opposition to the war. If (when) he is arrested next, he may face fifteen years in jail. Galina Rymbu was carried off by police twice in my presence in May of 2016 for organizing an event in solidarity with Russian LGBTQ+ activists. She moved to Ukraine a few years later in part to escape the political and psychological oppression in Russia and is currently in a bomb shelter in Lviv. Arseniev has left Russia. Osminkin has left Russia. Chukhrov and Skidan are exploring their options for leaving or staying in Russia. All are vocal opponents of the war in Ukraine.

On January 6, 2023, as I was editing this manuscript, the news reached me via social media that Dmitry Golynko—Mitya—had tragically passed. Our last exchange had been about the war, about his worries for Rymbu and others in Ukraine. He wrote then that he feared that "the entirely deserved stigmatization of Russia and Russians will continue for years, decades, if not centuries. I think the main thing now is to grit our teeth and keep working, no matter what." The pain of his loss does not lessen the truth of his words for those he left behind.

It challenges and threatens our understanding of Russian poetry to read it in real time, rather than, as was more often the case in prior generations, to arrive at the work decades later, after the biographies of dissident poets have become the stuff of legend. A not insignificant part of the story, as I realized upon writing this book, takes place in the endnotes, which are filled with the names of translators, poets, scholars, and activists responding to and disseminating work via independent presses, online publications, and academic workshops in a veritable performance of translocal solidarities. All of us too, one way or another, have been transformed by the newest Russian avant-garde—which refuses to be confined to the page, spilling beyond the literary histories that attempt to contextualize and contain it. I try to foreground these stories as well as the networked nature of scholarship: my readings of poetry here are contextualized through hours, years, indeed a decade of dialogue, translation, and collaboration.

Contemporary technologies have transformed global communities' awareness of one another in unprecedented ways, influencing both artistic and critical practices. Social media—along with (prepandemic, prewar) open borders and cheap international flights—have helped to subvert myths of critical distance and dated binaries of "Western" scholar and Slavic subject through the near simultaneity of exchange between academic and artistic, postsocialist and late capitalist, and politically varied milieus. Familiar methods of reading poetry contend with approaches borrowed from intellectual history and performance studies, among others. Today, scholars are in touch with artists and writers in real time: we invite the people we study to present at international academic conferences and to argue against our readings. The resulting debates at times alleviate and at others heighten fears of communication breaking down across dramatically different contexts. The shock of synchrony quickly makes evident the cultural baggage on both sides of the exchange.

But our changing environment brings with it too the escalating relevance of artistic and theoretical responses and demands attention to transnational intellectual exchange in our era of immediate, if mediated, communication. We cannot write post-Soviet literary history without interrogating global phenomena that implicate us as well as the untranslatable specificities of local struggle. One danger scholars of culture too readily fall into is assuming that the subjects of our research are less or belatedly theorized than we are—attributing their interests and influences to forms of critique popular in "Western" academe some years ago and since surpassed. I challenge scholars to be as well read in critical theory, in as many languages, as Golynko was to the end. If we shift from a defensive evaluative mode, we can instead study the spread and mutation of theory, finding in its divergent uses and interpretations new insights—through the translation, as it were—and read the work of Russian poets, artists, and thinkers with an eye to what they might tell us about our future.

AVANT-GARDE POST—

Introduction

RETURN OF THE RUSSIAN AVANT-GARDE

I don't believe that Russian history and culture have a special messianic mission, but I do know that from time to time the situation in Russia unfolds in such a way that it gives rise to a cultural-political leap, allowing us to "overtake" the West and present something genuinely new. . . . That's what happened with the political form of the Soviets that came out of the 1905 Revolution and was later adopted by many revolutionary and social movements across the world. The same thing happened with the Russian avant-garde. It's possible that we're experiencing a similar situation right now.

—KIRILL MEDVEDEV, 2013

*T*HERE ARE TWO STORIES TO TELL HERE, and they are intertwined. One is about the return to prominence of (primarily, political) poetry on a global stage, and the other is about the rise of a new post–Cold War left. I tell these two interconnected stories through the most paradigmatic case study I know: the newest Russian poetic avant-garde.

Contemporary poetry around the world has witnessed a proliferation of new forms and uses in the past two decades. From Cairo to Ferguson, from street slogans to Twitter, poetry has unexpectedly reemerged as a powerful and agile technology for political subjectivization and the conjuring of new collectivities. This book tells the story of that resurgence, a counterformation to total (or cognitive, late, disaster—as it has been variously called) capitalism, of which it is nevertheless fundamentally born. Following Theodor Adorno in essence, I consider lyric forms to exist in an uneasy, dependent relationship to contemporary capitalism and to imaginaries of the nation—and I posit avant-garde poetry as a recurrent form of internal resistance within the lyric.[1] A form so established seems fresh and vital once more, relevant in unexpected contexts across the globe—but perhaps nowhere more so than in

Russia, where poetry has maintained an exceptional status and political potency across several centuries.[2]

If post-Soviet Russia dared dream of joining the (former) West in the "after history" fantasy of the 1990s—reflected in the arts by the flattened horizon of ever-expanding postmodernism, and economically in the worst privatization-as-pillaging catastrophe across the former Second World—history returned to Russia with a vengeance in the twenty-first century.[3] I mark 1999 as the year of the sea change: the year of Putin's ascendance (as well as the year of NATO's bombing of Belgrade and the World Trade Organization protests in Seattle) or, in the literary sphere, the publication of Viktor Pelevin's prescient society-of-spectacle novel *Generation P*. Many (indeed most) cultural producers did not realize it yet, but the cease-fire was over. The decades that followed the precarious 1990s marked the return of the political repressed to Russian arts. Beginning early in the 2000s and building to a crescendo with the years of protest in 2011–2012, then again from the geopolitical events of 2014 and 2016 to demonstrations that braved Siberian winters and a global pandemic alike in 2020, and finally as of 2022, war, a once unimaginable war, the cultural sphere, like every other, moved swiftly in the direction of dramatic political polarization.

Under the slogan of stability and over the course of Putin's never-ending terms, an increasingly conservative and nationalist ideology came to dominate much of the country, drawing energy from the far fringes as well as center-right elite institutions. (In retrospect, the Russian right was a pioneer in this regard, modeling a stunningly effective strategy in subsequent decades for the right wing in many countries, including the United States. Indeed, Russia has emerged as a leading force in the paradoxical but prolific networks of international nationalism.) The most sizeable opposition to the flourishing right comes from what I will loosely term the liberal center, with a steady base in the intelligentsia and strong connections abroad. Against this familiar field, smaller movements have emerged in the last two decades, daringly oriented toward the left.[4] The cultural sphere is indeed *the* space for Marxist critique in post-Soviet Russia, particularly in cheaper (less funding-dependent, less monitored) arts like poetry and performance. For if earlier generations were shaped politically and aesthetically by the collective traumas of state socialist hypocrisy and repression, the generation that followed recognized in late capitalism no alternative. In the words of feminist socialist poet Galina

Rymbu (born 1990): "I'm sure no workers' children went hungry in the 1970s and 1980s. I grew up in a factory settlement in Omsk, in Siberia, and when I went to school, I often saw workers' children faint from hunger during class. I myself am the daughter of a worker and a schoolteacher, and they went years without receiving their salary."[5]

Russia has arguably never needed Marxist critique more. As political scientist Stephen Crowley suggests, the central irony underlying contemporary Russian socioeconomic structures and their systematic study is that Russian society requires class-based analysis more than ever in the wake of its official discrediting. The rapid transfer of property into private hands that took place in Russia in the wake of disintegration remains virtually unrivaled, even in eastern Europe:

> According to the World Bank, starting from a position of relative equality, Russia's increase in its Gini inequality index of 11 percentage points over a decade "is close to a record." . . . This concentration of property and wealth took place not during a period of economic growth, but one of dramatic decline, significantly worse than the U.S. experience of the Great Depression. One study of Russian social mobility—comparing class origins with class destinations—found that from 1990 to 1998, "downward mobility exceeded upward mobility by 30 percent," and that a downward shift, let alone of that magnitude, is highly unusual among mature economies. . . . By one estimate, the number of poor in Russia increased from 2.2 million in 1987–1988 to 66 million by 1993–1995, and a year after the 1998 crisis "four out of every 10 people slipped into poverty, unable to meet nutritional and other basic needs."[6]

Yet the taboo topic of socioeconomic class remains underexamined by Russian social scientists and mainstream political rhetoric alike. With the exception of the hardly progressive Communist Party of the Russian Federation (CPRF), there have been no successful political parties challenging United Russia from the left side of the spectrum.[7] Excluding decidedly anti-Marxist studies of the stabilizing potential of a near-mythical Russian middle class, or research declaring Russian exceptionalism to observed global economic patterns, theory has lagged behind the horrors of lived experience.[8] The notable exception has been the rise of political and socially conscious themes

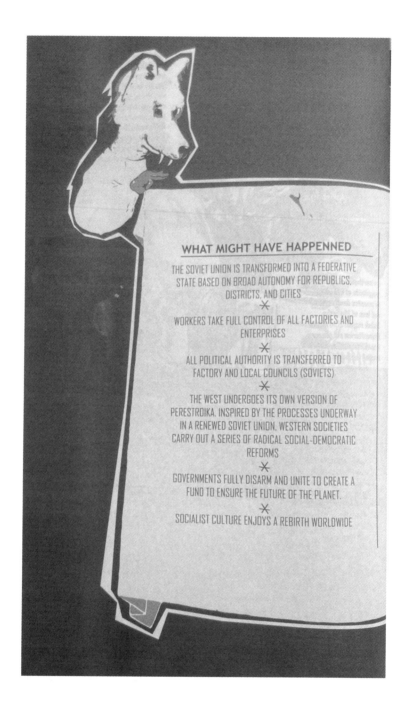

WHAT MIGHT HAVE HAPPENNED

THE SOVIET UNION IS TRANSFORMED INTO A FEDERATIVE STATE BASED ON BROAD AUTONOMY FOR REPUBLICS, DISTRICTS, AND CITIES

✳

WORKERS TAKE FULL CONTROL OF ALL FACTORIES AND ENTERPRISES

✳

ALL POLITICAL AUTHORITY IS TRANSFERRED TO FACTORY AND LOCAL COUNCILS (SOVIETS)

✳

THE WEST UNDERGOES ITS OWN VERSION OF PERESTROIKA. INSPIRED BY THE PROCESSES UNDERWAY IN A RENEWED SOVIET UNION, WESTERN SOCIETIES CARRY OUT A SERIES OF RADICAL SOCIAL-DEMOCRATIC REFORMS

✳

GOVERNMENTS FULLY DISARM AND UNITE TO CREATE A FUND TO ENSURE THE FUTURE OF THE PLANET.

✳

SOCIALIST CULTURE ENJOYS A REBIRTH WORLDWIDE

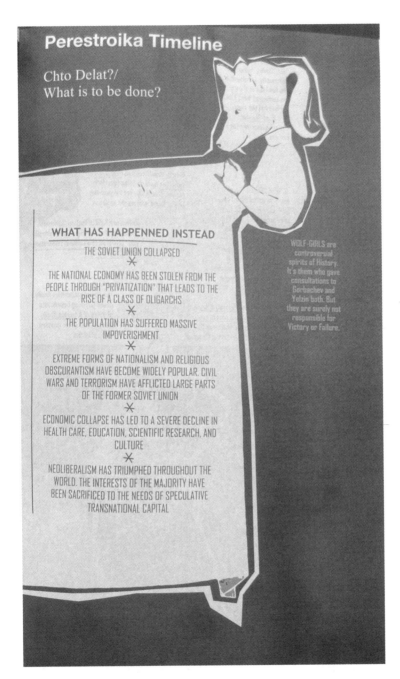

FIGURE I.1 Perestroika Timeline, Chto Delat artist collective. *FORMER WEST: ART AND THE CONTEMPORARY AFTER 1989* EDITED BY MARIA HLAVAJOVA AND SIMON SHEIKH (UTRECHT: BAK, 2017).

in art and literature.[9] The intellectual work of rebuilding class-based critique has emerged especially prominently in politically engaged poetry.

This book argues that Russia needed a new avant-garde poetics to create the language and forms adequate to contemporary experience: to identify the fault lines of the present, internally and externally; to begin the work of building communities with fellow thinkers; and to imagine different futures. Dropping the quotation marks around the term "Marxist" is not easy or quick work in many poststate socialist spaces. But this book also suggests that the rest of the world needs a new Russian avant-garde just as much as Russia does: that the powerful "and yet, let us sing 'Bandiera rossa,' again" gesture of a new Russian left holds symbolic significance across geographically distant parts of the globe.

In *Avant-Garde Post—: Radical Poetics after the Soviet Union*, I explore a radically revitalized and political Russian poetry through the intersecting praxes of seven protagonists: Kirill Medvedev (b. 1975), Pavel Arseniev (b. 1986), Aleksandr Skidan (b. 1965), Dmitry Golynko (b. 1969), Roman Osminkin (b. 1980), Keti Chukhrov (b. 1970), and Galina Rymbu (b. 1990). These poets are frequent collaborators, linked through the St. Petersburg journal *[Translit]*, several chapbook series, the Free Marxist Press, and events and collective actions in Russia and abroad. They are among the brightest stars in a broader contemporary constellation that shares an interest in the long history of the Russian avant-garde(s) and that conceives poetry as participating in a broader emancipatory project.[10] These seven poets in particular have been united by their overt political engagement and explicitly Marxist orientation: half the group are active members and de facto leaders of the oppositional Russian Socialist Movement political party.[11] They thus occupy a fraught position in poststate socialist time and space (as the lingering post-Soviet designation still signifies), forced into a heightened self-awareness vis-à-vis the mainstreams of Putin-era Russian culture and politics and "Western" formations alike.[12]

I conceptualize this circle (*kruzhok*) of poets as a contemporary avant-garde: hence the use of prefixes in my title, which gestures at the temporal paradoxes of a revived futurism. Following Mike Sell in *The Avant-Garde: Race, Religion, War*, I define avant-garde broadly as any "minoritarian formation that challenges power in subversive, illegal or alternative ways, usually by challenging the routines, assumptions, hierarchies and / or legitimacy of ex-

FIGURE I.2 Pavel Arseniev and Roman Osminkin read from issue 14 of *[Translit]*.
VITYA KUZNETSIA.

isting political and / or cultural institutions."[13] I view avant-garde poetry as
the recurrent return of the repressed of poetry, within poetry.[14] Moreover, I
argue that contemporary radical Russian poets seek in historical Russian
and Soviet avant-gardes an undetonated alternative to both the neoliberal
global present and to the discredited institutionalized left of the Communist Party. I read the latest return of the Russian avant-garde as drawing
on powerful local literary countertraditions, reimagined through global
critical theory—and all of it stitched through with a common red thread.
The twenty-odd years from 1999 and Putin's rise to power have been scruti-
nized through many lenses, but insufficient attention has been paid to this

hardly homogeneous period as giving rise to new republics of letters.[15] By looking at the praxes of poets and thinkers such as Medvedev, Arseniev, Skidan, Golynko, Osminkin, Chukhrov, and Rymbu together, we can trace the construction of a larger project, building on individual work but oriented toward a longed-for common political future.

The poets associated with the St. Petersburg–based journal *[Translit]* are radical in both political affiliation and in poetic form, although they explore their positions through dramatically different praxes. Their educations range from autodidact (Skidan, like Brodsky famously before him, never finished high school) to doctor of philosophy (Chukhrov, Golynko). Yet all members of the circle recognize a fundamental unity underlying the diversity of their approaches: a commitment to a global egalitarian future and to verbal art as a mode of critique, imagination, and struggle. Moreover, they revisit earlier waves of Russian avant-gardes across the twentieth century alongside the work of left-leaning artists and thinkers from around the globe—an unexpected part of the world culture to which Russian writers can now lay claim, due partly to the end of the Cold War and partly to the newly fast, cheap, and unchecked dissemination of texts and art online. As Keith Gessen asks in his introduction to Kirill Medvedev's translated collected volume, what did these newcomers see that the previous generation of Russian intellectuals—the generation of the fathers—failed to understand? "The very thing they thought they knew best of all: Marxism. Not the Soviet 'teachings of Karl Marx,' but the many intellectual heirs of Marx in the West in the postwar era. This was the Frankfurt School and Sartre and the Situationist International and Pierre Bourdieu and the Anglo-American thinkers around the *New Left Review;* but also such non-aligned thinkers as Barthes, Foucault, and Baudrillard."[16]

Medvedev corroborates the reading. Why is Russia still lacking a vibrant culture of literary criticism, he asks? Because "all the major critical theories of the West in the twentieth century passed, in one way or another, through Marxism. . . . Until the same happens in Russia, there won't be any criticism at all—not of poetry, nor of the authorities."[17] The global left is "buoyed by the entire cultural production of the past fifty years, from the Situationist Guy Debord to the avant-garde composer Cornelius Cardew to the leftist philosophers Bourdieu, Badiou, and Žižek, from Subcomandante Marcos, leader of the Zapatista resistance movement, to the Russian-born Israeli anti-Zionist intellectual Israel Shamir—in short, the Left has at its disposal practically the entire theoretical arsenal of the intellectual resistance of the past half-century. This, for Russia, is the legendary 'world culture' that the intelligentsia has been pining for all these years."[18] Through the revival and reappropriation of the still incendiary strategies of historical Russian and Soviet avant-gardes, as well as postwar European radicals and contemporary artists, intellectuals, and activists from around the globe, the *[Translit]* circle dares to reimagine politically engaged art for the twenty-first century. Such efforts, to think left-ward beyond the state socialist past to a global egalitarian future, challenge both Russian and oppositional "Western" narratives in our increasingly interconnected world.

The newest Russian avant-garde emerges against—and refreshingly complicates—a backdrop of dominant narratives about contemporary Russian literature and culture. The 1990s undeniably "precipitated a complete reshaping of the entire literary field," not to mention any stable notions of literary canon through the explosive publication of various kinds of (local and translated) literature.[19] A number of writers and critics have noted that, on the whole, the newly free market proved hardly fortuitous for experimental literature. While poetry and theater found ways to survive and innovate, forms more dependent on the market economy struggled to keep pace.[20] By the 2000s, Russian letters witnessed the solidification of a revanchist literary mainstream intolerable to all the protagonists of this book.[21] The influx of global Marxist thought meanwhile coincided with the long deferred local canonization of Russian historical avant-gardes, affording old and new, familiar and foreign models of resistance.

In *Avant-Garde Post—*, I study practices ranging from what I term the "poetics of refusal," when the critique of institutions makes traditional publication impossible and transubstantiates poetry into activism, to difficult philosophical poetry modeled after Arkadii Dragomoshchenko and inspired by his exchanges with the American *L=A=N=G=U=A=G=E* school. Nearly all my subjects recognize another recent and key precursor in the conceptualist Dmitry Prigov, who played the role of Russian poet as an extended provocative art performance, and nearly all borrow freely from contemporary art as well as from varied forms of collective theater. I am interested in the sites of publication and performance as contested, interdependent, and potentially contradictory, and in the reemergence of the avant-garde journal as a venue, art object, collective cause, and social network: today's avant-garde journal has an active presence both off- and online. Russian-language poetry merges with other languages, forms, and media: while poets test the limits of digital remediation, collective translation, and dissemination via social media platforms, they also embody their poetics in performances that insist on the physical presence of the poet, at times in dangerous or illegal circumstances.

Tracing the recurrent pulse of the avant-garde suggests an alternative narrative through twentieth-century Russian literature and shifts discussions of post-Soviet culture from stories of failed transition to renewed experiment and exportable dreams of futurity. I argue, moreover, that the newest Russian avant-garde stands in stark opposition to any mainstream phenomenon of Soviet nostalgia: the highly aware appropriations and remediations at play among these poets are in fact a reaction to official nostalgia for the imperial and militant aestheticized politics of the Soviet Union (e.g., the Putin regime's ready embrace of the cult of World War II). These renewed engagements with earlier avant-gardes range from appropriative to critical: a sharply self-aware and critical renewal of avant-garde energies demands important correctives, not least along lines of nation and gender.[22] The book indeed concludes by positing feminist and LGBTQ+ poetry as the next locus of interest and struggle in Russian—or better put, Russophone—poetry.

Using these Russian case studies, I try to show that contemporary poetry's marginalized position as a late-capitalist aesthetic production (differing dramatically from the market value of the novel or production costs of fiction film) contributes to poets' ability to imagine an outside to economic, political, and social mainstreams.[23] Russian poetry carries the added weight of a rare avant-garde tradition that, however briefly, infiltrated official culture and claimed the right to imagine revolution for all. I try therefore to reconceive for our own moment Adorno's critical insight from the 1950s: that the task of reading poetry is "to discover how the entirety of a society, as a unity containing contradictions, appears in a work; in which respects the work remains true to its society, and in which it transcends that society."[24] Ultimately, *Avant-Garde Post—* is about the persistent power of verbal art to imagine an outside to the apparatus and to forge communities of resistance—however imperfect or impermanent—against political, economic, and cultural injustice.

On Method and Frame

My book is structured as a theoretically motivated study of the constellation of poets, intellectuals, and activists whose practices have emerged as both innovative and paradigmatic of an extraordinary historical moment. My methods range from close readings to interviews with all the protagonists of *Avant-Garde Post—*, based on years of recurring fieldwork and hours of interview, conversation, translation, and collaboration. I borrow insights and approaches from intellectual history, anthropology, art theory, performance and media studies, and political philosophy, but I also try to highlight the collapse of some of these methods when working with contemporary material in a globally networked era. I consider the paradoxes an integral part of the story and the problem of method one of the major narratives of the book: the shock of synchrony between English- and Russian-speaking intellectuals (to eschew speaking of nationalities or the fraught term *intelligentsia*) has been inspiring and frustrating for both communities, but may afford new, if complicated, possibilities for resistance against the far more rapidly converging global political and financial elites.[25]

The readings that follow are not guided by hermeneutics of suspicion. While I address critique (and self-critique) when it seems productively insightful, I try to read instead in a way inspired by Ernst Bloch's midcentury opus *The Principle of Hope* as well as more contemporary praxes of sympathetic reading: to discover and describe the emancipatory vitality, the aesthetics and politics of hope, in each poetic project.[26] My own aesthetic and political position, after ten years of working closely with this poetry, has been so profoundly shaped by it that to position myself as master rather than student would be to miss the point.[27] Moreover, this is a story of cultural flow: of translations and the mutation and spread of ideas and forms; of translocal sparks and unexpected ephemeral collectivities; of shared and much-debated theoretical frames. I gave my copy of Bloch's *The Principle of Hope* to Kirill Medvedev a year or so after the 2012 protests. I first met Gabriel Rockhill, translator of Rancière's *The Politics of Aesthetics,* in Moscow around the same time. I was introduced to Jodi Dean at a conference by Alexei Penzin of Chto Delat. When I met Frederic Jameson in New Haven some years later, it emerged we had the same Russian friends. I discussed the art and politics of the new Russian left in Etienne Balibar's 2019 New York master class. I've struggled to articulate and differentiate trajectories for post-Yugoslav Marxism from that of Slavoj Žižek, who wrote the introduction to Oxana Timofeeva's (also of Chto Delat) recent book. To obfuscate or fail to mention these interconnections in a book fundamentally about coconstitutive uses of language (sometimes collaborative, sometimes clashing) would again, it seems to me, miss the point.

I will try to articulate some unifying premises for the readings that follow. This project is about the pursuit of subjectivization and new collectivities through new and borrowed language. I read *[Translit]* as paradigmatic of a larger trend in the (re)formation of postsocialist lefts across the former Second World. The closely related, and also St. Petersburg–based, *Chto Delat'* newspaper was founded a few years earlier in 2003, and Poland's *Krytyka polityczna* journal in 2002. In short, within a few years of 1999, similar projects started cropping up everywhere. The fastest way to conjure a new left, it seems, is to start a publication, and to begin translating primarily Western Marxist theory alongside new and emerging local work. The move seeks at once to catch up to the world and to accelerate local cultural production: it jumpstarts a new left-reading public, relying on foreign names to relegitimize Marxist language in places where local and direct continuities are problematic (as is especially striking and evident in the case of Poland). For the new lefts emerging across the former Second World, the dream of world culture, translated for the twenty-first century, means rejoining a global canon of Marxist thought and art. In keeping, translation—of critical theory as well as of poetry—is central to all the poetic practices explored in this book (most explicitly, perhaps, in the work of Medvedev and Skidan). I try less to "apply" foreign theory to raw Russian cultural ore than to trace, for example, the migration and mutation of concepts from thinkers like Foucault, Rancière, and Deleuze to Russia and to find motivation for the juxtaposition of poetry and theory in the material itself. The theoretical frames shift accordingly from chapter to chapter, but certain shared concepts hold. The fundamental commitment to a global egalitarian future rests on monuments like Marx and Wollstonecraft but also on more recent classics from the last quarter century that offer some way of thinking through late capitalism, the end of the Cold War, and the future of struggle. All seven protagonists of this book are engaged in an aesthetic response to Alain Badiou's communist hypothesis: "We know that communism is the right hypothesis. All those who abandon this hypothesis immediately resign themselves to the market economy, to parliamentary democracy—the form of state suited to capitalism—and to the inevitable and 'natural' character of the most monstrous inequalities."[28] All are dedicated to reconsidering the political and cultural legacies of the Soviet Union as well as other socialist experiments across the world. As has been powerfully articulated by Jodi Dean (especially in her 2012 book with Verso, *The Communist Horizon*) but also the political philosophers of Chto Delat—Oxana Timofeeva, Artemy Magun, Alexei Penzin, and others—the history of socialism cannot be reduced to several decades of Soviet Stalinism and is instead as dynamic, nuanced, and worthy of study as the history of capitalism.[29]

The most immediate political problem facing the new Russian left—and indeed, necessitating its rise—plagues much of the world. The whiplash-inducing rise of right populism (and its attendant aesthetics, reactionary postmodernism and new sincerity) necessitates a genuine alternative. The poets and thinkers explored in this book dare to say, if we do not become socialists, again, we will be fascists. But if the rise of Syriza in Greece and Podemos in Spain inspired hope for an inclusive left populism following Ernesto Laclau and Chantal Mouffe, as political theorist Benjamin McKean notes, Laclau's empty signifier is not as neutral as it seems.[30] In Russia, the problems with basing politics on "the people" are readily apparent, illustrating moreover the easy slippage of "people" into "Russian people." All the poets collected here struggle to imagine a more inclusive alternative—emphasizing their own and others' nonidentification, as Jewish, Ukrainian, Georgian, or Roma, as women, sexual minorities, and vulnerable bodies. The alternatives they imagine to Laclau's left populism are pluralistic, embodied in theory and practice in many ways (for example in the work of Chukhrov, who arrives at her position via Deleuze). Balibar provides a compelling umbrella articulation of such alternatives in the *Citizen Subject,* with a dialectical understanding of subjectification, citizenship, and universality.[31] Balibar's dialectic offers no guarantees but struggle, no definitive victories, and instead the knowledge that even "our achievements may be links in the historical sequence through which our defeat is realized."[32]

Drawing from the same well, essentially all the protagonists of *Avant-Garde Post—* are incisive readers of Rancière (published in Russian translation in the first issues of *[Translit]*) and share an understanding of aesthetics and politics as interrelated a priori, rather than needing to commandeer (dangerously or productively) one for the other. Politics revolves around aesthetics, for, in Rancière's terms, aesthetics is most broadly a delineation of "the visible and the invisible, of speech and noise, that simultaneously determines the place and stakes of politics as a form of experience."[33] If aesthetics delineate the distribution of the sensible, Rancière writes, its disruption is politics. To sidestep a number of dead-end "vain debates over the autonomy of art or its submission to politics," the relationship between aesthetics and politics should be understood at this level, "the level of the sensible delimitation of what is common to the community, the forms of its visibility and of its organization."[34] The project of the artistic avant-garde, Rancière concludes, is simply the aesthetic anticipation of the future.

What, then, do I claim in the following pages that the poetry of the new Russian avant-garde can do? For clearly, I do not mean to evaluate one poetic project against another for success as measured by political opinion polls or social media likes, nor for their efficacy in removing Putin's party from power. What poetry can do is occupy its marginal position to imagine an outside to the apparatus of power. In a corollary move to some of my protagonists, Sianne Ngai builds on Adorno in "The Cuteness of the Avant-Garde" to claim that poetry's powerlessness in commodity society reflects "its distinctive ability to theorize powerlessness in general."[35] The question of how art's theorization of powerlessness might become the source of aesthetic / political power must be answered again and again in different cultural and political contexts. Ngai foregrounds cuteness ("simple or formally non-complex and deeply associated with the infantile, the feminine, and the unthreatening")[36] as one subversive way forward—which will prove relevant to Roman Osminkin's work, as explored in Chapter 5. Without exception, and despite their otherwise divergent styles and forms, all the protagonists of this book frame their poetics as explorations of powerlessness.

Poetry can also spark the work of subjectivization. Again I will borrow from Rancière (but see also Foucault, Arendt, Deleuze) for a commonly shared working definition: "The logic of political subjectivization, of emancipation," Rancière writes, is "never the simple assertion of an identity; it is always, at the same time, the denial of an identity given by an other, given by the ruling order of policy."[37] Closed formulations of identity pin people to places, to work, to brutalizing limitations and political impotence; politics, on the contrary, is built of "misnomers that articulate a gap and connect with a wrong."[38] The idea of subjectivization then refers to a continually deferred "becoming" subject, never unique or primary, but immersed in a process or movement—the recognition of which allows for emancipatory politics. By giving language to the incomplete identities of self and others, poetry opens the space for new identifications. It aids, amplifies, models, and inspires collectivity formation: the coming together of a temporary "we" who reads, who argues, who shares texts.

I explore the work of seven individual praxes here, then, but through the readings try to tell the collective story not only of a journal but of a movement that is still growing, changing, and evolving. Ultimately, I offer a collection of readings about the flow of ideas, translated in and out of languages; about the spread and mutations of concepts and forms—with the full humility, à la Balibar, that the future may reveal many moments of false consciousness, and that we never know when we aid future defeat in the celebration of current achievements. But we grit our teeth and we work, we learn, and we hope.

Russian / Avant-Garde

There are many problems with the term avant-garde; there are problems with the term Russian, and more still with their combination. Nevertheless, my usage is overdetermined. I will try to show why rehabilitating the term is useful, particularly given the unique and potent cultural tradition afforded by the Russian avant-garde.

Ambivalence and anxiety are woven into the fabric of international critical discourse on the avant-garde. Art typically identified as avant-garde takes as its central tasks liberation from automatized perception and the exposure of ideology, often most pointedly in relation to artistic production and institutions.[39] While this position in a sense won, and aesthetic critique largely continues to rest on a distinction between cultural productions that estrange and that enthrall, the notorious avant-gardes of the early twentieth century largely failed to realize the full demiurgic ambitions that marked their historical beginnings. The term itself has been accused of not only losing all combative potency in the many decades since but indeed also of obfuscating the absorption of radical art into the institutions it once sought to topple. Or so the familiar argument goes, for critics have been heralding the death of the avant-garde for the better part of a century. An artistic avant-garde, many believe, must accompany political revolution—and we live in an epoch of defeat and retreat.[40]

Peter Bürger's *Theory of the Avant-Garde* (1971), for example, differentiates what he identifies as the authentic historical avant-garde from mere modernism and from later imitations: modernist literature might well present "an attack on traditional writing techniques, but the avant-garde can only be understood as an attack meant to alter the institutionalized commerce with art."[41] A Frankfurt School melancholy (reflecting core theoretical influences) haunts his treatise: Bürger shows reluctance to concede a future to politically engaged aesthetic practice at all.[42] He argues that it is only in the sense of fetishizing novelty and the consumption of art that the historical avant-garde entered the cultural mainstream; under such conditions, however, art "ceases to be an instrument of emancipation and becomes one of subjection."[43] So many critics and theorists have responded in kind that Paul Mann turns the inquiry on its head in *The Theory-Death of the Avant-Garde* (1991). The death of the avant-garde has been proclaimed so many times, Mann suggests, that we must "grasp the avant-garde as the production of a death-theory, a seemingly inexhaustible discourse of exhaustion."[44]

How can we learn—and then depart—from such broad critiques? Mike Sell draws attention to the dominant narrative of the avant-garde as itself delimited by a "remarkable" but hardly unassailable group of critics, from Bürger to Roland Barthes, Michel Foucault, Clement Greenberg, and other twentieth-century luminaries.[45] Writing nearly two decades after Mann's metacritique—and two decades after the end of the Cold War—Sell notes that all these remarkable men

> emerged from and engaged with the ideological end game between bureaucratic communism and laissez-faire capitalism—the Cold War. It is hard to imagine any other topic that could earn such unanimity ... but they agree that the avant-garde has been neutralized by the affluence-inspired tolerance and style-consciousness of the haute-bourgeoisie. They agree that Stalinism, National Socialism, Maoism and the mass-

murdering regimes of Pol Pot and other despots demonstrate the inevitable consequences of vanguard logic. . . . They also agree that the avant-garde's power as a catalyst for social transformation has been permanently disabled by the split between radical art and radical social movements institutionalized during the era of High Modernism.[46]

However, theirs need not be the only narrative: Sell takes as his starting point the premise that a theory of the avant-garde that excludes ongoing "subaltern and minority artists and communities creating radical culture and theorizing it as a historical and critical tendency" proves only that we need a new theory of the avant-garde.[47]

Yet the critiques do warrant real and recurrent consideration: theory and practice alike must grapple with a century of limitations and blind spots, Eurocentrism, corruptions, and appropriations, as well as intermittent slides into outright fascism. Such histories explain the prevalence of readings that view the first avant-garde as tragedy, as in Boris Groys's bleak vision, and subsequent echoes as farce.[48] In an era of total spectacle, with militancy co-opted to every side but the left, to what fresh horrors might aestheticized politics and delusions of elite vanguardism lead? Sell invokes Chris Burden's infamous performance piece *Shoot* (1971) as symptomatic, embodying the fear that "vanguards past have devolved into the self-referential mumblings of the navel gazer and the spectacular horror of mass destruction . . . unable to find a way out of the hall of mirrors, unable to distinguish between political engagement and the glamour of death."[49] The grand critiques of poststructuralist theory contributed to our collective suspicion by pointing out that, while the avant-garde may have forcibly expanded the canon, the resulting pantheon still "looked and sounded pretty much like it had before the radicals arrived": white, male, Euro- and fine arts–centric.[50] Our enthusiasm was further "chastened," as Hal Foster puts it, "by feminist critiques of revolutionary language and . . . postcolonial concerns about the exclusivity not only of art institutions but of critical discourses as well."[51] It has become increasingly difficult to ignore or claim as coincidental the fact that some of the most visible and successful aesthetic / political vanguards fall squarely on the far right of the political spectrum.

One way out is to consider the avant-garde, as Sell does, "less as a substantive entity in history . . . the canonical avant-garde of countless syllabi" than as a mode or "perspective from which we might examine a wide variety of sites, moments, creations, and critical methods that produce a culture that is 'political' in some fashion, that challenge in some way the structures and flows of power."[52] Rather than ask, Is this avant-garde? of a given work, we might ask, What are the benefits of considering this subject in terms of the avant-garde?[53] Foster's *Return of the Real* (1996) presents a similarly compelling psychoanalytic reading, sketching a dialectic of the avant-garde as the ever-returning repressed real of art institutions. What Bürger failed to recognize, according to Foster, was the importance of the art of his own time ("a fatal flaw of many philosophers of art").[54] But the explosion of ambitious art since the 1960s rediscovered and put to new use "avant-garde devices (e.g., the constructivist analysis of the object, the photomontage refunctioning of the image, the readymade critique of the exhibition) to contemporary ends," seeking through past practices a disconnect with the present.[55] Ultimately, Foster advances that, "rather than cancel the historical avant-garde, the neo-avant-garde enacts its project for the first time—a first time that, again, is theoretically endless."[56] He develops the analogy of revived avant-gardes as a return of the repressed to argue that such work is never effective in its initial occurrence precisely because it is "traumatic—a hole in the symbolic order of its time that is not prepared for it, that cannot receive it, at least not immediately, at least not without structural change."[57] Necessarily repressed, historical avant-gardes continue to return—as it were, from the future.

If one thrilling return of the avant-garde clearly swept the world in the 1960s and 1970s, artists and thinkers all over the world are recognizing a new wave in the past decades. Again, I want to make the claim that the shift in the critical perception of the avant-garde today reflects (and shapes) a political sea change: the end of the Cold War has given us a chance to reimagine leftist politics and aesthetics on a global scale. Groundbreaking publications in political philosophy such as Antonio Hardt and Michael Negri's *Commonwealth* (2009) and Badiou's *Communist Hypothesis* (2010) proposed new foundations for a global egalitarian future just as protests erupted all over the world.[58] With the end of both the discredited state socialism of the former Second World and a "free West" that defined itself in opposition to gulags and socialist realism, philosophers, activists, and artists of all stripes dare reimagine old / new ground. The theory-death of the avant-garde may fall the way of the imagined (dead) end of history: as a brief and historically specific fantasy.[59]

Is there a recurrent "avant-garde idea" that corresponds to the communist idea? Our very willingness to use the term (particularly without qualifying prefixes) seems an index to our era's politics. Studying the dramatic global resurgence of politically engaged art, Marc Léger finds that "forms of critical art practice, associated with social and political movements, autonomous collectives, and alternative media, bear a striking resemblance to what was once referred to as the avant-garde."[60] The list of participants returning to the term in Léger's anthologies *The Idea of the Avant-Garde and What It Means Today* alone speaks volumes: many of the theorists (Andrea Fraser, Hal Foster, Laura Mulvey, Marjorie Perloff, John Roberts, Boris Groys, etc.) and artists (Alexander Kluge, Lyn Hejinian, Vitaly Komar, Krzysztof Wodiczko, Dmitry Vilensky of Chto Delat, etc.) united on those pages are recurrent characters in my study as well.[61] In an era of cultural productions shaped by the biopolitics of total capitalism, these figures are increasingly interested in reengaging with the "pleasure and radical potential of the avant-garde."[62]

* * *

THE TERM AVANT-GARDE maintains a particular valence and power in Russia—the one place where the historical avant-gardes, however briefly and however partially, infiltrated and helped shape official revolutionary culture. The early twentieth-century Russian avant-garde captured the attention of the world in a way that has been matched only by the universally translated great Russian novels of the nineteenth century and the global phenomenon of Russian ballet.[63] In the crucible of prerevolutionary St. Petersburg, visual arts detonated traditional aesthetics while Futurist poets scandalized the bourgeoisie with manifestos and language experiments that slid from the "word as such" to "tropes of anarchic rebellion, sexuality, violence, war, urban life, and revolution," and pioneered performance art (*avant la lettre*), frequently to the point of scandal.[64] Literary productions emphasized the materiality of the word, borrowing from sister arts: the poetry of *zaum* (trans-sense, or beyond-sense) mimicked abstraction, and looked to transform the word

FIGURE I.3 Roman Osminkin performs in front of projected text at *n+1* headquarters
in New York City on December 5, 2015. *N+1.*

into autonomous form through "rhetorical equivalents."[65] Poetry played a
distinctively central role in the development of the Russian avant-garde, and
zaum arguably put the Russian Futurists ahead of even the Italians in radical innovation.[66] The names of Aleksei Kruchenykh, Velimir Khlebnikov,
and Vladimir Mayakovsky would make their way around the world.

Many artists and writers now associated with the historical Russian
avant-garde never used the term, which grew over time to encompass and
contextualize a range of practices:

> As a result of the First World War, with the sudden public awareness
> of military *avant-gardes* and *arriere-gardes,* the avant-garde became
> common currency and, no doubt, evoked the kind of associations that
> the cubo-futurist detachment relished—bravery, exploration, action,
> and aggression. This military and cultural alliance produced a number
> of artistic phenomena that took advantage of the new consciousness—
> from Tatlin's creation of his counterrelief by analogy with counterattack
> to the journal *Avangard* of 1922 (Moscow, one issue only), which ran,

simultaneously, statements by Trotsky (people's commissar for military affairs) and Georgii Iakulov (an avant-garde painter and designer).[67]

Far from emerging ex nihilo or merely imitating more western neighbors, the Russian avant-garde developed the preoccupations of nineteenth- and turn-of-the-century Russian literature.[68] The symbolist belief in the transformative power of language and the utopian strains of the nineteenth-century novel (à la Nikolai Chernyshevsky's 1863 *What Is To Be Done?*) shaped the Russian take on that "branch of modernism" that saw in art a vehicle for social change.[69]

Along with the dream of a new language, a new man, and a new world, the artists and writers of what we now term the Russian avant-garde shared a fascination with the scientific and technological innovations of their era. Julia Vaingurt writes that new technologies promised a "mode and product of creative action" capable of driving change rather than "passively contemplating its effects," and points out that "*Techne*, the etymological root of 'technology' . . . is a mode of cognition through making."[70] Technological development enabled new forms of experimentation in aesthetic production (and vice versa), but also modeled ways of thinking and making.[71] Moreover, the technological boom felt deeply compatible with an increased emphasis on collectivity: many of the early collective projects, including familiar forms such as anthologies of art and poetry, in retrospect "seem like the incubating laboratories for the emerging avant-garde."[72] Nina Gurianova writes that the Russian Futurists saw themselves as anarchists "throwing books as if they were bombs" in pursuit of the "radical liberation of the human spirit" and of "a method of cognition, or new epistemology, a conscious expansion of artistic space through the deconstructing of aesthetic cliché."[73]

One story of the Russian avant-garde seemed to end in 1922, the year of Khlebnikov's death as well as tectonic shifts in early Soviet cultural politics, but others persisted and new ones began: although "hostility toward all forms of creative rebellion and aesthetic experimentation was to solidify in the 1930s, avant-garde innovations survived in clusters of individuals and in efforts by some who worked in quiet isolation to be rediscovered much later."[74] The writers of OBERIU (the Union of Real Art, or Association for Real Art)—Daniil Kharms, Aleksandr Vvedensky, Nikolai Zabolotsky, among others—carried the avant-garde torch well into the 1930s, this time pushing against the Soviet state as political backdrop. OBERIU manifestos pushed on ideas sparked by Futurism to claim a new relationship to words and things alike. Moreover, the OBERIU poets were performers: their fundamental understanding of language as an event rather than a record of events went on to shape an alternative understanding of Russian literary arts well into the twenty-first century. What Aleksandr Skidan calls "the resistance of / to poetry" (an "insolvable dual meaning" that includes a "guarantee of a more demanding and possibly a more real failure") reads as a rearticulation of the OBERIU struggle against the limits of life and art.[75]

Even in the decades after OBERIU, while the banner of socialist realism flew high, quiet continuities persisted with earlier generations of the avant-garde.[76] Poets and artists in Leningrad especially understood art as existing in a complex relationship to power: in the Thaw era and after, unofficial literature flourished in Russia's most bohemian city.[77] The precursors to Conceptualism (Ian Satunovsky, Vsevolod Nekrasov) were born of such circles; and many underground writers were honored by the country's oldest and most prestigious nonstate literary award, the Andrei Bely Prize (ongoing since 1978 and heavily represented by [Translit] poets today).[78] Arkadii Dragomoshchenko in particular became a standout hero of the Leningrad poetic underground, a status formalized by the institution of the Dragomoshchenko prize in 2014 for innovative poets under the age of twenty-seven: as Skidan writes, Dragomoshchenko's "significance snapped into clearer focus after his death in 2012. . . . His relentlessly curious mind, his knowledge of philosophy and other poetic traditions, and his prolific poetry as well as prose had already made him an important poet for the younger generation in post-Soviet St. Petersburg. He modeled a kind of wide-ranging poetic creation, poetic translation (notably of American L=A=N=G=U=A=G=E poets), deployment of free verse, and absorption of contemporary theory."[79]

In Moscow too, a new wave of literary rebels turned aggressive play against state clichés: their poems "drew on the language of slogans or public discourse, rendered either as grotesque repetition or as fragmentary delusion, but almost always as radically minimalist utterance."[80] In 1979 Groys introduced the term *Moscow Conceptualism* to set apart this emerging trend in late-Soviet nonconformist art.[81] The group included Dmitry Prigov but also Ilya Kabakov,

Erik Bulatov, Viktor Pivovarov, Andrei Monastyrsky, Lev Rubinshtein, and Vladimir Sorokin. The even more radical new "actionists," such as Alexander Brener, Oleg Kulik, and Anatoly Osmolovsky, explored increasingly outrageous provocations through performance.[82]

How do we make sense of such evolving, overlapping, and at times competing avant-garde formations? Evgeny Dobrenko suggests a genealogy in three waves, following Prigov's own model:

> Discussing the genealogy of "avant-garde art-producing," Prigov distinguished its three "ages": "futurist-constructivist," which was replaced by "reaction against the mechanicalness and planned euphoria of the first," by an attempt to prove "the absurdity of all levels of languages," but nevertheless these figures (the OBERIUty) were, according to Prigov, the "cloudy unreflecting bearers of the avant-garde ideology of the first age." And only in the third age ("pop art / Conceptualist") did the "completion of the triad" take place, "the removal of the opposing mutually-directed linguistic positions of the first two ages . . . the affirmation of the truth of each language within the limits of its axiomatics . . . and the declaration of the untruthfulness of totalitarian ambitions."[83]

But the past two decades have brought a response to Conceptualism in turn. Building from Prigov's dialectic sketch, we can add a fourth turn: the post-Soviet left avant-garde builds from and against Prigov as a father, as poets with such divergent styles as Skidan and Medvedev both suggestively call Prigov in their essays.[84]

What kind of avant-garde legacy, then, have the poets of *[Translit]* inherited? I imagine it as a pulse beating sometimes strongly, sometimes weakly throughout the last century (and more, given the avant-garde's Romantic roots), offering up a history of interrupted projects and unrealized possibilities. Igor Chubarov defines the left avant-garde not as the "historical realization of a certain artistic project, the development of trends or genres of art" but as a still relevant and intelligible idea, "a counter-realizable historical opportunity."[85] I try to show in what follows seven distinct poetic praxes that lay claim to that tantalizing, lingering opportunity.

Avant-Garde Post—

I tell the story of radical poetics in Russia today through the vivid examples afforded by seven protagonists, each a central hub in a larger constellation. The book is about the *[Translit]* circle, but grounded in close readings of experimental poetry, contextualized in turn by each poet's theoretical and political essays, translations, performances, and other aesthetic practices. Each of the seven poets in this book explores the political power of literary labor, and some venture into very direct forms of political activism. All of them, in one way or another, refuse to *work:* that is, all (try to) engage in some form of Marxist refusal to "sell" aesthetic productions resulting from alienated labor and instead seek to experience poetry as a form of nonalienated labor. Each occupies a slightly different point on a spectrum of avant-garde poetry as political possibility even as they explore their own and others' deep suspicions of that prospect. Their differences cast their praxes as pieces of a larger puzzle—the "avant-garde post—" of my title—even as their work together makes it possible to conceptualize the group as a circle adumbrating leftist aesthetics and politics in contemporary Russia.

The chapters that follow are not arranged in chronological order by poet's age (as would, for example, emphasize generational difference), but are in an order that describes the emergence of a movement as such, its many aspects and influences, and potential futures. Each chapter is organized thematically, while dedicated to an analysis of one poet's work. I begin with the end of the ceasefire, as declared by Medvedev amid the cultural and economic free fall of Russia in the early 2000s, and with Arseniev's central role in founding the unlikely new Marxist literary journal *[Translit].* I end with a coda on Rymbu, who in many ways already reads as a post-*[Translit]* poet and the forerunner of new directions in radical Russophone poetry. Each chapter begins by introducing and contextualizing its protagonist and thematic frame with an eye to the ever-present question of audience (including local and international reception); each ends with a summary of the poet's most recent challenges and redirections.

Chapter 1, "The Poetics of Refusal: Kirill Medvedev," opens with one of the earliest and most militant case studies of the book. I argue that the return of a politically radical Russian poetic avant-garde began when Medvedev vowed to stop publishing poetry in the literary institutions and emerging neo-liberal marketplace of 2000s Russia. Initially hailed by Moscow literary society as an extraordinary translator of Charles Bukowski into Russian and as an innovator of documentary tendencies and free verse form, Medvedev distanced himself through a series of refusals from a world that had, as he put it, polluted the Word. His refusal to publish and his transubstantiation of poetry into other forms and actions shaped Medvedev's poetics. Inspired by the years of protest and new venues that he himself helped build, Medvedev has since returned to poetry: his collection *March on City Hall* (2014) promptly if controversially won the Andrei Bely prize. Increasingly, Medvedev casts both his poetic experiments and political organizing as expressly tied to the cause of independent Russian labor unions. He imagines today's avant-gardist quite directly as the vanguard of tomorrow's citizenry.

Chapter 2, "The Avant-Garde Journal 2.0: Pavel Arseniev and *[Translit]*," turns to the journal that quickly became the heart of Russia's avant-garde revival, and to the André Breton–like leader of the group. Inspired by the leftist art collective Chto Delat, the first such group to take shape in post-Soviet Russia, Arseniev joined with Osminkin (whom he met in Dragomoshchenko's underground poetry seminar, as if literalizing a genealogical metaphor) to found a poetry and critical theory journal dedicated to their shared aesthetic and political convictions. Twenty print issues later, *[Translit]* has won numerous awards and published international leftist luminaries; the journal's blog, meanwhile, sees weekly updates and features online multimedia works such as Arseniev's video-poetry experiments. Arseniev's own poetics cannot be understood outside the context of the collective endeavor: he is a curator and remediator of words across languages and media, best known nationally for political slogans that took center stage in the 2011–2012 protests. Moving fluidly between print and online platforms, *[Translit]* reimagines the avant-garde journal for the twenty-first century and reclaims Marxist world culture for contemporary Russia.

Chapter 3, "Language Poetry Is Leftist: The Long Durée of Aleksandr Skidan," emphasizes the revival of late-Soviet underground practices through the work of the most senior and storied poet publishing in *[Translit]* and the Kraft series. A founding member of Chto Delat, the poetry editor of the prestigious *New Literary Review,* an extraordinarily difficult and erudite poet, and a St. Petersburg cultural institution in his own right, Skidan, like many romantic heroes of the underground, worked as a stoker in a boiler room in the last years of the Soviet Union. He serves as a living link between the late-Soviet underground, the legacy of Dragomoshchenko, and the younger generation of poets behind *[Translit]*. His understanding of leftist poetry resembles the American *L=A=N=G=U=A=G=E* school far more than it does the overtly political and relatively accessible work of Medvedev, whom Skidan nevertheless tirelessly champions. Fiercely resistant to national and international trends of new sincerity, Skidan's poems search for emancipation within a defiantly, if only relatively, autonomous sphere of art. His newest work moreover suggests a reverse influence from the younger poets he has mentored over the years, and who evidently inspire Skidan with hope for the future.

Chapter 4, "Dmitry Golynko: Writing Poetry for Zombies," uses the work of the group's seminal poet-theorist to study the increasingly prevalent understanding of experimental poetry as a form of contemporary art. Golynko, a precariously poised academic specializing in media studies and with roots in St. Petersburg's ever-productive bohemia, follows Prigov in the metamorphosis of the Russian poet into a global artist. Golynko's long combinatorial poems and polemical essays (such as the manifesto "Socially Engaged Poetry," inspired by the Polish artist Artur Żmiewski's "Socially Engaged Art") expose the linguistic and psychosocial horrors of the global present even as they circle around attempts to forge new subjectivities and collectivities through aesthetic practice. Golynko defines what he terms "monstrology" as a key analytic practice of our age, and calls for a reverse identification that reveals the emancipatory potential of the modern monster. Breaking with poetic subjectivity in 2002, Golynko tries to imagine instead a poetry that engages with the monstrous as the political: he writes poetry for zombies.

Chapter 5, "Poetry in the Age of Digital Reproduction: Roman Osminkin," develops the growing importance of performance to Russian political poetry through a study of the work of Golynko's former student and Arseniev's partner in cofounding *[Translit]*. The inimitably charismatic Osminkin follows in the Prigov vein but takes the performance of his poetry to new lengths, through Technopoetry and his many other musical groups, parodic YouTube videos, and sheer graphomaniacal output on Facebook and other social media. More than any other poet in this group, Osminkin constantly uses social media to draft, edit, and disseminate his poetry. At the same time he insists more than any other on the body of the poet, moving through multiple roles at readings, from St. Petersburg poet (black glasses and beret) to street thug (*gopnik*) or self-conscious activist galvanizing a crowd of protesters. Such poetic practices rely on audience presence and participation, and site-specific experience: Osminkin's work refracts the widespread influences of performance and feminist art, exploring the local transformative potential of what Sianne Ngai termed the "cuteness of the avant-garde."

Chapter 6, "Art Must Be Communist: The Voices of Keti Chukhrov," moves to the contemporary archaic, and to poetry as drama and song, through the work of one of the women central to the *[Translit]* constellation. Born Ketevan Chukhrukidze in Tbilisi, Soviet Georgia, Chukhrov moved to study literature and philosophy at Moscow State University. Chukhrov's intellectual and political interests and extraordinary erudition are in evidence in her poetic works, which tend toward long dramatic verse forms and collect the voices of Moscow's various subalterns: migrant workers, sex workers, and precarious surplus populations. Chukhrov's work demands collectivity-building staging and remediation through form while conjuring post-Soviet political subjects in content. If previous incarnations of the avant-garde reveal a recurrent tendency to slide from left to right along the twin channels of nationalism and masculinism, Chukhrov probes socialist feminist and post-Soviet (not only Russian) strategies.

The coda, "The Passion of Galina Rymbu," closes the volume with a reflection on the collaborations, collective actions, and shared alliances that unite the poets of *Avant-Garde Post—* into a recognizable, if fluid and open, aesthetic and political phenomenon. I conclude with a look at an extraordinary and more recently acclaimed poetic voice. The young and talented Rymbu stole the attention of Russian literary society in 2014–2015 with poems such as the untitled "the dream is over, Lesbia, now it's time for sorrow." Through classical references, sliding pronouns, and oblique treatment of grammatical gender in Russian, among other formal play, Rymbu's work highlights gender and sexuality in courageous reflections on the region's histories and on contemporary possibilities for cultural and political change. As the world polarizes, the Romantic lyric—of all forms, and after all dismantling—seems paradoxically fresh, queer, and dangerous once more. Rymbu takes us beyond St. Petersburg and *[Translit]* circles: *Avant-Garde Post—* thus concludes in Ukraine and with an argument for the increasing centrality of gender-based critique to the aesthetics and politics of the new Russophone left.

The poets and poetry explored in *Avant-Garde Post—* inevitably face familiar critiques: that this work is not poetry (being for the most part suspicious of virtuoso displays of craft and traditional conventions of rhyme and meter); that it is not Russian (embracing global influences in aesthetics and politics, incorporating other languages freely, and indeed written against Russian nationalism in content and form); and that it is not politically effective (being doubly marginalized as avant-garde and poetry). Each of the poets studied in the pages that follow grapples in her or his own way with these external and internalized accusations; each at times rejects and at others agrees with accusations of inutility and complicity; and in the end each arrives at a distinctive and dynamic marriage of experimental form and content.

This book ranges across two decades demarcated by 1999 and ending with the double full stop of the global pandemic in 2020 and invasion of Ukraine in 2022. What comes after this moment—politically, aesthetically—seems like it must be fundamentally different, even as what the creative vanguards responded to at the turn of the century is dragged into visibility for the rest of us: the deadly consequences of inequality and globalization, as of nationalist and technological "revolutions." In March 2020, *Nozh* (knife.media) published the responses of Pavel Arseniev and several other Russian poets to the pandemic in verse. Arseniev writes:

нам придется закрыть университеты
(когда еще будет такой повод),
отменим мероприятия:
ни культурных, ни спортивных
ни даже религиозных.
друг к другу
не приближаемся,

we will have to close the universities
(when will there be such an excuse again),
we will cancel events:
cultural, sports
even religious.
we won't get close
to one another

[. . .]

кашляем в кулачок,
плохо себя чувствуем,
остаемся у себя,
звоним по номеру
кризисной службы.
спасибо тебе, коронавирус,
наконец все получило
хоть какое-то объяснение

we cough into fists,
we feel unwell,
we stay home,
we dial the numbers
of crisis hotlines.
thank you coronavirus
at last it all has
at least some explanation[86]

The pandemic provides the state with an excuse no police mastermind could have dreamed up: to shut down institutions, forbid public assembly, and isolate citizens into crushing and self-imposed home arrest. Everything is forbidden in this fresh hell of biopolitical dystopia: touching, kissing, shaking hands, all public life, mere proximity to other humans. Arseniev's politicizing punch line asks: But haven't we been living this way for years?

1

The Poetics of Refusal

KIRILL MEDVEDEV

OVER THE PAST DECADE, Kirill Medvedev (born in Moscow, 1975) has become one of the most recognized voices in contemporary Russian poetry, for Russophone and international readers alike.[1] Russian critics caught the significance of the Moscow poet early on: Ilya Kukulin named Medvedev the most important "poet of reportage" at the turn of the century and described his work as the most vivid example of the new aesthetics and ethics emerging in Russian poetry.[2] Aleksandr Skidan declared, "Over the heads of his immediate precursors and teachers . . . Medvedev actualizes the seemingly long-discredited and botched tradition of politically engaged poetry."[3] After playing an active role in the oppositional protests in Moscow in 2011–2012, Medvedev made a number of appearances on popular Russian television shows such as *The School of Slander and Aloud.*[4] His rock band's rendition of the protest song "The Walls" became an anthem of what has been called Russia's long year of protest—and rang out again recently in Belarus during those bloody demonstrations in 2020.[5]

The next image is a still from a video recording of Medvedev and other members of the group Arkady Kots singing "The Walls" (Lluis Llach's famous 1968 Catalan protest song "L'Estaca," remade into "Mury," the anthem of Polish Solidarność in the 1980s, now "Steny" in Medvedev's Russian translation) inside an *avtozak,* or armored police van, when they were arrested while protesting outside the courtroom during the Pussy Riot trial. As it was for so many, 2012 was a watershed year for Medvedev, politically rousing and bringing him into direct contact with new audiences. Unlike the rest

FIGURE 1.1 Kirill Medvedev and members of his protest-rock band Arkady Kots sing in a police van after their arrest during the Pussy Riot trials. VLAD CHIZHENKOV, WALLS, ARKADY KOTS IN A PADDY WAGON. YOUTUBE.

of his generation, however, Medvedev had been preparing for revolution for years.

The impromptu music video of the arrest, one of several versions available on YouTube, is striking not only for its demonstration of the longevity and political vicissitudes of the tune but for the power of Medvedev's presence. It suggests a conscious political utilization of the (recently dismantled) cultural capital of the poet in Russian society: given Russia's traumatic past, even riot police are reluctant to "squander" poets.[6] The video and its accompanying images serve as an introduction to the paradoxes that plague the contemporary Russian political poet: Medvedev speaks of a "weak heroism" necessary in an era when cultural figures feel called to social responsibility and to action while remaining profoundly suspicious of heroic posturing and of the elevated status of cultural elites.

International readers discovered Medvedev through the first volume of his work in English translation, *It's No Good,* published in 2012 through the efforts of the Brooklyn-based *n+1* and Ugly Duckling Presse.[7] Medvedev's essays on politics and aesthetics have since made their way into such publications as the *New Left Review,* the *Guardian,* and the *London Review of Books.* Interviews and reviews have appeared in the *Independent,* the *Nation,* the *New Inquiry,* the *Boston Review,* the *Chicago Review,* the *Paris Review,* the *Los Angeles Review of Books,* the *New Yorker,* and the *New York Times*—to name a few. In *BOMB Magazine,* Chris Cumming points to the striking fact that

> a Marxist activist and free-verse poet who writes only for his own blog, should get as much attention in America as Medvedev has—including a favorable review last week in that mouthpiece of socialism and experimental poetry, *The New York Times.* No doubt this reflects the tireless publicity work of his publisher, *n+1.* But there's more to it: many people in America are disgusted by our politics and depressed by our literary culture, and Medvedev's central subject is the miserable marriage of these two. . . . his own life, even his Russianness, give his opinions a legitimacy on these subjects that American writers' lack. He has behind him a tradition of Russian artists who combine political and aesthetic radicalism, something American writers don't really have.[8]

The insight is excellent, if the conclusion doesn't entirely read right; and the problems with this alleged Russian authenticity are too close to the surface to need much pointing out. Medvedev has behind him indeed a tradition of Russian radical poetics, but also an unprecedented arsenal of global models— some very much American.

It is moreover unsurprising that Medvedev found champions in *n+1* and Ugly Duckling Presse, both of which emerge, in some sense, out of Russian New York. Keith Gessen writes: "As I read Medvedev's critique of the Moscow literary and intellectual world, what struck me above all was how it answered so many of the questions my friends and I had been struggling with in New York. Here we were, writing about the depredations of multinational corporations—how they dodged taxes, off-shored work to places with lax or no labor laws, and destroyed the environment—and then publishing our books or articles with places that were owned by . . . multinational corporations. . . . Medvedev cut through all this."[9] Medvedev visited New York during the height of Occupy Wall Street and was deeply moved by what he saw. Within the year he would use the "human microphone" call-and-response technique at Moscow protests; a year later he was organizing Occupy Abai.[10] In the years since, Medvedev has returned to the United States several times for readings and festivals building on the collaborative energies and exchanges sparked in 2012.[11] But Medvedev's fairly astonishing popularity attests to more than personal connections: decades after the end of the Soviet Union, Russian and international audiences alike desperately needed a revival of *Russian* leftist poetry.

It could be tempting for critics to conclude that Medvedev and other *[Translit]* poets indeed write for an audience of Western academics and fellow travelers. But the moment we accept such a binary of national versus international art, we have fallen into a trap. I see such arguments as akin to the dangerously cynical "two Russias" cliché, applicable in so many other national contexts. As Ilya Matveev argues, the "two Russias" theory of a cosmopolitan and West-oriented Moscow and St. Petersburg versus a barely literate wild East "constructs a veritable 'ontology' of Russian politics, naturalizing differences in ways of life, behaviors and tastes that otherwise could be critically explained by social and economic conditions ... into 'primordial,' eternal qualities, forcing their bearers into an ahistorical and unresolvable confrontation."[12] Just as the two Russias model is an ideologically motivated construction that hides as much as it reveals and serves a political purpose, so too is the reflexive division of art practice into international and academic versus national and authentic precisely calculated to invalidate global solidarities.[13]

In this chapter, I argue that Russia's newest poetic avant-garde—indeed, the poetry of the new Russian left—was born out of Medvedev's highly public refusal to write for the literary institutions and emerging marketplace of 2000s Russia. That refusal (to comply, to be complicit, to remain in an elite silo, to perform Russian poet as expected) has colored his entire career. Skidan gave his 2006 review of Medvedev's poetry the prescient title, "The End of the Cease-Fire: Notes on the Poetry of Kirill Medvedev."[14] Initially hailed by Moscow literary society, Medvedev, through a series of public refusals, turned his back on a world that had polluted language itself.[15] In the years since, inspired by recurrent outbursts of political action and by the success (in the field of symbolic, not actual, capital) of the new venues for publishing that he helped build, Medvedev returned to poetry.[16] His collection *March on City Hall* (2014) promptly if controversially won the Andrei Bely prize for poetry.[17]

His collaborations with the other poets central to the St. Petersburg–based journal *[Translit]* in turn helped shape the group's identity and formulate their shared vision: a commitment to a global egalitarian future and to verbal art as a mode of critique, imagination, and struggle—poetics of political subjectivization and collectivity formation. Medvedev's cease-fire signaled that Russia had a new, post-Soviet cultural left and that it had something to say on a global stage.[18]

*   *   *

MEDVEDEV BEGAN DISTANCING himself first from the literary marketplace and then from the Moscow literary scene as early as 2003 (a few short years into Putin's new "stability"), soon after publishing two well-received books of poetry. In "Communiqué," a manifesto first posted on his personal website, he described post-Soviet Russia's new book market as a "clique of half-literate publishers" flirting with "the most monstrous and disgusting ideologies": "You have what are in effect a few cultural lobbies waging a nasty and primitive battle for cultural influence; the disgusting speculation of critics and journalists earnestly serving their masters; or other critics, forcing their half-developed, half-conscious cultural viewpoints down readers' throats, or propagating their cultural or other types of xenophobia and pseudo-religious quasi-fascism."[19] Medvedev found all of this intolerable: "I don't want to have even a tangential relationship to a system that has so devalued and cheapened the Word."[20] Crucially, Medvedev's manifesto articulated not a vague stance against commercialization but a pointed challenge to writers and publishers willing to share shelf space with increasingly chauvinist tracts. As Greg Afinogenov notes, Medvedev's withdrawal was motivated by an early and perceptive recognition of "the Putinist literary intelligentsia's refusal to examine its own political function. . . . the descendants of Brodsky were gradually becoming complacent 'cultural bureaucrats.'"[21] All of this occurred against the backdrop of nearly unfathomable growth of income inequality after the dissolution of the Soviet Union. Medvedev's first grasps at a post-Soviet left poetics articulate an early critique of emerging cultural and economic formations while formulating a new human ecology of want.

Medvedev's many manifestos and essays on the political function of literature invariably return to this point. In the provocatively (and prophetically, given the precipitous rise of Russia's alt-right in the years since) titled "My Fascism," Medvedev writes: "We need to do away with this false notion of 'literature as a private activity.' Because poetic language in Russia, even the most refined and individualized, is, sorry to say, far from being your private business."[22] Through the illusion of the autonomy of literature, and through the very real complicity of journals, presses, prizes, and reviewers with the apparatus of power, a writer is trapped into either legitimizing corrupt institutions or giving up the few platforms available that might allow for some impact on society. Faced with an impasse, Medvedev instead began looking for a way to live in the world as a poet without creating appropriable products or intellectual property.

Refusing any involvement in literary projects sponsored by the government or its cultural bureaucrats, as well as public readings and publication even in journals allegedly sympathetic to his politics, Medvedev declared that from 2003 on, he would only publish in such venues as he could put out with his own labor and money.[23] In 2004 he voiced his opposition to copyright entirely and demanded that his work be republished only "in a PIRATE EDITION, that is to say, WITHOUT THE PERMISSION OF THE AUTHOR, WITHOUT ANY CONTRACTS OR AGREEMENTS, which must be indicated in all the publication data."[24] Picking up the gauntlet, Moscow's preeminent literary journal and publishing house, the *New Literary Review* (*Novoe literaturnoe obozrenie, NLO*) took the legal risk and provocatively published a collection of Medvedev's writings—without contacting the author—in a volume titled *Kirill Medvedev: Texts Published without the Author's Consent*. As the (more liberal than leftist) *NLO* followed up with a symposium and a public discussion, Medvedev hesitantly concluded that if the episode had prompted "even a minimal amount of thought" about the questions he had hoped to raise, it could be deemed a success.[25]

Medvedev's energies in the subsequent years went to translating political and aesthetic theory and to organizing for political activist groups such as the Russian Socialist Movement (Rossiskoe sotsialisticheskoe dvizhenie; RSD). In 2007 he opened his own independent publishing venture, the Free Marxist Press. Initially staffed solely by Medvedev, the press's first releases

FIGURE 1.2 Kirill Medvedev performs at protests for internet freedom in Russia.
KRASSOTKIN / WIKIMEDIA COMMONS.

were stapled chapbook translations of Western Marxists such as Herbert
Marcuse and Pier Paolo Pasolini.[26] In 2010 the Free Marxist Press joined
forces with *[Translit]* to establish the Kraft poetry chapbook series and began
publishing fellow left-leaning experimental poets including Skidan, Pavel
Arseniev, Roman Osminkin, and Keti Chukhrov. The same year, along with
the sociologist Oleg Zhuravlev and the artist Nikolai Oleinikov, Medvedev
founded the protest rock group Arkady Kots, named after the Russian Jewish
socialist who translated "The Internationale." Arkady Kots, fittingly, would
help Medvedev reach the broader audiences and more direct political utility
he longed for, putting creative talents and critical thinking honed through
decades of poetry to new use.

Medvedev's poetry and public persona alike were shaped by his early and
dramatic gesture of refusal, illuminating the shared ethical drive behind his
aesthetic and political actions. And whether publishing poetry or not, he has

devoted himself to the work of activism with no sign of exhaustion. In 2017, Medvedev even ran for local political office in Moscow (municipal deputy in the Meshchansky district): he did not win, but the energy around his campaign brought in 11 percent of the vote and mobilized a younger generation into political action, resembling recent campaigns in the US northeast by the Democratic Socialists of America (DSA).[27] One more recent example of his many arrests, in turn, was just in September 27, 2020, for a demonstration and micro-concert (given the challenges of Covid-era activism) in solidarity with fellow protestors in front of the Belarus Embassy in Moscow. Driven by stubbornness or farsighted vision, and even when faced with the clear impossibility of success—even in the years of global pandemic, even in war— Medvedev has found ways to work, and to organize.

I read Medvedev's paradoxically productive poetics of refusal as reflecting the position of poetry under disaster capitalism, linked in unholy marriage to the rise or revival of twenty-first-century nationalism. Writing about the unexpectedly convergent conflict evident in the work of the American poet Anne Boyer (born in 1973, not incidentally nearly exactly of Medvedev's generation), Walt Hunter sees that the poetic subject "has no choice but to write within the conditions set by global capital," however unwillingly: "There is a double bind here, enacted by the poem. . . . To speak with, or in, 'conditions' would be both to assume the impossible language of the liberal, universal subject, the language denied to the precarious—to 'bare life,' evacuees, refugees, prisoners, women, and colonial subjects—and also, at the same time, to reject the process by which precariousness might become subsumed under capital."[28] Boyer's 2015 collection *Garments Against Women* makes it painfully clear that by "garments," she means the linguistic forms that enclose her. Medvedev shares with Boyer that fraught, adversarial relationship to his medium. He knows intimately that poetry can be (and has been, in Russia of all places) both transformative and emancipatory, but in practice sees it all around as obfuscatory, hypocritical, and revanchist. In the post-Soviet Russian context, Medvedev must contend moreover with the complicity of leftist literature with, in his words, "the tragic story of Russian socialism which began long before 1917, suffered a defeat in the early 1990s, and continues today."[29] The only way forward for leftist poetry, as for politics, is not to start blindly anew but to face that past and push through, using whatever language the poet is able to cobble together in order to think, to see, to free. If he cannot see a path forward, he must be mute; when he does write, he must foreground his noncompliance in other ways. As Skidan recognized, Medvedev was among the first to dare revive Russia's "botched" tradition of political poetry, and to dare suggest it could contain a powerful response to the looming tragedies of the twenty-first century.

Viewed through the lens of a revived Russian avant-garde—in precisely the militant sense of the term, scouting for the citizenry of the future—Medvedev's poetic and political actions spring into focus as parts of a larger unified project. His poetry, translations, social media posts, manifestos, music, videos, actions, arrests, and campaigns all interrogate the role of cultural institutions in the ideological apparatus of power and try to generate alternatives to those institutions. Beginning with small, relatively insular circles but extending his range and influence through translation, music, and direct political involvement, Medvedev has remained at the center of progressive Marxist literary and political communities since he first announced his rejection of the contemporary cultural mainstream.[30]

Translating on the Edge

Before protest, before the disavowal of literary institutions or gradual cautious returns, where did Medvedev come from? The son of a relatively well-known late-Soviet journalist, the Moscow-born Medvedev emerges out of a literary-minded urban culture he understands brutally well. The poem opening Medvedev's first published book of verse *It's No Good* (2000) is an ode to, or a lament on, the art of translation.[31] In "I'm tired of translating . . . ," the first poem of a first book, a new voice announces an entrance: we see a story of origin, problematized and deferred from the start.[32] Medvedev suggests that his poetry was born out of translation—of which he has since grown sick. But he made great discoveries when translating Charles Bukowski into Russian. Boldly he claims:

но там есть просто гениальные куски
я в этом уверен

there are really brilliant passages
I'm sure of that

[. . .]

когда я переводил стихи
чарльза буковски
мне казалось
что я делаю
лучшую современную поэзию на русском языке

when I was translating the poems
of charles bukowski
I was convinced that I was writing
the best poetry then being written in russian

We can guess what Medvedev saw in Bukowski: working-class realia as
populist subject matter, and a pedestrian language and formal freedom
atypical of Russian verse. Conjuring a Russian-language Bukowski clarified
for Medvedev what was missing in his own language and poetry, and what he
needed to do.

Bukowski remains a relatively marginal figure in scholarly accounts of
American poetry, although his assimilation too is underway. In 2010 the
Huntington Library held the biggest retrospective of his work to date, *Charles
Bukowski: Poet on the Edge*. The retrospective's title is interesting in itself:
Bukowski felt more "edgy" than avant-garde to a generation of readers that
had little interest in the latter. As the exhibit stressed, the high-culture industry, like the critical establishment, is concentrated on the East Coast, and
Bukowski was a Californian. It has accordingly taken Bukowski far longer to
enter the literary mainstream than, say, Norman Mailer, despite relatively
similar politics and doses of violence and misogyny in their writing. But Bukowski was unapologetically a working-class writer who wrote in a language
and on subjects that still had little place in high literature. He never bought
into national fantasies like the American dream—or the nuclear family—and
proved harder to clean up than the Beats. Worse yet for his prospects of highbrow assimilation, "the people" actually read him: Bukowski found a cult
following with readers during his lifetime and after, if not a place with arbi-
ters of the canon and the *Norton Anthology of American Literature*.[33]

Just as an earlier generation of Russians knew John Steinbeck and Jack London better than most Americans, so too is Medvedev a displaced Bukowski fan.[34] What happens between the two is a kind of charged literary chemistry:

это был самый настоящий контакт—
когда два совершенно разных человека
начинают вдруг понимать друг друга
по-моему такой контакт
это и есть самое настоящее событие
искусства и жизни

I think it was genuine contact—
when two different people
begin to understand one another
in my opinion this
was a real event
in art and in life

Despite Bukowski being "far from the poet's ideal" (charl'z bukovski eto daleko ne moi ideal), despite being "two completely different" (dva sovershenno raznykh) bodies as well as bodies of work—through inspired translation they come to merge and occupy the same space, in language that smacks of erotic innuendo:

мне кажется что им стоит заниматься
только тогда
когда ты можешь
полностью слиться
с автором
подписаться
под каждой его строчкой
подхватить и усилить
его крик

I think it's only worth doing
if you really feel

you can become one
with the author
sign on
to every line
pick up and amplify
his cry

Medvedev did not betray his poet: this translation constituted genuine communion, a real event "in art and in life" (iskusstva i zhizni). We notice that pervasive pairing: real contact must take place in both; the real event must disrupt both, allowing for an interpenetration of art and life. At the same time, the very phrasing separates the two terms through the conjunction, highlighting paradoxes of autonomy and entanglement.

The poem opens and closes with the declaration that the lyric persona will "probably" stop translating entirely. Translation is ultimately too easy of a pleasure, and hence one the poet must deny himself now that he has seen the extent of the difference:

потому что перевод
это сладкий сон
а творчество
это мука

because translation is like
a sweet dream
whereas actually creating something
is torture

Some of the other oppositions set up in the poem include true versus false translation; American versus Russian literature; and vampiric profiteering versus selfless dedication and love. The kind of translation Medvedev means to give up, we realize, is the commercial work he has been pushed into, such as translating a detective novel by John Ridley for the journal *Foreign Literature* (*Inostrannaia literatura*). The young, African American Ridley seems a promising and talented fellow outsider, but he too made the compromise with the market that serves as one way out of a creative writer's perpetual dilemmas: lack of money, lack of readers, lack of relevance and utility. Ridley's clever, self-referential fiction offers something

чем-то похож на фильмы квентина тарантино
там есть сатира на голливуд
и критика нравов голливудского
истеблишмента
но с использованием
все те же старых голливудских уловок

like a tarantino film
a satire of Hollywood
and a critique of
the hollywood establishment
but with the use of
all the same old tired hollywood clichés

Russifying this kind of work rather than Bukowski's poetry (likely never to be published, due to lack of interest and profitability) leaves Medvedev equally "at the service of the bourgeoisie" (na sluzhbe u burzhuazii) as Ridley.

Medvedev would later pen a similar critique of Vladimir Sorokin, whose early texts he admires but whom he now considers declawed postmodern entertainment. Medvedev sees Sorokin's "transformation into a trendy plaything of the mass media" as "coincid[ing] with the decline of Conceptualist artistic principles that had sought to clarify the meaning and mechanisms of art's power over the individual."[35] The market adapts quickly and provides mainstream elites with safer, watered-down versions of similar techniques. As Medvedev puts it, "I don't like it when former victims, rebels, and avant-gardists become themselves masters of the culture. . . . This is an old and boring story."[36] He tries to resist such appropriation, even if that means transubstantiating his work into unassimilable forms. If we read Medvedev's refusals as performance, à la Prigov (a closer Conceptualist father figure than Sorokin) playing the role of "Russian poet," in Medvedev's case the performative act is specific, explicitly political, and comes with instructions for interpretation. In Putin's Russia, Medvedev lets us know, a real Russian poet should be defiantly mute.

One way to avoid the danger of commercial or rightist appropriation would be to write only for a small group of fellow insiders—to become a sectarian, which has its appeals: "You say, 'I only publish in these places, I have five readers, no one else reads me, but at least I am honest, and uncompromising, and consistent.' That to me is a very sympathetic position; I, in fact, like that position very much. But I also recognize that insofar as I am part of a political movement and we need to get our message out, we do need to consider these questions of political tactics."[37] Hence Medvedev's other projects, including the Free Marxist Press, pick up where his poetry leaves off. Just as observers have noted the seeming impossibility of going to a protest in Russia without finding Medvedev there "marching, handing out leaflets, fronting his protest-rock band Arkady Kots, or, often, being punched and / or arrested," so too have Medvedev's efforts as a translator and editor seemed inexhaustible.[38] The translations, which began with the likes of Pasolini, Žižek, Jean-Luc Godard, Herbert Marcuse, and Terry Eagleton, have expanded to include poetry as well as more recent leftist theory (a selection from the work of American historian and activist Mike Davis in 2016, for example; and another planned with the feminist Marxist political scientist Jodi Dean).[39]

One particularly vivid Free Marxist Press project is a book of Victor Serge's poetry in Medvedev's translation published in 2015.[40] The revolutionary Marxist, born in 1890 in Brussels to Russian exiles, wrote poetry in French. In Medvedev's hands, the text reads implicitly as a translation "back" into an original Russian Serge *might* have written under other circumstances. Medvedev mines Serge's language and forms for an alternative road to Russian poetry, finding in an imagined Russian-language Serge another, better forefather. The Serge translation in particular clarifies the stakes of Medvedev's larger project when it comes to poetry: to rewrite Russian poetic history from the position of the new left—and in the process to enrich contemporary Russian language and literature as much as possible. What Serge in particular has to offer are the "amazing optics" and incomparable perspective that arises from a lifetime spent trying to combine "political passion with objective detachment, bitter irony with that 'principle of hope' that Ernst Bloch was trying to formulate at the same time through philosophical language. In essence, it's free verse with a spontaneous, seemingly random rhyme—uncharacteristic for the Russian poetic tradition even now, not to mention in the 1920s–1940s, when these poems were written."[41] Far from foregrounding the originality of his own work, Medvedev goes to great lengths to discover and promote his influences (Serge, Bukowski, Pasolini, Bloch), as if to stress that his voice is one of many speaking truth to power, now as ever. Through his essays, translations, and literary activism, he puts forward an alternative canon: required reading for Russia's new left.

(Killing) Fathers

One of Medvedev's early poems, "I recently ran into the poet Lvovsky..." from his second collection *Invasion,* vividly describes the crescive, tempestuous Russian literary society of the 2000s from which Medvedev emerged and diverged.[42] This poem too centers on a moment of contact between two poets with an affinity for each other's work but moves sharply to a critique of cultural capital in its contemporary Russian manifestations. The narrator runs into fellow poet Stanislav Lvovsky in the subway:

львовский ехал вниз, а я вверх;
я жевал жвачку
и в тот момент
когда мы увидели друг друга
я как раз надувал
огромный пузырь;
мы встретились глазами
и улыбнулись друг другу;
мне стало интересно, о чём он подумал,
глядя на меня

Lvovsky was going down and I was going up
I was chewing gum
and at the moment
we saw each other
I was blowing
a giant bubble;

our eyes met
and we smiled at one another;
I was curious what he thought
looking at me

Kukulin describes Medvedev's characteristic style, evident in this poem, as "long free verse with an abundance of enumerative constructions and an energetic, at the same time almost breathless, intonation."[43] These long digressive poems experiment through their subject matter, lexicon, and very willingness to be prosaic: ruminations on cheap pâté merge with discussions of political theory. The form still felt atypical for Russian poetry: indeed, Mikhail Gronas argues that while free verse in Russian is "represented among the younger poets who became known in the 1990s and 2000s . . . such as Kirill Medvedev, Stanislav L'vovsky, Aleksandr Anashevich, Andrey Sen-Sen'kov, and Dmitry Kuz'min," the vast majority of contemporary Russian poetry is still written in rhyme and meter.[44] But it is Skidan who identified Medvedev's form as locally politically charged, drawing a line of continuity with more radical, alternative Russian traditions while stressing Medvedev's humanizing, comradely innovation: "Using free verse, like Brener and Magutin before him, which had until then been in the Russian context mostly an elite form, a form of social escapism and / or sabotage, Medvedev equally turns to 'diaristic,' intimate utterance. . . . He is more human, more democratic, more normal."[45] What is surprising formally to Skidan is the absorption of an earlier, more marked technique into a poetics of the present everyday—as if lived reality had caught up to experimental form.

Long, digressive free verse is far more typical of American poetry after the 1970s than of Russian verse, as Medvedev's own genealogical ruminations are quick to point out. In "Weak Narrativity: The Case of Avant-Garde Poetry," Brian McHale traces the distinctive formation of a rambling, "weak" narrative structure in contemporary English-language poetry and reads it as a response to modernist lyricism: "Postmodernists recoil from the modernist recoil. But of course it is too late now to return naively to premodernist forms of narrative poetry. Instead, postmodern poets resort to various strategies of having their cake and eating it too, of telling stories without committing themselves to the master-narratives wherein such stories are inscribed. . . . An alternative strategy, one that is harder to describe, seems to evoke narrative forms of coherence without fully submitting to them."[46] The main narrative may be weakened and deferred through various disruptive strategies, incorporating "a proliferation of 'minor' narrative genres: anecdotes, gossip and hearsay, jokes, dream narratives, ekphrases of paintings with a narrative content."[47] Weak narrativity emphasizes that these stories are told "poorly," evoking narrative coherence while undermining it through a wide range of formal and discursive strategies. The plot goes on, but it can only do so visibly accompanied by the writer's self-doubt.

McHale's weak narrativity offers a tantalizing aesthetic counterpart to the weak heroism Medvedev deems necessary in contemporary political activism: clearly, both emerge scathed from a postmodernist horizon. While Medvedev's poetry diverges from McHale's description by virtue of an explicitly charged contextual immediacy and unflinching political clarity (written, after all, twenty years of global trauma later than some of the works McHale analyzes), the common features offer a backdrop against which to read Medvedev's early works. The poet begins by undermining confidence in his own voice, technique, and unique subjectivity—and from there, begins to search for the political truth behind his experiences. The poetic "I" never vanishes from Medvedev's poetry, unlike in the works of some of his friends and collaborators (Golynko and Chukhrov in particular). Some subject material always remains, beyond each subjectivizing removal and (failed) identification.

Catching himself after a series of digressions, Medvedev writes:

этот текст должен был быть посвящён проблеме общения
и центром его композиции должен был стать пузырь
но потом всё как-то сдвинулось
и перемешалось

this text should be dedicated to the problem of communication
and the core of this composition should have been the bubble
but everything shifted somehow
and got mixed up

The giant chewing-gum bubble returns unexpectedly as the forgotten secret heart of the poem, a center that refuses to hold. Something bigger still, an invisible force, keeps the two poets apart and breaks down the possibility of human communication. Medvedev guesses what Lvovsky may have been thinking about: the gossip spread about Medvedev online, murmurs that Lvovsky nobly tried to shut down. Clearly, the quality of Medvedev's verse was the subject of discussion, but look how he chooses to express it:

[. . .] *когда медведев был юн,*
то его отец продал свою огромную библиотеку
и мальчик остался
без регулярного образования
и без знания истории
русского верлибра

[. . .] *when medvedev was young*
his father sold off his huge collection of books
and the boy was left
without a good education
without an awareness of the
history of russian free verse

Italics set off the reported or imagined trolling. The gambler father is a recurring trope; the lost inheritance, in this instance, is a library of Russian literature.

Medvedev's intelligentsia roots run deep and form an important, if ambivalently valenced part of his literary autobiography. His early LiveJournal blog, zoltan-partosh.livejournal.ru, took its name from Medvedev's great-grandfather, a Hungarian poet, translator, pediatrician, and dedicated communist who fled to the Soviet Union in 1919 after the Hungarian revolution was quelled. Partosh was briefly arrested and then released during the purges of the 1930s: none other than György Lukács wrote a letter vouching for him. Kirill's father, Feliks Medvedev, was in turn a popular perestroika-era journalist: in 1987, "amid a media blackout, he courageously announced at the Soviet Union of Writers in Moscow that Brodsky had won the Nobel Prize. . . . a cheer went up through the building."[48] But Kirill looks over the heads of recent generations to claim his great-grandfather's as his most relevant legacy. The youngest literary Medvedev indeed views Brodsky as the most exceptional yet paradigmatic example of the fathers' generation's shaky intelligentsia ideals. Brodsky, he writes, "had an enormous influence on the literary scene from his earliest poetic experiments, and was subsequently nominated by a large and in its own way influential intellectual milieu for the poetic representation of its own values. . . . As far as I'm concerned, a person like that cannot be a private citizen."[49]

Oedipal tensions echo in both poetic and biological genealogies. According to Medvedev fils, he and his mother lived in relative poverty due to the father's gambling. In a perfect metaphor for generational ressentiment, the legacy has been gambled away by the fathers, performative *intelligents* and lapsed idealists.

> The '90s-era Russian liberal intelligentsia had one supreme goal. It wanted to catch up to its Western counterparts, acquiring and digesting the works of postwar Western culture that the Soviet Union had suppressed, and it wanted the modernist heritage from the first half of the Russian century (Akhmatova, Nabokov, etc.) returned to its rightful place. From there it hoped to create a truly "competitive" national culture and ideology. But once it had received . . . its cultural inheritance, the liberal intelligentsia refused to evolve. It continued to debate questions that had been solved long ago, like whether you should consider Malevich's "Black Square" art, and so forth. . . . Regressiveness, provincial ambitions, and a parochial vision of the world ruled the day. What never emerged was a class of intellectuals—that is, people who see their duty in a disengaged critique of Authority, in a non-identification with any official discourse.[50]

This passage sketches the stagnation of one generation and outlines the program for another and is entirely illustrated through examples of cultural inheritance. Medvedev names iconic names—Akhmatova, Nabokov—identified explicitly as Russia's modernist heritage. When he brings up Malevich in the next breath, he highlights the ignorance with which the old debates provoked by the historical avant-garde are relegated to facile, oblivious discussions (could a child have painted better?).

In place of the missing giant collection of books (the second "huge" in the poem; for the huge bubble blocking the narrator's ability to communicate

with his fellow poet might as well be the lost library of literary precursors),
we have more genealogical signposts:

и дело тут конечно не в том что я например не представляю
   себя
НЕ ПРЕДСТАВЛЯЮ СЕБЯ
МАЯКОВСКИМ
БОЛЬШИМ СИЛЬНЫМ ЗВЕРЕМ
ЗАТРАВЛЕННЫМ МЕЛКОТРАВЧАТЫМИ
СОВРЕМЕННИКАМИ

and the issue here isn't that I, for example, imagine I am
IMAGINE I AM
MAYAKOVSKY
BIG POWERFUL BEAST
NAGGED AT BY MY PATHETIC
CONTEMPORARIES

Just as the poet claims he does not pretend or imagine himself to be Mayakovsky, he evidently, if self-mockingly, begins to do just that, in five unmistakably central lines of capital letters.

Poetry, far more than the visual arts, remains inseparable from its linguistic
medium and cultural context. While Medvedev does not often describe himself as avant-garde, on occasion the term bursts out of him. He uses *poet* and
avant-gardist interchangeably in one passage: "I am a poet. And we poets do
not want to be victims of history, we do not want to be dissidents, the very
thought depresses us, we are talented, we are avant-gardists, we want to be
that which no one has ever been before."[51] Elsewhere he uses the term *vanguard* historically, as in another passionate defense of Mayakovsky for the
Chto delat'? newspaper:

We are against determinism: we know that history is not foreordained,
that it could have turned out differently. And if we assume even a little
that the fate of the Revolution could have been different, then we understand Mayakovsky's fate was determined not by his choice (the only

choice worthy of man and poet like himself), but by the fact that the
Party in the end was transformed from a vanguard into an obstacle to
social revolution in our country. It's another matter to what degree Mayakovsky's own position was capable of impacting the overall political
dynamic. Given the example of Victor Serge, who wholly associated
himself with the Revolution and worked for it but nevertheless (or rather,
precisely for this reason) criticized various aspects of Bolshevik policy
and Party life, we can say that, yes, it was possible to fight for the Revolution and thus fight for one's poetry and for one's life.[52]

This reading too sets up Mayakovsky as the quintessential example of revolutionary poet, matched only by "dissident among dissidents" Serge, and offers yet another manifesto by proxy for Medvedev's own revived avant-garde
project.[53]

Chris Cumming notes that Medvedev's poetry draws on multiple traditions:
"American free-verse poetry from Whitman through Bukowski"; diverse leftist
writers across Europe; and a lesser-known Russian tradition that, in his words,
"combines absurdist art with an aesthetic that's similar to punk rock. This is a
tradition that stretches from the Oberiu group of the 1920s to artists and activists like Edward Limonov, Alexander Brener, and Sergei Kuryokhin (he of the
famous pseudoscientific proof that Lenin was a mushroom) who flourished
in the '80s and '90s, and is now represented by groups like Voina and Pussy
Riot."[54] I would emphasize the avid, hungry attention to recurrent waves of
Russian avant-garde poetry, which indeed fed all the more notorious figures
Cumming mentions. Medvedev's poetic lineage stems from revolutionary avant-
garde poets; the Soviet-era avant-gardes; nonconformists and unofficial poetry
throughout the Soviet period; and the Conceptualist artist-poets who brought
contemporary performance and art theory into Russian verse. And now Medvedev, like other poets of his generation, faces the question of what next, after
Conceptualism (and more generally, Russian postmodernism)?[55]

Medvedev is unequivocal about the need to move forward after ingesting
the best of the past. He finds in Prigov another poetic father, naming him as
one of the great postwar poets, along with Brodsky and Vysotsky, in an unusual trinity: "These are three genuine, immortal faces of the anti-Soviet discourse—the intellectual-critical, the intelligentsia, and the democratic."[56]
Medvedev rejects Brodsky but tries on the mantle of both Prigov and Vysotsky

in his dual roles of poet and modern bard. What he finds in the Conceptual-ists is a clear-sighted intellectualism, missing in his own era of ascending "new sincerity."[57] Distancing himself from what he also terms the *new emo-tionalism,* Medvedev suggests that such discourse rejects not only the worst aspects of postmodernism ("elitist jargon and its opposition to grand narra-tives and global concepts") but also the best: critical engagement and sophis-ticated thought.[58] Indeed, a decade before populism and its discontents swept popular and academic discourse alike as *the* political and aesthetic problem of the twenty-first century, Medvedev identified uneasy family resemblances between aesthetic tendencies attributed both to antifa and to the other side. If new sincerity is the aesthetic wing of new fascism, as he fears, avant-garde po-etics must include a marker of distinction from right populism and must fight to establish a starting point for interrogating and expanding on those differences: namely, Marxist theory.

For poetic models of how to look back to move forward, Medvedev in-evitably returns to the enormous (looted, embezzled, now fortunately en-tirely if illegally online) library of Russian literature. He identifies Vsevolod Nekrasov (1934–2009) as another landmark of Russian poetry who "paradox-ically combines uncompromising aesthetics and a unique, deep demo-cratism."[59] Medvedev suggests Nekrasov teaches us how to rejuvenate and vivify by drawing from the past: "Nekrasov looks for what is alive in everyday life and in everyday speech. . . . That's how he always explained and excused his love not only for the early Soviet Mayakovsky, Khlebnikov, Mandelstam, but also for the late Soviet 'official' contemporaries."[60] By looking at example after example, Medvedev attempts to repeat the move for a younger genera-tion, simultaneously curating a countercanon and exploring the new vistas it opens.

The group Arkady Kots also regularly performs the poetry of controver-sial actionist Alexander Brener, forerunner to the likes of Voina, Pussy Riot, and Petr Pavlensky, among others. Reading Brener's brutal performances as a total reaction to the "collapse and degradation of the Russian intelligentsia," Medvedev explains his generation's attraction to a figure who "turned him-self into a ticking, internal time bomb":

Finding himself face to face with a situation in which the poetic word had exhausted all its force—in the West naturally, because of new technologies of entertainment and a powerful critique of logocentrism; in Russia unnaturally, because of the violent archaization of the Russian literary language under the Soviets—Brener announced his utter creative impotence in advance and began to practice direct, radical actions. To protest the war in Chechnya he went into Red Square with boxing gloves, to challenge Boris Yeltsin to fight him; to protest the commercialization of Russian revolutionary art he spray-painted a giant green dollar sign on a Malevich in the Stedelijk Museum in Amsterdam, for which he received a six-month sentence in a Dutch jail.[61]

Brener's actions bring to the surface the violent desire to reclaim and reradicalize a declawed Russian avant-garde artifact that had been utterly absorbed by the institutions of the international art world. At this point, any new Russian avant-garde must reclaim its past not only through but also *from* the mediation of Western art and theory. While there is little in common on the surface between Brener's performatively masculine violence and Medvedev's warmer, feminist and LGBTQ+ supporting persona (again, in Skidan's words, Medvedev is "more human, more democratic, more normal" than much of the preceding avant-garde tradition), Medvedev recognizes the power of Brener's quite literal attack on art as institution.

Militant Aesthetics and Political Violence

After years of international protest, and after the unexpected success of his publishing house and the journal *[Translit]*, Medvedev returned to poetry nearly a decade after his first gestures of poetic refusal. His style had changed with the times: the newer work is shorter, to the point, sure-footed even on dangerous ground. One such poem, "On the way to defend the forest..." (2011), directly addresses the ambiguities and ambivalence inherent in resuming the Russian avant-garde project after the historical disappointments of state socialism and the collapse of the Soviet Union.[62] Written about the real protests over the planned highway construction through the heart of the Khimki forest, "On the way to defend the forest..." marks one of Medvedev's spontaneous returns to poetry. It moreover literalizes the metaphor at the heart of my inquiry: the avant-garde, with all its military etymological origins.

In this poem, a smaller group of activists quite literally moves in advance of a larger force. Initially, we expect this bunch of "student-pacifists, / useless intellectuals and local pensioners" (studentov-patsifistov, / propashchikh intelligentov i mestnykh pensionerov) to be no match for the OMON riot police sent out against them. With all the cinematic logic of a spaghetti western—or of a Quentin Tarantino film—a machine gun appears in the midst of our heroes and fells the OMON "like the trees of Khimki forest" (kak podrublennye derev'ia Khimkinskogo lesa). The unlikely victors gaze at the pile of bodies and discuss the relative degree of bloodshed vis-à-vis the October revolution over a little vodka. As they toast in the hope, this time,

> полиция и армия
> перешли на сторону народа,
> то есть на нашу сторону,

> for the police and the army
> to come over to the side of the people,
> that is to say our side,

at that very moment they see

> в виде бойцов ОМОНА
> одетых в камуфляж цвета свежего леса
> к нам идет подкрепление.

> dressed up as OMON fighters
> in camouflage suits the color of the forest,
> our reinforcements were on their way.

At first, the short piece reads as wish fulfillment and revenge fantasy. In the summer of 2010, Medvedev joined Evgeniia Chirikova and other eco-activists in the Khimki protests. Violence did indeed erupt—but in a more typical turn of events, the activists were attacked and beaten by neofascist youth. Not unlike Tarantino in recent projects, we might conclude, Medvedev reimagines history in favor of the victims and reallocates the weaponry.[63] However, despite seemingly firmly drawn battle lines, the poem is really about disconcerting ambiguities and abrupt reversals. The narrator first muses on the "old idea" (staruiu ideiu) that weapons signify powerlessness. The psychoanalytic reading is too close to the surface to need much pointing out; the word "powerlessness" (bessiliie) repeats four times in the first stanza, as does the phallic "weapon" (oruzhie). In as many as six instances, one of the two neuter nouns is the last of the line. The effect is intensely repetitive, lexically ascetic, and oddly but compulsively rhythmic for free verse. The narrator's first idea is followed by a "very earthly and real feeling of powerlessness" (vpolne zemnogo chelovecheskogo bessiliia) when he sees the OMON. Yet another borrowed idea from a more combative theoretical text reverses the earlier stance. Weapons, the poet "thought" (podumal; the first stanza takes place almost entirely in his thoughts), would allow for great philosophizing about pacifism. Yet he is already able to philosophize—he can only philosophize—even without weapons and in the face of the approaching OMON.

Or is he weaponless? "And then suddenly from this apex of our powerlessness a weapon appeared" (i vdrug v etoi vysshei tochke nashego bessiliia poiavilos' oruzhie): a weapon appears born of thought and theory, even as it physically parts "our side," that is, the side of the student-pacifists, fallen intellectuals, and pensioners. A more interesting inversion still flips the two factions. They (i.e., we) who have come to defend the forest cut down the police like trees. And in the last line, when reinforcements arrive in the guise of more OMON, it is hardly clear which side they are coming to join. Translator Keith Gessen clarifies and interprets by assigning these reinforcements a possessive pronoun in English, "*our* reinforcements were on their way." The original, however, gives the spare and more ambiguous "toward us move reinforcements" (k nam idet podkreplenie). Has the toast come true, just like that, and the police come over to the side of the people, "that is to say," as Medvedev adds with a good dose of self-irony, "to our side" (to est' na nashu storonu)? Or have the defenders of the forest become indistinguishable from the troops sent out against them? Were they the vanguard of a revolution to come, one that will be bigger than October? (The narrator claims: "There were fewer people killed during the October Revolution than there were today" [Vo vremia oktiabr'skoi revoliutsii bylo ubito men'she narodu, chem segodnia].) Or have the idealistic activists been absorbed into the forces against which they made a stand, "our side" lost in the disguise of camouflage suits the color of fresh trees? The moment the machine gun appears, enemy bodies metonymically replace the endangered trees.

Encoded in this terse and, compared with Medvedev's earlier work, narratively linear poem, we glimpse all the central paradoxes: the tangle of thorns around an avant-garde that trails behind (failed) revolution; the questionable possibility of a stand against dominant institutions in the face of an all-assimilating culture industry; and the disturbing proximity of the other side. The military metaphor dances on the surface, tangible; and the poem betrays and elicits mixed emotions over the exposed violence of the utopian vision. It is no coincidence that one of the first Western Marxists Medvedev chose to translate for his press was Pasolini, who famously and unpopularly pointed out the central irony in the 1968 clashes between Italian student protestors and the police: the long-haired leftists fighting for social justice were for the most part children of well-educated middle- or upper-middle-class families and brought up in relative comfort and affluence, whereas the short-haired police who met them with batons actually came from the working class.[64] In 2010s Russia, with the clichéd divide between sophisticated, cosmopolitan, and digitally savvy Moscow and the rest of the country only growing in the popular imagination, Pasolini's observation might seem cuttingly apropos.

In the post-Soviet context, more so even perhaps than anywhere else, "neo"-avant-gardes can all too easily read as farce; as aftershocks of the misspent revolutionary impulse of the twentieth century, a priori discredited by the violent disappointments of state socialism.[65] Moreover, the dominant and growing strain of radicalism in post-Soviet Russia has been right populism, not inclusive democratic socialism. Concerns over the distinction manifest themselves across Medvedev's oeuvre, openly in essays like "My Fascism," and in poetic imagery like the machine gun of the avant-garde that emerges so unexpectedly amid the pacifist protestors. Calling attention to these problems himself, Medvedev nevertheless rejects such vivisection of the population into insurmountable silos. Arguably, all of his poetry beginning with the 2014 collection *March on City Hall* has been dedicated to imagining alternatives to such divides and reaching out for new alliances. If the earlier poems, especially read retroactively, allow us to witness the politicization and radicalization of Kirill Medvedev as poetic subject, after 2012 he writes almost entirely in the service of new collectivities.

Medvedev's longing for broader audiences has always been about an aesthetics *of* and *for*—calling into being, conjuring—a new political subject. But what does leftist populism look like in Russian arts today? The restrictions placed by the Russian state on its entertainment industries make it nearly impossible for any serious critique of Russian society, let alone Marxist (unless defanged as "Russian classics"), to reach truly broad audiences. Capital-intensive cultural fields such as television or cinema remain far more difficult—and dangerous—to infiltrate. When anti-elitist, anticorruption themes do erupt, their tendencies toward a populism "of the Russian people" easily slide from left to right in the hands of less politically grounded cultural producers. The "new sincerity" that Medvedev often critiques—but with which he has also been associated—reads increasingly as the aesthetics of twenty-first-century populism. For example, the filmmaker Iurii Bykov (whose early hits *The Major* in 2013 and *The Fool* in 2014 led audiences to place him as at least a vaguely progressive, socially engaged millennial auteur) shocked left / liberal fans when he directed the first season of the nakedly nationalistic Channel 1 television show *Sleepers* (Spiashchie) in 2017.[66] Seduced by the so-called Crimean consensus and a growing sense of opposition between "the Russian people" and elite pro-Western liberal intelligentsia, Bykov—who clearly sees himself as a man of the people—represents the kind of populism so successfully co-opted by the state in recent years.[67] He is far from alone: the writers Zakhar Prilepin and Sergei Shargunov have followed a similar trajectory, from critique of Russia's socioeconomic realities and calls to revolt, to full identification with Russian foreign policy and active participation in the war in Donbas. When I asked Medvedev what he made of Bykov and the *Sleepers* scandal, he responded thoughtfully: "His sincere pain for the country is somehow combined with a wild fear of falling into liberal discourse. But he doesn't see a third option. . . . I tried to invite him a few years back to a festival of Art for Unions, but things didn't work out."[68]

In the post-Soviet world, where the "working class" has been economically restructured beyond recognition and defanged as a political category through decades of Soviet-era misuse and lasting liberal hostility, leftist artists today try to locate that subject in pluralistic (more inclusive, less patriarchal) visions of "the people."[69] All seven poets featured in this book reject dominant aesthetic modes like new sincerity and reactionary postmodernism. And if in some fundamental way, fascism (most broadly construed) cannot tolerate self-doubt, then poetry, as Medvedev understands it, should be the perfect site for struggle. As Medvedev puts it: "I know I need to write a poem when I see that no other medium will work for it. That is, I don't have a clear polemical argument that I can express in an article or essay. I can't express it through direct speech; I can't sing it in a song. Then there's nothing left but to write a poem."[70] Medvedev does not make it look easy: each poem is in some way about his fears of losing his footing on ethically treacherous ground, about finding himself in the wrong company, about failing to do enough. And yet, as a crucible for subjectivization and a laboratory for trying out new collectivities, poetry offers Medvedev a technology of cognition, of research—a way to reach toward what he cannot yet name.

In the early review "The End of the Cease-Fire," Skidan recognized in Medvedev's poetry a sign of political sea change and the revival of a long revolutionary lineage in arts and culture.[71] Eight years later, in his 2014 afterword to *March on City Hall,* Skidan tries again to summarize the significance of Kirill Medvedev for Russian poetry. Medvedev's "open, public, democratic" project, he writes, simply "shames those skeptics who do not believe in the feasibility of a project of self-critical, reflexive and simultaneously popular left culture. . . . Left poetry, and therefore politics, is not just possible, but is possible here and now, in the very heart of the heartless world."[72] By 2023 the courage of Medvedev's open and unwavering political position is self-evident if all the more remarkable.

Songs for the Working Class

Ultimately, Medvedev's poetics must be understood in the context of the dramatic anti-utopian positioning of twenty-first-century Russian culture. State and mainstream cultural establishments alike embraced the all-excusing "Stability" as their slogan, as if "not terrible" were the only goal and all alternative forms of social organization had been permanently discredited. Medvedev's montage of poetry, critique, and action pops against the backdrop of a society that has unlearned how to dream. The return of the repressed emerges as a shocking resumption of Russian avant-garde energies, conceptualized through the (reimagined, at times strangely appropriated) Western Marxist theory that had been, in turn, so inspired by the original Russian avant-gardes.[73] Is it really possible that poets might again serve as the vanguard, as early agents and symptoms of political change? Is it possible in Russia, of all places? In answer, Medvedev grabs whatever tools are available (Serge, Bukowski, Bloch, Pasolini, Occupy, and Black Lives Matter) and tries them on as Russian free verse to search for gaps and interstices where protest, opposition, and utopianism remain viable.

Interstices appear in all manner of new collaborative projects, independent presses, and journals. Medvedev's experiments have as much to do with occupying digital as physical spaces, in an attempt to imagine for our age something like Walter Benjamin's "Author as Producer." Indeed, Medvedev and his friends and collaborators, especially the [Translit] poets Arseniev and Osminkin as I will argue in subsequent chapters, reimagine poetry and politics for the age of digital reproduction. An early adapter to new technologies and to the platforms of Web 2.0 in particular, Medvedev has made prolific and contrarian use over the past two decades of—to give a partial list—his personal website, LiveJournal, commercial giant platforms like Facebook, VKontakte, and YouTube (see, for example, his YouTube channel "Allende"), as well as, for a while, Dmitrii Kuzmin's vavilon.ru and litkarta platforms. Poetry, perhaps more than any other literary form or genre, has been transformed by digital remediation and modes of dissemination in Russia and globally.[74] Via social media, politically engaged poetry is not only readily reposted but also quickly translated, illustrated, and amplified. Remediations lean on "universal languages": guitar poetry, video poetry, and physical performance in many cases reach broader and more diverse audiences than print forms.

Over the past decade, including during his hiatus from traditional publishing, new poems continued to appear on Medvedev's Facebook page, to be reposted, copied and pasted, published, and translated from there. Some have been made available on his website; and many found their way into the collection *March on City Hall*. I close this chapter with a look at one final poem, "The wife of an activist who died under strange circumstances . . ." (zhena aktivista, pogibshego pri nevyiasnennykh obstoiatel'stvakh), a text that first appeared, to my knowledge, on Medvedev's Facebook page. Only a few signs mark the untitled piece as poetry at all—although once recognized as such it was reprinted (without permission) and is now included in both Medvedev's Russian collection and in Gessen's translated anthology.[75] That the original post was a poem is indicated only by an introductory line of ">>>," a nod to amateurism and to the radical democratization of poetry online.

The poem begins with another set of oppositions, displacements, and conflations. The wife of a dead activist turns to our narrator for help—thus framing the entire text as a dialogue between a man and a woman, beginning with questions and ending with a lullaby. She asks what should be done, not for her own husband (for it is too late to help him by the first line of the poem) but for N, another jailed activist. Medvedev too is an activist who might be jailed, extending the chain of replaceable male bodies: in jail, as in the army, bodies are identical units of exchange. Something must be done: international campaigns are failing, so action must be taken locally. As in melodrama, time is of the essence, for an activist in jail is a ticking clock.

> Я говорю, что вижу два варианта—либо терпеливое
> строительство профсоюзов . . . а если нет тогда надо совсем
> жестко действовать, потому что никакие радикальные
> художества тут не помогут,
> не проймут этих козлов,
> да, говорит она, ну а что? террор?

> And I say, we have two choices. Either we patiently build the
> labor unions . . . or we have to do something really ugly
> because no radical art actions are going to help here,
> are going to get through.
> And she says, yes, and then what? We commit a terrorist act?

Terrorism is one possible child of the avant-garde. The "slow building" (terpelivoe stroitel'stvo) of a new culture, one labor union at a time, is another. If we follow inclusive definitions of the avant-garde as any minoritarian formation that challenges power, humble organizers might serve as another set of forerunners of the future—the human face of the new avant-garde.

> всё так медленно . . .
> сколько же еще времени потребуется,
> впрочем, наверное, это и правда единственный путь.

it's all
so slow . . .
How long will it take,
although, it's true, it's the only way.

The final lines seem to integrate poetry with the slow construction of a new world. Night comes, the lines shorten; somewhere warm, a pretty mother sings to a well-fed child:

спи спи мой сладкий
спи мой малышик

sleep sleep sleep my little one
sleep my baby child

[. . .]

спи крепче набирайся сил
много сил потребуется
храбрые крепкие мужественные бойцы будут нужны рабочему
    классу
тяжелые впереди времена

sleep tighter my little one
gather strength
you'll need lots of strength
the working class needs brave strong tough fighters
there are difficult times ahead

We end with poetry embedded in life-practice in an unexpected place and unexpected way, both tender and menacing, lightly ironic and deeply heart-felt—a militant lullaby. Poetry will return and in varied camouflage: as fight song, slogan, social media post, embodied theory, and internal intervention. Ultimately, in Medvedev's vision, creative workers can only empower themselves as political subjects by letting go of elite, individual status for the sake of collective struggle and collective labor. The avant-garde poet is but a harbinger of the future citizen.

Following Medvedev's career for over a decade, I have witnessed his return to poetry on his own terms, always in parallel to activism and political organization (he does not dismiss the possibility of running for office again), labor unions (support for long-distance truck drivers), and international leftist networks (LeftEast among others).[76] Medvedev has risked arrest and injury in shows of solidarity with LGBTQ+ and feminist activists, as with Ukrainian and Belarusian comrades. As he recounted to me in a 2015 interview, it was a breakthrough moment when his group Arkady Kots recorded an album commissioned by independent labor union organizers, titled simply "Songs for the Working Class." Laughing, Medvedev said that it was the best present he could have hoped for, because now he had the perfect answer for the cynics who inevitably ask him what use "the people" have for his work: they commissioned it.

What kind of Russian avant-garde legacy does Medvedev bring to the surface, for himself and for fellow thinkers and readers? As Medvedev phrased it in another interview, in the language with which I began this chapter:

> The goal of Russian art today must be to find new ways of interacting with politics, pushing off in part from the achievements of our 1920s avant-garde, and in part from the experience of the West in the 20th century, which was in many ways ignored or marginalized in the USSR. I don't believe that Russian history and culture have a special messianic mission, but I do know that from time to time the situation in Russia unfolds in such a way that it gives rise to a cultural-political leap, allowing us to "overtake" the West and present something genuinely new, or else to give our very specific (but at the same time universal) answer to a problem that the West has been wrestling with. That's what happened with the political form of the Soviets that came out of the 1905 Revolution and were later adopted by many revolutionary and social movements across the world. The same thing happened with the Russian avant-garde. It's possible that we're experiencing a similar situation right now.[77]

At the time of that interview, Medvedev was still fresh from the optimistic moment of the 2011–2012 protests. The years since have seen that rush of hope supplanted by more difficult phases, by demoralization and the dissolution of once promising institutions and political organizations. Even *[Translit]* has threatened to run out of steam. Its editorial board has scattered in the First Wave of twenty-first century emigration. Ever the futurist, Medvedev responds with seemingly unshaken political commitment and faith in the next generation. By the second half of the 2010s, as poet and critic Kirill Korchagin notes, the Russian cultural sphere had changed as irrevocably as the political terrain: the motivations for social engagement had grown self-evident and political art itself "respectable." But the first explanation Korchagin offers for the cultural change is that "a generation came to literature for whom Medvedev's poetry had the status of practically a classic. . . . Authors such as Galina Rymbu and Oksana Vsiakina already feel no need to justify why they write political poetry."[78] With the rise of young radical feminist initiatives and a flood of activity from Russia's "provincial" cities, reinforcements were indeed on their way.

2

The Avant-Garde Journal 2.0

PAVEL ARSENIEV AND *[TRANSLIT]*

*I*N A 2014 essay for the Poetry Foundation blog, David Lau asks, What has happened to avant-garde poetry? Experimental writng, he claims, has been "increasingly incorporated into neo-liberal capitalism's hegemonic public-private cultural institutions, with their known track record of normalizing and neutralizing even sometime political or artistic antagonists."[1] Running through the declawed forms and archives that today co-opt the legacies of the avant-garde, Lau concludes with a glimpse of hope for the future:

> But there is also some new song (that old bad thing) slouching out of the megacity today, a left *political* aesthetic development forged in the crucible of perilous circumstance. . . . Today another sort of avant-garde poetry is emerging, steeled in post-financial crisis anti-austerity struggles, like those in 2009 that preceded Occupy on UC campuses and other parts of the public sector, but one that is also global in reach, a "post-crisis poetics," as Brian Ang calls it: from Moscow's Kirill Medvedev, and the young Pavel Arseniev in Saint Petersburg's poetry and activist video scene.[2]

The very first examples of a new and living left poetics "forged" in crisis are Russian: Kirill Medvedev and, in the next breath, Pavel Arseniev. Unlike in the United States or Europe, reemergent avant-garde energies in Russia—in poetry, in particular—have hardly been co-opted by capitalist institutions or by a commercialized mainstream: the liberal elite, neoconservative, or openly fascistic agendas that Medvedev, Arseniev, and their circles attack either ignore the avant-garde entirely or treat it as (primarily visual) stylized historical kitsch. Radical Russian poetry, in other words, not only has the strength of an incomparable national tradition behind it but (for a moment at least) reads as comparatively independent and spontaneous.[3]

When other writers, artists, and critics talk about Arseniev, they usually begin with the alternative institutions for which he is largely responsible. Arseniev (born in Leningrad, 1986) has served as the backbone behind the journal *[Translit]* from its modest beginnings in 2006 to its broader legitimization with the Bely prize in 2012 and international presence today. In 2008 he organized the Street University in St. Petersburg to protest the forced closing of the European University.[4] In April 2020, he was lecturing in a new "*[Translit]* Laboratory" for the Covid-era initiative, the Moscow School of New Literature.[5] Arseniev's mission, as Molly Blasing summarizes in a review of his bilingual anthology *Reported Speech* (published in 2018 by New York's Cicada Press), appears to be "to continue the legacy of the Russian avant-garde and factographic movements of the 1920s" while simultaneously "working to fill a void left in the wake of the collapse of *samizdat* culture of the 1970s."[6] The surprisingly tenacious and well-received journal *[Translit]* serves both goals, while Arseniev's own writing, remediations, experiments, and provocations push the boundaries of Russian poetry to the edge of recognition. In 2017, for example, Arseniev sent in the following biographical note for a nomination to the Arkadii Dragomoshchenko prize for poets under twenty-seven: "Dora Vey is a poetry machine that uses the technology of spamdexing, based on Markov chain algorithms (doorway). . . . Dora Vey's poetry book is about to be published in the Kraft series. Dora lives and works in St. Petersburg."[7] While central to nearly every discussion of left-oriented poetry in contemporary Russia, Arseniev has consistently, as Sergei Zavialov notes, done "everything he could to distance himself from the role of 'poet'; from a Soviet-era tradition that sticks closely to the rules of pseudo-bourgeois intellectual snobbery."[8]

This chapter focuses on the journal at the heart of St. Petersburg and Moscow's poetic avant-garde revival and on Arseniev as the Breton (or Diaghilev) figure anchoring the group. Inspired by the Chto Delat collective, among the first independent and progressive Marxist initiatives in the post-Soviet art scene, Arseniev joined with Osminkin and other kindred spirits to found a poetry journal based on shared aesthetic and political convictions. Their desire to generate more thrilling and relevant poetry than was being published elsewhere in Russia merged with a pragmatic need to work through a library of global critical theory. While the first issue of *[Translit]* dates to 2006, according to Arseniev the journal found its collective voice and mission in 2008 with issue 4, known as the first political issue.[9] The release of that volume—which includes writing by Skidan, Osminkin, and Chukhrov, as well as Medvedev and Arseniev (Golynko was on the board of advisers; Rymbu would join some years later)—marks a watershed moment in the formation of a new Russian literary left. By issue 8 in 2010, the journal was publishing original dialogues with the likes of Giorgio Agamben.[10]

In an interview with Denis Larionov, Arseniev recalls the immediate backlash inspired by the journal's openly Marxist stance, such as the response of one critic who "threateningly waved his arms at a PEN center presentation, predicting our rapid demise and degradation."[11] Yet once *[Translit]* found its footing, Arseniev and his comrades hardly looked back. Sixteen years, twenty-five issues, and numerous side projects and offshoot publications later (including the Kraft poetry chapbook series, *démarche* critical theory editions, and Kraft_audio CD recordings of Roman Osminkin's techno-poetry and Keti Chukhrov's oratoria), *[Translit]* has won prestigious cultural awards and attracted an international fan base.[12] Its print run resides in archives and libraries including the Beinecke Rare Book and Manuscript Library at Yale University. From its inception, the journal has published leftist luminaries from around the world alongside original Russian-language essays and poetry, taking as its (eminently St. Petersburg) mission to bring the world to Russia and Russia to the world. The innovation, and break from previous generations, is the kind of "world culture" Arseniev and others longed to join. Drawing on the nearly infinite sources available in the 2000s, primarily via pirated "shadow" libraries and other online archives, the *[Translit]* group found tremendous productivity in intercutting local experimental poetics with an international canon of Marxist art and theory.[13] Many texts excerpted in *[Translit]* were otherwise unavailable in Russian, or else the new translations (of Jacques Rancière, Michel de Certeau, and others) and juxtapositions were intended to provoke hitherto missing applications and debates. Indeed, the theoretical side of the project threatened to eclipse the poetry: Arseniev reports, "I was very upset about this until I came across an interview with

Lyn Hejinian, in which she says that she 'found that when we engaged in theory, we were more stimulated . . . than when we were writing poems.'"[14] With Hejinian's reassurance that they were in good company, the group forged ahead.

They borrowed from other postsocialist artists like Artur Żmijewski as readily as from West European Marxist philosophers and left-leaning American poets: the last were indeed introduced into Russian verse through the efforts of Arkadii Dragomoshchenko (Skidan's most important mentor and, more briefly, Arseniev's as well) and his creative exchanges with Hejinian.[15] As if to make the genealogy even harder to miss, Osminkin and Arseniev, founding editors of [Translit], met in Dragomoshchenko's last home seminar—making them something like the literary grandchildren of the most generative love affair between the American L=A=N=G=U=A=G=E school and the Leningrad underground. We accordingly see elements of discourse poetry, found fragments of language, and other globally familiar poetic techniques reflected in their work: the preformed locally performed, as it were. As Arseniev explains, "Issue No. 13, called the 'School of Language,' almost entirely consists of translated texts—both analytical and poetic—by representatives of the English-language 'language school,' with whom we were able not only to catch up but also to establish a dialogue in real time. . . . I also entered into correspondence with Charles [Bernstein], who is keenly interested in our work, including (due to old publishing habits) our production process, checking, probably, whether we were less independent and self-organized than what he and Bruce Andrews did with the journal L=A=N=G=U=A=G=E."[16] Arseniev is quick to enumerate the connections between [Translit] and L=A=N=G=U=A=G=E, including direct collaboration as well as inspiration for the Kraft and démarche series. The language of "catching up" is also telling: Arseniev means not to imitate but to quickly absorb older international models, all the while producing a poetics perhaps less distinctively Russian than specific to the ever-bohemian city of St. Petersburg.

A crucial part of the appeal of [Translit] lies in its inseparability from its city-palimpsest setting.[17] Skidan, to whom I turn in the next chapter, provided the journal a tangible link to the Leningrad underground. Skidan (born in 1965) bridges two eras: one under the aegis of late-Soviet counterculture and another defined by the generation that exploded into view in 2012. He witnessed the end of a civilization in the 1980s, disintegration in the 1990s, and crisis after crisis in the new century: he practically personifies the radicalization of the Leningrad underground from apolitical by principle (in defiance of the hypocrisies of the Soviet state) to actively hostile to global capitalism and its local nationalist formations. A father figure of sorts to Arseniev, Skidan cements the bond between Chto Delat and *[Translit]* as a foundational member of both collectives. If Chto Delat's most significant contribution to Russian culture is their recurrent unofficial School of Engaged Art—an on-ramp to artistic life for generations of younger artists—Arseniev and *[Translit]* might be considered their greatest success story.[18]

Alongside the print publications and related public events, the *[Translit]* blog and social media pages see weekly, even daily updates and showcase unpublishable multimedia content. Arseniev's work with the Laboratory of Poetic Actionism and other new media experiments combines digital forms with the familiar features of the infinitely adaptable avant-garde journal as platform and medium. If Medvedev's poetics of refusal were the first to catch the public eye, locally and globally, Arseniev's efforts via *[Translit]* and related publications, discussions, festivals, and on- and offline outreach have done the most to forge the connective tissue binding the seven individuals featured in this book (each in turn a central hub in a growing network that includes many other artists, curators, activists, translators, and scholars) into a distinctive cultural phenomenon. Medvedev's thrown gauntlet to the existing literary institutions of Putin's Russia sparked a new left Russian poetry, but Arseniev made it a movement.

*   *   *

MORE SO EVEN THAN THE REST of the *[Translit]* circle, Arseniev's own texts, creations, and collaborations are riddled with references to historical avant-gardes. Indeed, they primarily derive from such material as infinitely rearrangeable building blocks. As Kevin Platt notes, "Arseniev's own innovations frequently engage with and build on past traditions of politically committed poetry. In the Russian context, these include avant-gardists like the Futurist Vladimir Mayakovsky, the Productivist 'factographic' author Sergei Tretyakov, and late Soviet nonconformist authors like Vsevolod Nekrasov and Andrey Monastyrsky."[19] More so too than the others, Arseniev repeatedly probes the ironies inherent in his paradoxical position as avant-garde *post—*. He understands well that the avant-garde has been thoroughly co-opted—in the former Second World by Stalinism (or so Boris Groys has argued), and in the equally former First World by "the commercialization of modernism and its eventual politicization as a tool of Cold War politics."[20] Contemporary avant-gardes (returning to Mike Sell's definition, minoritarian formations that challenge "the routines, assumptions, hierarchies and / or legitimacy of existing political and / or cultural institutions") build on historical precursors with practices ranging from increasingly sophisticated conceptualism to direct action.[21] Like others of his generation, Arseniev must respond and differentiate himself from both the totalizing violence of early avant-gardes and the flattened horizon of seemingly infinitely expandable postmodernism. More overtly referential and "meta" than his friend and collaborator Medvedev (and less directly engaged in political organizing outside of the arts), Arseniev responds to the same sense of political and aesthetic entrapment by taking a different tack. As he puts it archly in the poem "Slightly Edited," in language reshuffled from critical descriptions of his work: "'The machine of irony,' surfacing in relation to my poetic texts, / blurs the tracks of the Soviet past with its gigantomania" ('Mashina ironii', vsplyvaiushchaia v otnoshenii moikh poeticheskikh tekstov, / sakrugliaet sledy sklonnogo k gigantomanii sovetskogo proshlogo).[22]

Arseniev's path forward might be summarized as resting on ingenious remediations of avant-garde material for a new political and technological era, via the alternative network created through *[Translit]*. The journal's motto, printed on the cover of every early issue, borrows Robert Frost's line in English: "The best way is always through."[23] The allusive title, in turn, with its enigmatic bracketing, suggests translation, transliteration, trans-sense, but also quite specifically "translit": informal romanizations of Cyrillic from earlier days of computing.[24] For Arseniev, a self-described Chomsky fanatic, that way "through" always refers to language itself, which he holds at a seemingly permanent distance and discovers anew each time as a profoundly alien object. Even Arseniev's own poetry, as *Reported Speech* made clear to international audiences, relies on the found language of others: "Its ethos," as Giuliano Vivaldi writes, "is often a documentary one, rescuing found footage, found speech and writing to offer what Kirill Medvedev calls a 'subversive materialist exploration' of reality in post-Soviet Russia."[25] Blasing suggests that Arseniev's strengths as an "editor, curator, DJ" allow him to use language from the streets, public transportation, police stations and court-rooms, social media, and nationalistic journalese alike to "dismantle the idea of poetry as narcissistic, individualistic self-expression and instead . . . to cap-ture and convey aspects of human social experience in the world through the multifaceted voices of the collective."[26] Arseniev's language games, both re-viewers recognize, are politically charged in form as well as content.

Arseniev's most famous line of poetry to date remains one of the most rec-ognized and remediated slogans of the 2011–2012 protest movement: "You don't even represent us / You can't even imagine us" (Vy nas dazhe ne pred-stavliaete), playing on the two meanings of the Russian verb *predstavliat'* (and itself a loose translation of the Spanish Los Indignados slogan, "No Nos Rep-resentan").[27] The line, emblazoned across a red banner, photographed and reproduced in galleries as well as online news, became a stand-in for the wit and youthful energy of the protests as a whole. The pun in Russian borders tantalizingly on the conceptual: you do not represent us politically, you cannot even imagine our generation; but words also fail to represent or be fully com-prehensible as meaning, they are deferred through an endless chain of signi-fiers, and even the tape font on cloth standing in for language grows strange and textured the more it is examined. And yet, the Magritte-like ("Ceci n'est pas une pipe"), poststructuralist, or Conceptualist-adjacent language game nevertheless reads as highly legible and politically meaningful in its partic-ular context. The slogan and its subsequent incarnations are representative of Arseniev's strategies as a poet, which have been called "simultaneously both highly political and highly formalist."[28]

As the striking and differently legitimizing combination of Bely prize and protest slogan fame suggests, Arseniev's work cuts straight to the relation-ship of aesthetics and politics in contemporary Russia. Arseniev's main tool, Platt suggests, "in overcoming the critical positions he refuses to accept (that politics in poetry is nothing more than a pose; that poetry is a poor tool for mobilization; that all political art is doomed to be co-opted) is to write po-etry about them, internalizing critique and incorporating it into a dialogic meditation on its own overcoming."[29] Why is such an intervention and rescue project even necessary, especially in Russia? What foreign readers might fail to grasp is that, despite the long tradition of political poetry envied and imitated by many nations, after the Soviet era political poetry came to be "derided

FIGURE 2.1 Pavel Arseniev's banner design in protest context, featured photo on *Colta.ru*.
PAVEL ARSENIEV.

as neither good poetry nor effective politics. Or it is simply denounced as insincere—a damning accusation both for poetry and politics."[30] Armed with a "machine of irony" and a shadow library of models, Arseniev rejects his era's fixation on sincerity as impoverishing and, worse, as reeking of a thoughtless, everyday fascism. His work is most powerful when it makes alternatives (e.g., confessional lyric poetry that takes the "rich inner world" of its liberal subject and categories like gender, sexuality, and nation as given) seem not only ridiculous but impossible, self-parody. Armed with wit, tenacity, a peculiar organizational genius, and an agent's eye for talent, Arseniev uses his own remediations and collective initiatives alike to try to reboot the political potential of a century of Russian literature. As he warns at every stage, he has no idea whether the effort is doomed a priori—but with such material on hand, he has to try.

The Avant-Garde Journal as Social Network

[Translit] is far from alone in rediscovering the avant-garde journal (or similar experimental literary periodical: little magazine, zine) as not only foundational for twentieth-century culture but fully adaptable to the global

present. The deceptively simple technology of the little magazine, Erik Bulson writes, "has lived a rich and varied life on five continents throughout the twentieth century, and it managed to do something that no book or network of books ever could. . . . Frederick Allen, who contributed to the first comprehensive history and bibliography on the subject of little magazines, estimated that the number of post-1912 writers cosponsored by the commercial book business was somewhere around 20 percent, leaving 80 percent to the little magazine start-ups. And this percentage, it should be added, only took account of the American titles."[31] The medium flourished in response to advances in technology and transportation that "enabled the formation of an increasingly interconnected (but not totalizing) global infrastructure" as well as to the geopolitical upheavals of the century: the form's very "littleness" reflects its budget, print runs, duration, and audiences—and nevertheless offers an astonishing alternative to hegemonic publishing industries, even today.[32] A growing number of critics, deeply interested in journals, magazines, and their more recent online incarnations, claim such periodicals as the enabling form (but also medium, platform, and network) behind the cultural achievements of global modernisms and avant-gardes.

If literary and art histories alike tend to tell individual stories—neatly delineated, narratable histories of generals—a shift in focus to the places of publication adds dimension, sound, and color. According to Suzanne Churchill and Adam McKible, literary critical practices typically engage in "strip-mining," extracting individual artists "from the heterogeneous terrain in which they first published . . . [to be] singled out as the elite geniuses of modernism," but what characterizes the little magazine is nearly always a radical emphasis on collective creativity.[33] As Mike Sell puts it, "The avant-garde group and journal provided the forum to develop, experiment with, and experience a performative conception of intellectual practice. The group . . . became itself the practical focus of transformative intellectual experimentation in which the theories imported from the social sciences played a crucial role."[34] A social network *avant la lettre,* the avant-garde journal derived cultural capital and political significance through the collectivities it brought into being.[35] Brent Hayes Edwards, in one powerful example, singles out the journals, their "translation practices—and transnational coverage," as central to the fabric of twentieth-century Black print culture. "Black periodicals," he writes, "were a threat above all because of the transnational and

FIGURE 2.2 *[Translit]* journal covers 8 and 21 and Pavel Arseniev's chapbook from the Kraft series, 2011. *[TRANSLIT]*.

anti-imperialist linkages and alliances they practiced."[36] Rebellion clings to the very form.

Old and new avant-garde journals alike try to slip through global economies of culture and commerce. Never part of a totalizing world system such as world literature or entirely of "the art world," historically, literary periodicals have always been either the work of "a small but dominant class of high-minded intellectuals and artists looking abroad for . . . alliances," or else that of a similar "but dominated class of intellectuals and artists reacting against a more localized political and social situation."[37] Inevitably, they turn toward voluntary collective labor and away from the book market: such projects, almost by definition, cannot turn a profit through sales. If we link the rise of the novel and fall of poetry in capitalist modernity to the far greater suitability of the former to sale (of the book as consumer object, produced in bulk), we have another explanation for why the experimental periodicals became the refuge of poetry, fueled by poetry.

While typically still produced in culturally powerful global capitals and inevitably embedded in the social totality of their eras, journals and magazines nevertheless provide

> an alternative model of the literary field that emerged during and after modernism, one that was *decommercialized, decapitalized, and decentered.* There was never a single city to monitor or regulate movement. . . . There was never any unified infrastructure between them, no international cadre of editors or translators or publishers with the power to regulate the flow of texts in every direction. And while it is true that individual writers and critics were blocked from some magazines and cities and embraced in others, the stakes were very low. Not only was there no capital involved in the little magazine world, but there was really no prestige either.[38]

The decentered and disconnected nature of the form explains as well why "world magazines" never really came into being: the medium was tightly bound to "local, regional, and national contexts and print cultures, which were, in turn, defined within and against international and transnational processes."[39] Even today, despite the seemingly centripetal forces of digitization and online dissemination, online journals and zines exist in a different field of cultural production than the global marketplace of books (by now virtually synonymous with one name: Amazon).

The inspirations behind the twenty-first-century St. Petersburg avant-garde journal *[Translit]* include the storied periodicals that forged the international twentieth-century avant-gardes, the local incarnations of *Avangard, LEF,* as well as Soviet-era samizdat such as *Syntaksis* and *A-ya.*[40] More recent additions and collaborating constellations include the *Chto Delat'?* newspaper and arguably the Polish journal *Krytyka polityczna.*[41] Like other post-Soviet-era publications, *[Translit]* publishes (at constant financial loss) work that does not need to curry favor with consumers or make it past elite, state-appointed or state-adjacent gatekeepers. To survive, the journal relies on the collective drive of its community, using the periodical's network potential to grow and reinforce locally rooted yet globally connected collectivities. *[Translit]* thus presents us with a Russian avant-garde / samizdat journal, now as then: experimental, self-published, reimagined for the twenty-first century, but still fundamentally similar to century-old models. Indeed, the beloved but digitally updated form could stand in for the larger mission of the new Russian literary left: picking up where dead poets were cut short, but mining the technological, political, and economic possibilities of the present.

According to Arseniev, the collective behind *[Translit]* consciously aims not only to reclaim local traditions (to try to revive them as they once were would be naive) but to write the next chapter of St. Petersburg's radical cultural history. He sees the steady stream of "critical, mostly leftist, theory" that the *kruzhok* imbibes as informing their practices in real time—and next to that theory stands a practice of pragmatic, collective decision-making. Nearly all of it is enabled by the platforms of Web 2.0: "The editing process of the journal (and in part the book series Kraft, Kraft_audio, and *démarche*) is governed by the editorial council, whose membership consists of a closed mailing list. . . . Of course, the whole big circle of *[Translit]* is formed via a group on Facebook, where we discuss candidates for publication and coordinate literary and artistic events in different cities."[42] Despite hovering permanently on the edge of bankruptcy, *[Translit]* editors manage to update the blog frequently on the major social networks, broadcasting a wide variety of information about the journal and its participants, as well as kindred international efforts, publications, and events of interest. Editorial board member Natalia Fedorova noted in an interview that, as she was based for a time in the United States, the journal's online resources allowed her to remain enmeshed in a Russian-language community, serving as a "window to St. Petersburg."

If an earlier generation of online experimenters believed "internet art excluded local community practices," Arseniev and the *[Translit]* circle grasp what Warhol "understood so well . . . literary time doesn't begin once the computer screen is turned off, but continues throughout."[43] While the Kraft books and *[Translit]* journal appear in hard copy, most of the materials are readily found online: archived in PDF form on the *[Translit]* blog; reprinted on poets' individual websites; and often available via Facebook, VKontakte, and YouTube. Digital publication and dissemination shape every step of our interaction with this material: we search for it, read it, share it, and reference it online. Hard copies meanwhile provide a tangible focalizing point and make publications into events: print serves the purposes of collecting, gathering, fundraising, or signing, personalizing, and gift giving. On- and offline worlds interact with and necessitate one another to forge a new, pragmatic, and political poetics.

The fluid on- and offline existence of *[Translit]* puts the St. Petersburg project in line with many new periodicals proliferating around the globe, created by the same generation and often with similar politics—not least the Brooklyn journals *n+1* and *Jacobin*. But again, the Russian cultural context provides a unique and provocative backdrop. Just as post-Soviet computer virtuosos drew on late-Soviet tinkering culture and extraordinary public education in mathematics to flourish around the world (as has been made notorious by recurring Russian hacker scandals), so too were the literati creative and quick to adapt to online possibilities. The *[Translit]* blog thus begs comparison not only with contemporary international models but with a very early and prolific scene in Russian online poetry. Russian poets proved early adapters since the 1990s, when "authors' blogs, internet-based magazines and portals such as the *Vavilon.ru* archive of contemporary poetry, *The Literary Map of Russia, OpenSpace.ru, Colta.ru,*" and others provided "venues for constant everyday interaction between writers and their readers, a place for publication of both the newest texts and critical reflection on them."[44] The most important precursor, Vavilon.ru, began as a poetry anthology that Dmitry Kuzmin developed into a web-based publication, "dramatically expanding both its reach, its frequency of publication, and its

archival potential" as early as 1997.[45] The curated encyclopedia presented by
Vavilon.ru or its successor, New Literary Map of Russia (launched in 2007),
in turn pops against the larger, anarchic, at times disturbing backdrop of
free web poetry. Medvedev has called web poetry a "concentrated portrait
of the Russian unconscious, a collection of its most painful neuroses," that
sometimes "manifests itself as an inert, conservative, and very aggressive mass."[46]
Parts indeed have congealed into nationalistic online platforms, resting on
carefully curated selections from the Russian classics alongside recent material responding with patriotic fervor to the annexation of Crimea or other
current events.[47]

Such a politically polarized background complicates matters for the new
Russian literary left. While Arseniev, Osminkin, and Rymbu especially read
as "digital natives," all of the poets of the [Translit] circle recognize Web 2.0
(like the Russian state, for that matter, or Trump's America) as enemy-
controlled terrain. By the second decade of the twenty-first century, no one
misses the ironies of using Facebook to organize anticapitalist protests or of
turning to Amazon to preorder the latest Verso book. The sharpest techno-
pessimist thinkers have convincingly argued that the so-called technological
revolution was less revolution than a coup, ushering in the reign of a new and
incomprehensibly powerful oligarchy. Jonathan Crary leads a swelling chorus
of critical voices when he argues in 24 / 7: Late Capitalism and the Ends of
Sleep that the vast majority of digital usage is based entirely in consumption,
and that only a small (he would add, negligible) minority of savvy producers
make use of online possibilities in "progressive" ways—say, for some form of
activism or genuinely original cultural experimentation.[48]

While digitization certainly enables wider circulation than ever before, the
historical avant-garde journal in its physical format provided an alternative
model of the literary field that was easily dispersed and virtually profitless.
Bulson worries that the age of "digilittle" magazine brings with it something
else entirely: "In the past decade or so, libraries, universities, and museums
have begun to digitize their collections, making little magazines more accessible, and indeed less ephemeral, than ever before. Because of this aggressive
remediation phase, the little magazine is beginning to assume a shape that
not even Marinetti or his fellow Futurists could have imagined."[49] Moreover,
funding for such projects comes from academic and government institutions
that bring their own interests, selections, and access limitations to the table:

"The more deeply embedded in the institution a subject or field becomes, the less open it is to unorthodoxy, opposition, and surprise."[50]

More generally, it is striking to follow the dramatic and global turn from techno-optimism—as late as 2011, when many appeared to believe that social media were fueling global revolutions—to the techno-pessimism that followed 2016 and Brexit, the US and Russian presidential elections, and subsequent accusations of election tampering and filter bubbling. Amid the last decade's surge of international protest, BBC journalist Paul Mason wrote an enthusiastic overview of the functionalities of social media platforms for contemporary activists: "Facebook is used to form groups, covert and overt—in order to establish . . . strong but flexible connections. Twitter is used for real-time *organization* and news dissemination, bypassing the cumbersome 'news-gathering' operations of the mainstream media. YouTube and the Twitter-linked photographic sites—Yfrog, Flickr and Twitpic—are used to provide instant evidence of the claims being made."[51] In the space of just five years, we moved from imagining the internet as making direct democracy an imaginable possibility (not to say inevitability) to wondering whether democracy can survive the internet age. But while the complicity and embeddedness of social media platforms within the apparatus of power and economic domination is by now old news, Mason wasn't wrong: artists and activists around the world continue to use the tools available to their own ends—sometimes remarkably effectively. Online platforms cannot be written out of the stories of protest culture, at this point. Even allowing for such a stark divide between consumers and producers as Crary suggests (which in practice we know to vary over time and shades of gray), minoritarian cultural formations continue to imagine alternative modes of social organization and push back against a predetermined future, online as well as in person. Here, in other words, is another space open for avant-garde practices to anticipate future networks and internet usage outside of cognitive (or total, or disaster) capitalism.

All of the poets studied in this book have evolved highly self-aware praxes for the age of digital reproduction. Nearly all try to actively lay claim to their own online presentation and digital archives—something Arseniev does especially masterfully: Russian poetry merges with other forms, media, and languages through digital remediation, collective translation, and immediate dissemination. I return to some of the possibilities and limitations of online avant-gardes in Chapter 5 with Osminkin's work but will offer a few brief examples of *[Translit]* poetics online as illustrative of the group's aesthetic use of social media (several use the same platforms directly for political organizing in the more straightforward ways outlined by Mason and others). Different kinds of work, all linked under the aegis of the journal and its central collective, combine image and text across the major social media platforms. In one, Osminkin, alongside other playful Facebook posts in which he calls himself "master of the meme," posts a draft of the poem "a little class warfare" (nemnogo klassovoi bor'by) on his timeline on August 2, 2013. Later that day, he adds several more lines through the comment function, before returning to the text fragment on August 5 to add the chorus, and then to post a YouTube clip of himself singing the piece, accompanied by Medvedev on guitar, while walking the streets of Moscow. The clip was shot on the previous day and the words appear to be at least partly improvised. The next day, Osminkin adds them to the original posting. The final version of the poem (if it makes sense at all to think in such terms; rather, the text he later performs and sends on for translation as a poem) includes all the lines listed above, with a few minor textual and formatting changes.

Medvedev's video poetry on YouTube (reposted on VKontakte), in turn, tries a different approach. The remediated poem "3%," which Medvedev wrote in 2005, was montaged in collaboration with Iakov Kazhdan in 2010. A finished and previously published poem is put to images—less "illustrated" than expanded and recast for the new medium. The street setting and a car passing in slow motion hardly translate the poem's language into visual media, but instead invite us to contemplate the incomprehensible 3 percent of the poem even in this unremarkable scene—or so one potential reading might have it. The text is read in a neutral male tone (not Medvedev's own distinctive reading voice) and simultaneously presented in supertitle fragments, oddly resembling speed-reading teaching applications but to opposite effect. If Osminkin begins collaboratively, with multiple media, and ends with an Osminkin poem, Medvedev moves into online coauthorship to expand the life and reach of his earlier text.

Both cases, however, begin or end with a recognizable poem—something that resembles an abstract, Platonic ideal of a poetic text. The last example, one of Arseniev's video-poetry pieces, carefully does neither. In "A Translator's Annotations," Arseniev selects found language from Ludwig Wittgenstein's notebooks, translated into Russian, and picks out fragments that suit him in

FIGURE 2.3 Pavel Arseniev creates found poetry from a Russian translation of Wittgenstein's works. CHTO DELAT.

real time, "censoring" the rest with a thick black marker. The evocative work thus exposes the "poem" (or artwork, or performance) as always by another—indeed, by a receding chain of others—and incorporating violence, censorship, and betrayal in its composition. Notably, this work of found and performed poetry (discourse poetry, in terms established by the *L=A=N=G=U=A=G=E* school) can only be published in video format, here embedded in the *[Translit]* blog. What makes Arseniev's work distinctive too from most discourse poetry is that he does not begin with commercial or ideological texts that he exposes through manipulation, but rather with a text he considers central to his own canon of progressive, emancipatory intellectual thought. The added frame of digital remediation challenges our preconceived uses of the framing platform just as it does the manipulated content.

Ultimately, the poets of the *[Translit]* constellation maintain an active and creative presence online, even as they remain deeply skeptical of the neoliberal and surveillance potentialities inherent in Web 2.0 technologies. In Foucauldian terms, the location of resistance is the same as that of power: *[Translit]* frequently features essays critical of "evil media" even as many in the group push the boundaries of poetic remediation and online dissemination.[52] As the rich history that precedes their attempts would lead us to expect, the aesthetic experiments of Arseniev and other *[Translit]* poets are shaped by the collective work and network provided by the journal itself.

In Pursuit of Pragmatism

It is far from enough for contemporary leftist poetry to stop at experimental form or to ascribe to progressive political stances in its content. Instead, Arseniev argues in "The Pragmatic Paradox as a Means of Innovation in Contemporary Poetic Speech," radical texts should be "built on what can be called the *pragmatic paradox,* which gives a poem the properties of a speech event, a self-fulfilling prophecy, or an archive that unpacks itself. . . . This requires *(self-)critique of the utterance's ability,* included in its very production. . . . [*Such* texts] rebel, as it were, against being read in traditional institutional circumstances. Only texts that invent anew each time a pragmatic frame for their realization . . . have the right to be called experimentally poetic."[53] Arseniev looks to serial music, concrete poetry, and even 1990s-era code for a continuation of Sergei Tretyakov's "literature of fact" (*literatura fakta*) and Dziga Vertov's "film truth" (*Kino-Pravda*).[54] The great early Soviet contributions to world culture, he writes, aimed to apply dialectical montage to life itself by introducing "accidental material into the work, like pierced holes in a representational system."[55] So too now, the only practices that interest Arseniev are ones that fundamentally change—and challenge—the rules of the game. Moreover, they should be impossible to appropriate or assimilate, even on the level of structure and form: this, to Arseniev, is avant-garde. It is also nearly impossible to achieve, much less maintain.

Arseniev's own Kraft chapbook *Colorless Green Ideas Furiously Sleep* (2011) takes its title from Noam Chomsky's 1957 *Syntactic Structures,* where the phrase is offered as a textbook example of a sentence that is grammatically correct but semantically nonsensical.[56] Yet Arseniev's book opens with a poem that appears more political than formalist, suggesting the impossibility of trying to distinguish between the two modes in his work— or of ever trying to look at language separately from politics. "A Poem of Solidarity and Alienation" tells the story of the peaceful resolution after the forced closure of the (progressive, internationally oriented) European

University in St. Petersburg in 2008 (not for the last time).[57] At that time, the university was under attack ostensibly for fire code violations, but more believably for questioning Russian electoral law and for generally serving as a hotbed of political freethinking within the increasingly conservative state.

Возвращайтесь в аудитории,
они защищены от пожара.
Из искры, нет, не возгорится—
приняты все меры,
более-менее искренне.[58]

Return to your classrooms.
They are fireproof.
No, a spark will not set them ablaze.
All measures have been taken,
More or less earnestly.

The poem's opening stanza establishes the recurrent imperative refrain: an implicit "you all" (the second-person plural *vy*) are called back to the university's classrooms. The crisis has been averted, the school reopened, and the alleged fire code violation addressed. In a move familiar to the point of parody, Arseniev runs with the conceit of fire as revolutionary fervor; he also skips any expected critique of the state to challenge the academic community's willingness to play along in order to preserve an autonomous place from within which to (safely) critique the system. It is the university, not the oppressive state, that the poet takes on, and the self-justifying academic fear / hope that

[. . .] Ведь пожар в одной голове
всегда может перекинуться на другую.
И тогда полыхнет весь город.

[. . .] a fire in one head
Can always spread to another.
Then the whole town will go up in flames.

Meanwhile, we need safe, fireproof classrooms, just as the state demands:

> Только в аудиториях священное исследовательское
>   негодование
> можно будет без утечки направить
> на подробное описание всех нарушений и попраний.
> Состроить немой упрек системе.

> Only in the classroom can the researcher's righteous indignation
> Focus, without fear of brain drain, without fear of leaks,
> On a thick description of all violations and abuses of rights.
> To send the system a silent reproach.

The splendid facades of the university's architecture keep out such external "vexations" (nadsady) as outlined in a grim list of contemporary Russian horrors: "daily murders of ethnic minorities" (ezhednevny[e] ubiistv[a] natsmenov), fluctuating oil prices, homelessness, "the regime's truncheons" (dubin[ki] rezhima)—all of that "Centralized postmodernism" (tsentralizovannyi postmodernizm).

Like so much of the (reactionary, commercial, debased or actively dangerous) postmodernist culture Arseniev despises, the "generous liberal soul" (shirokaia liberalistskaia dusha) he imagines populating European University classrooms is performatively ready to question everything except its own complicity.

> Вы не хотите играть в подковерные игры,
> но вы оставляете нетронутым сам ковер
> и оставляете возможность вызвать вас на него.

> You don't want to join the fighting under the carpet.
> But you leave the carpet itself intact
> And the possibility you will be called on it.

> Возвращайтесь в аудитории,
> и вправду, не май-месяц.

> Return to your classrooms:
> This really is not the month of May.

The readily drawn contrast is between the safety of academic rebellion and what it would take to actually shake the system: from sweeping things under the carpet to challenging the ground the university, too, stands on, which in the next line is transformed into the location of exposure. It is not the month of May yet, citizens—one of the officially sanctioned times for political spectacle and empty shows of solidarity.

Arseniev's piece initially reads as a familiar leftist critique of liberal elites: rendered as Russian verse, it inevitably takes on literary and historically charged undertones. The spark (*iskra*) of the opening stanzas cannot but invoke Lenin's socialist émigré newspaper (*Iskra*, 1900–1903, run by Georgii Plekhanov and the Mensheviks until 1905). The recurrent imperative recalls the rhetorical constructions of a young Mayakovsky (e.g., in "And Could You?" [A vy mogli by?] of 1913). The entire text arguably echoes the "My University" section of Mayakovsky's *poema* "I Love" (Ia liubliu) of 1921–1922. Unlike a young Mayakovsky, however, Arseniev leaves one side of the political and aesthetic dichotomy blank: perhaps no clear distinction between bourgeois and revolutionary culture seems imaginable in the 2000s. If Mayakovsky explodes against his drab hypocritical strawmen with an ever-expanding, all-encompassing revolutionary "I," here there is no poetic subject at all, only a muted adjectival form of the first person presented in negation: "It is not my reproach, it is no one's reproach" (ne moi i nichei). The political position of the missing self remains ambiguous: while the plural "you all" is clearly guilty of rarified abstractions of rebellion, there is no contrastive "I" of poetry, or of the street—and no mention of the actual street university Arseniev started in real life.

The speaking subject is instead subsumed into the scene described, and poetry's role in the old binary of intellectual versus revolutionary remains suspect at best. Lines later, the phrase "raising our voice" (vozvyshaia svoi golos) again recalls Mayakovsky's "At the Top of My Lungs," ("Vo ves' golos," 1930). But while the language borrows from Russian revolutionary verse, the poem leans more toward Conceptualist play with the purposefully threadbare fire-fervor metaphor and the collapsed distinction between progressive intellectualism and repressive state. Vivaldi suggests that Arseniev's writing is indeed constructed around the contradictory desire to "break out of those fireproof, noise proof classrooms that the privatization of experience constructed in the 1990s" and the recognition that there is no longer any clear role for the poet outside such spaces.[59] (Arseniev, who publishes theoretical articles in Russian, English, and French, defended in 2021 a PhD in Switzerland. While savvy at navigating academia and academic interest in his projects, he remains vocal in his poetry about the desire to remain, as much as possible, on the outside.)[60]

Whither, then, the pragmatism to which Arseniev's critical prose so frequently returns? What does Tretyakov offer Arseniev that the more overtly Romantic Mayakovsky doesn't? In "Sergey Tretyakov between Literary Positivism and the Pragmatic Turn," Arseniev interrogates the legacy of the precursor who has most powerfully shaped his own ideas about the written word. The Literature of Fact (*literatura fakta*) occupies a privileged position for Arseniev, who frequently writes about the historical significance it held for Russian and Soviet literature: "Life was built from scratch, from the atomic level, and together with the new man a new language was created; a language which also had to be re-created at the atomic level. This language could not borrow either common phrases or idiomatic expressions from the previous bourgeois epoch, and it was crucial that it did not borrow techniques from fiction, as these were laden with obsolete ideology."[61] Arseniev identifies Tretyakov as the embodiment of the Russian avant-garde in literature, following a framework very close to Peter Bürger's and Walter Benjamin's: he defines the avant-garde mode as "self-criticism of the institution . . . that aims not at former styles, but at the very institution of art (as it has developed in its material apparatus of production and distribution, as well as in its prevailing practices of reception)."[62] In words that bleed into the language of his other essays and manifestos, Arseniev understands the battle cry of the avant-garde to be less for the "restoration of socially important content in literature, but the invention of a new functional modus: its new *pragmatics.*"[63]

What Arseniev finds revolutionary and beyond compare about the Literature of Fact is the unprecedented, if brief, sense of total possibility that that cultural moment represented: only when language "is immersed in praxis (especially directed towards socialist construction—according to the Literature of Fact), there is no rupture between language and reality."[64] Several of Arseniev's essays conclude with the Bürger-like suspicion that today, even if formally similar techniques periodically crop up in experimental literature, they cannot hope for a similarly direct impact on life. However, occasionally, as in the essay "Performative Knowledge" for the *Chto delat'?* newspaper in 2008, Arseniev offers a more cautiously optimistic, future-oriented vision (and his very productivity around *[Translit]* belies some of the pessimism expressed elsewhere). Beginning with J. L. Austin's definition of the performative utterance as a statement that not only describes but changes social reality, Arseniev concludes that forms of knowledge can be performative. Related to (and derived from) utterance but with the additional implication of accumulation over time (of information, skill, comprehension, collective memory), knowledge too can be "identical to action insofar as it alters reality."[65] In the heyday of the Soviet-era opposition, the paradigmatic form of ideologically charged, performative knowledge was the written word. Today, Arseniev is most interested in differently public and collective forms: by "performative," he clarifies that he means less "discourse that is aware of its own engagement" than "knowledge engaged in action, in the collective action of protest."[66] His own slogan-poem, "You don't even represent us," might serve as the best illustration of what he is after.

Moreover, Arseniev observes that performative forms long meaningless in Russia are once again gaining currency, linking his experiences of Putin-era protests to Austin's insights from the philosophy of language: "Nowadays . . . no one is forced to take part in demonstrations. This form is rising again from its discredited status, and politics might return to the street. This doesn't mean the current state of things is predisposed to a politics 'from below,' but only that the regime of social representation creates the structural possibility of such a politics."[67] Arseniev's task for his own poetry, broadly understood— as well as for the poetic practices that he curates, archives, and promotes through his startlingly prolific publishing and intellectual programming— is to probe the possibilities unexpectedly left open by state and capital and their seemingly pervasive apparatus. At the very least, avant-garde poetry, as a form of performative knowledge, must remain vigilant, and ready. A new poetics must marry pragmatics—the linguistic study of language in use— with inassimilable experimental forms.

Not (by Word) Alone

Skidan's seminal essay in issue 4 of *[Translit]* bore the provocative title "Poetry in the Age of Total Communication." As if in illustration, Arseniev published in the same issue a manifesto poem, not incidentally his "calling card," or *vizitka,* on the online platform "New Literary Map of Russia."[68]

Продается б / у Маяковский
на новой торговой площадке Рунета.

Рекламные ссылки.
Добавить.
Послать ссылку другу.
Найдутся все.
Неограниченный трафик.
Чем заняться в свободное время.
Картинки.
Еще.

A used Mayakovsky for sale
on a new site on the Russian web.

Advertising links.
Add to cart.
Email this link to a friend.
Everything is searchable.
Unlimited traffic.
What to do in your free time.
Pictures.
More.[69]

As is typical of Arseniev's work, it is difficult to definitively identify "Mayakovsky for Sale" as either a poem or the textual component of a composite artwork. It is and has been both: "Mayakovsky for Sale" was published as a poem in *[Translit],* labeled "From the cycle *Ready-written*" (the latter term in English, highlighting $L=A=N=G=U=A=G=E$ influence). The corresponding video has been published online as an art piece and performs its composition. Screen-captured video shows the "narrator"-cursor logging onto his (its?) email account and running a word search for Mayakovsky. (The login information shows Arseniev's actual email address.) The cursor hovers over

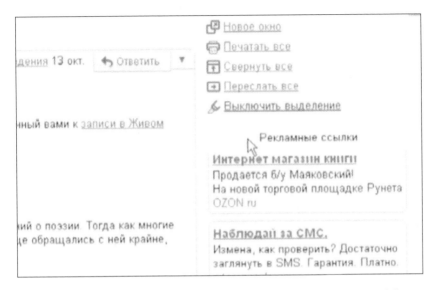

FIGURE 2.4 A screen capture from Arseniev's online video of "Mayakovsky for Sale."
LABORATORY OF POETIC ACTIONISM.

but quickly skips past the content of an email exchange that mentions Mayakovsky. If the viewer pauses, rewinds, and replays the video, it is possible to read fragments of an exchange with a LiveJournal blogger regarding Arseniev's ideas about avant-garde poetry. The cursor, however, heads for the advertisements and miscellaneous textual effluvia hovering at the screen's edges. While the movable indicator selects the words and phrases that make up the poem (or "poem"), Arseniev's digitized voice reads aloud the oddly evocative words.

From the title to the execution, as Platt notes in an introduction to his work, Arseniev directs our attention to the "subjugation" of avant-garde poetry to the market.[70] Considerably less violently—and therefore also repeatably, scalably—the move nevertheless echoes Brener's graffiti defacement as intervention. The video captured as a still above, meanwhile, offers a glimpse into Arseniev's characteristic play across media, collaborative poetics, and digital technologies. The piece crosses smoothly from an individual to collective creation: the poem is by Arseniev, as single auteur; the video piece is by the Laboratory of Poetic Actionism, a collaboration with Osminkin and poet Dina Gatina. Poem and art object coexist in offline and online formats, taking advantage in each instance of the particular contexts of their framing. The piece is therefore *about* the absorption of avant-gardes into the quicksand of total capitalism even as its form playfully subverts common tools of communication and commerce into serving something very much like Roman Jakobson's poetic function.[71] In other words, we are forced to pay attention to the message as such (*l'art pour l'art*), to how the code is used—and in turn to see that as inseparable from social totality, or modes of production in the widest sense.

Much of Arseniev's practice is dedicated to pushing well past the limits of the page in ways impossible with pen and paper alone. Key works include video graffiti poetry, varied forms of performance and public installation, and seemingly endless permutations of play with found and manipulated language. More often than not, the medium is the message (as in Marshall McLuhan's prophetic 1960s-era vision): Arseniev's experiments with form defamiliarize both language and technology and suggest an inevitable if metonymic link from such deformations to political deconstruction, à la Lyn Hejinian. The poets of the $L=A=N=G=U=A=G=E$ school too sought to lend physicality and "heft" to words using a range of techniques including performance and installation. Hejinian spoke for an emerging movement when she advocated for the open text and active reader theory, wherein "the writer relinquishes total control and challenges authority as a principle and control as a motive."[72] By rejecting the authority of the writer over the reader, such poetry, as if by analogy, questions other social, economic, and cultural hierarchies. If refusal and labor organization shape Medvedev's vision for the poetry of the new Russian left, Arseniev sees his path forward through remediation and networks. More so even than the other poets of *[Translit]*, all of whom are acutely aware of (and to varying degrees, electrified or alarmed by) our era's digital metamorphosis, Arseniev never ceases to think about aesthetic productions as code.

Why are remediations so central to Arseniev's own poetry? In part the answer lies in his recognition of the difficulties literature faces when reaching toward avant-garde critique. In his writings on Tretyakov (whom he inevitably brings up as the paradigmatic example of a literary avant-garde), Arseniev raises the subject of technological determinism. For example, he writes, "Benjamin derives the possibility of art's self-critique entirely from changes in the technology of (re)production and distribution."[73] This model, which privileges changes in technological capacity over intellectual innovation, is hardly promising for "such 'low-technological' artistic industries as literature. . . . In literature, one can hardly find such technological innovation of recording devices, whose impact can be compared to the appearance of photography in visual art's history."[74] Or so it seemed until relatively recently: the internet and Web 2.0 have brought about just such a transformation in textual recording, dramatically transforming the production, dissemination, and reception of literature on nearly every level. For all his necessary critique and suspicion of contemporary techno-optimism, Arseniev indeed seems to follow Benjamin in his fascination with new technological possibilities and more radically democratic forms of production and distribution. While Arseniev has few illusions about the forces driving the "technological revolution," or perhaps more accurately, technological coup, again he appears to follow the motto of his own avant-garde journal 2.0: the only way forward is through.

Arseniev's most interesting interventions remediate avant-garde legacies in both lo- and hi-fi ways: computer poetry and cardboard alike are code.[75] The image below, for instance, offers a glimpse of another paradigmatic Arseniev work, taken from a carefully crafted video moving through an outdoor installation of Vsevolod Nekrasov's minimalist poetry. A companion piece of video poetry depicts sequential flashes of cleverly placed graffiti (the original site-specific poetry, as it were) to spell out a text by Andrei Monastyrsky—both figures evident inspirations for Arseniev's own hybrid poet / artist identity.[76] Both experiments create a visual work of art out of text; both toy with public and presumably private modes of reading and consuming poetry; and the latter especially invites viewers to look with new eyes at other "found" street text. From a stance of "the avant-garde is over" (or even, for some, "the avant-garde was always already over"), Arseniev retrains us to see the avant-garde everywhere. The avant-garde is dead, long live the avant-garde.

Anna Landikhova compares Arseniev's work with the Laboratory of Poetic Actionism to cinema: a "synthesis of literature and theatre" accessible to nonparticipants through the mediation of video. All the careful construction work of genealogy is there on the surface, as is Arseniev's palimpsestic experience of living in a world covered in the (at times barely discernible) traces of Russia's greatest art. *Where* can we find Mayakovsky now, and Nekrasov,

FIGURE 2.5 Pavel Arseniev and the Laboratory of Poetic Actionism festoon Gorky Park
with the words of Soviet underground poet Vsevolod Nekrasov.   PAVEL ARSENIEV.

and Monastyrsky? Casting Arseniev's practice as exclusively a "machine of
irony" misses some of the sense of genuine wonder at encountering these
traces anew in unexpected places or situations—and in recreating the wonder,
and surely significance, of that discovery for others. More the unabashed
pedagogue than Medvedev, Arseniev means to emancipate his spectator: he
ensures that each poetic performance also takes on the mantle of social
commentary, responding recognizably to current political events.[77] For critics
like Landikhova and Schellens, Arseniev reads as a militant offshoot of Russian Conceptualism, adapting the techniques of Soviet-era forefathers into
an instrument of contemporary critique and thereby proving the earlier interventions hardly dated but indeed "key to making political art" in Putin's
Russia.[78]

Like nearly all the poets of the *[Translit]* circle—which he, more than any
other, has generated and sustained against all odds—Arseniev is as suspicious
of the role of Russian poet as he is interested in mining the alternative potentialities of Russian poetry. He is, if anything, even less interested than the
others in forging a recognizable, unique poetic practice as such. Arseniev
therefore constantly foregrounds the unoriginal and collective aspects of cre-

FIGURE 2.6 Pavel Arseniev at the Festival of Poetry, St. Petersburg.   SERGEI YUGOV.

ativity: whether by remediating the works of others, collaborating with contemporaries, or through the editorial and organizational work of bringing together the communities of *[Translit]*.[79] Such a practice reveals poetry as always already produced through familiar acts of collective labor (editing, typesetting, publishing, printing, disseminating, discussing), and has the added benefit of perpetually introducing Arseniev to new potential collaborators, comrades, and converts.

The Future of Paper Utopias

In the end, Arseniev's oeuvre, his self-conscious archive of paper utopias, might best be described as based on the twinned premises that you must still try to build better things with language, and that the contemporary intellectual has a duty to rescue the avant-garde from aestheticized politics (with a nod to Walter Benjamin)—even and especially on his own side. In 2014 an international art world scandal took place over the Manifesta Biennial, held in St. Petersburg's Winter Palace mere months after Russian's forced annexation of Crimea. Chto Delat challenged the aging European star curator Kasper König to take a political stand on the event, given the biennial's planned St. Petersburg location and Manifesta's politically progressive aura. Chto Delat ultimately withdrew from the biennial in response to what they saw as a fundamentally condescending and ultimately spineless corporate response.[80] Many Russian and some East European artists planning to participate in the biennial followed suit. As the St. Petersburg event nevertheless took place, a number of mediating actors (including respected-by-all-sides Polish curator Joanna Warsza) organized local interventions and conversations around Manifesta's presence. The *New York Times* journalist Sally Mc-Grane encountered a familiar set of characters active on the scene:

> "Whether Manifesta is here or not, it is really important for us to include our view and our voices in the public space, because this possibility could end," said Pavel Arsenev, a poet and activist based in St. Petersburg. . . . Last month, as part of Manifesta, Mr. Arsenev organized a day of "poetic actions" in the city. On a Saturday morning, young volunteers wearing sandwich boards handed out poems by Bertolt Brecht at metro stations. . . . Later, in the shadow of the Peter and Paul Fortress—once home to an infamous political prison—Kirill Medvedev, a poet, singer, and literary critic, read aloud from the poetry of political prisoners.[81]

Asked by another interviewer whether, in urgent and difficult times, art might have less time for ambiguities, Arseniev did not waver: "Even during times of war art has to be ambiguous."[82] Arseniev's response to the end of the cease-fire is to imagine—and to prop up, via institutions created nearly ex nihilo—a Russian political poetry whose complexities and contradictions are as tangible as the storied streets of St. Petersburg.

One of the seemingly least emotionally detached poems in Arseniev's oeuvre, "Russia Day," narrates his 2013 arrest by the police during the celebrations of Russia's independence day. The story of Arseniev's only politically motivated arrest to date made quick rounds of Russia's new left: the chief irony being that Arseniev was not detained for direct political action (as Medvedev and Rymbu have been many times) but for reading a poem with "non-normative language" no longer legal in the presence of children and families under Russia's increasingly restrictive legislative changes. Arseniev tells the story in an uncharacteristically straightforward documentary style that seems closer to Medvedev's mode of narration:

в тот день я решил все-таки заехать на митинг,
хотя велосипед так и не удалось починить,
на марсовом поле собралась типичная политическая
тусовка:
немногочисленные фрики, ратующие за отделение
ленобласти от россии,
еще какие-то психоделические флаги—
было видно, что протест выдыхается:
люди уставали и одновременно
начинали опасаться ходить на митинги.
меня попросили прочитать стихотворение
в поддержку узников 6 мая[83]

That day I decided to go to the rally after all,
though I still hadn't fixed my bike,
the typical political crowd gathered in Mars Field:
a few freaks, advocating for the Leningrad region to secede from
    Russia,
a few more psychedelic flags—
it was clear that protest was flagging:
people were growing tired and simultaneously
starting to be afraid to go to rallies.
I was asked to read a poem
in support of the May 6 political prisoners

Warned by his colleagues that the authorities were "displeased" (nedovol'ny) with what he was reading, Arseniev responds initially with disbelief:

я рассмеялся этой старомодной опасности,
в уме пронеслось словосочетание

«третье отделение» и другие
ностальгические фантазии на тему «поэт и власть»,
и тут ко мне действительно подошли
двое представительных
и, разумеется, не представившихся мужчин в форме
и предложили пройти с ними.

I laughed at the old-fashioned danger,
words came to mind like
"third department" and other
nostalgic fantasies on the theme of "poet and power,"
and then toward me actually came
two representative
men in uniform and, it goes without saying, without introductions
suggested that I go with them.

It is unclear who is more embarrassed by this turn of events, the officers
muttering their directive in "muffled voices" (priglushenno govorili) or Arseniev himself at the "chanted slogans / about freedom of thought and all
that" (ot skandiruemykh lozungov / o nepodsudnosti mysli i vse takoe—)
that fill the air behind him. Part of the irony is that Arseniev was not even
reading his own work, but that of a *[Translit]* colleague—another slippage of
self, and of voice.

Almost immediately, the narrator (for once it might be fair to say, lyric
hero) starts feeling solidarity with all the wrong elements. Among the police
he encounters members of the post-Soviet precariat, bored and embarrassed
that "ten men in the service had been riding in the heat in a dusty bus"
(desiat' sluzhivykh muzhikov edet po zhare v pyl'nom avtobuse) over non-
normative poetry. After flipping through his Kraft booklet and questioning
Arseniev about who was publishing the chapbooks and their circulation
numbers, the uniformed gentlemen grow evidently more disappointed still.
The reigning mood for all is a mix of boredom, embarrassment, and vague
disbelief as police and poet seem to find themselves acting out a Soviet-era
script without any inclination to do so on either side. At the station, the poet
catches a glimpse of a different cross section of Russia, deeply familiar and
estranged at the same time:

по приезде в отделение я узнал еще больше о своей стране в
    день ее независимости. кадровый состав в основном состоял
из скучающих мужчин и женщин,

when I arrived at the station I learned even more
about my country on the day of its independence.
the staff consisted mainly
of bored men and women

коллектив был поистине многонациональным,
как народ страны, покой которого они охраняли:
узбеки, славяне, тувинцы, армяне,
одинаково расслабленно расхаживали в серой форме с
    какими-то бумажками,
и было видно, что никому не хотелось ничего делать. во всем
    царила беззаботная усталость и
предпраздничная атмосфера.

the collective was truly multinational,
like the people of the country, whose peace they guarded:
Uzbeks, Slavs, Tuvinians, Armenians
all in gray uniforms and in a relaxed manner moved around
with some papers,
and it was clear that no one wanted to do anything.
a carefree weariness and pre-holiday atmosphere reigned over
    everything.

After being treated rather well by everyone, Arseniev is freed by his overquali-
fied lawyer, whose unnecessary and noble defense of literature on trial bores
the judge and strikes the defendant, again, as *not modern*. After a day charac-
terized by a journey seemingly more into a different time than a different place,
the poet returns home to a collective with much the same agenda as the one he
left behind: to put the entire business behind him and enjoy the holiday.

некоторая литературоведческая дискуссия
все же состоялась, тем более что в качестве адвоката

мне достался
человек с серьезными гражданскими амбициями,
в результате чего литература вновь рисковала
стать предметом морального осуждения (и оправдания),
чего с ней не случалось уже давно.
но судье это быстро наскучило,
она была намного более современным человеком, чем мы.
наконец при выходе из здания дзержинского суда,
что на восстания, 38,
меня встретили ухмыляющиеся товарищи,
которые давно уже мечтали перестать переживать
по телефону и хотели просто отметить
сегодняшний день россии.

some literary discussion
did take place, especially as I got as my lawyer
a man with serious civil ambitions,
as a result of which literature again risked
becoming an object of moral condemnation (and absolution),
which hasn't happened to her for a long time.
but the judge quickly grew bored of all that,
she was a much more modern person than us.
finally leaving the building of Dzerzhinsky's court,
on Uprising Square, 38,
I was met by snickering comrades,
who had long been dreaming of stopping worrying
and making phone calls and just wanted to celebrate
today's Russia Day.

In equal parts weary and warm, "Russia Day" casts a simple contemporary narrative against the historic Leningrad backdrops of Dzerzhinsky's court and Uprising Square. Arseniev reduces the much-mythologized persecuted Russian poet to bored buffoonery and bureaucratic malfunction.[84] And yet, in between various sets of shattered expectations (his, ours, the police's), forms of collectivity do emerge: we end with more camaraderie and compassion than before. Poetry and police met with some kind of thought-provoking clash after all, and one that—crucially—shares little with romanticized dissident narratives of previous generations. There is no hero, no villains, no martyrdom, no exalted suffering, no gulag, no hidden interrogation room of horrors: only a shared history of clichés, bureaucracy, and exhaustion. The radical poet Sergei Zavialov describes Arseniev's poetry as having Marxist analysis at its very core and sees Arseniev's major artistic discovery to be the central character in these more narrative poems: "the modern Russian . . . a product of anthropological disintegration and the latest forms of Internet conformism."[85]

The productivity of the intervention, and of the vision behind it, comes through in the speed with which Arseniev responds to current events with new projects and original work. One recent demonstration was the quick ode to the coronavirus pandemic, published in March 2020, with which I ended the introduction of this book:

> спасибо тебе, коронавирус,
> наконец все получило
> хоть какое-то объяснение
>
> thank you coronavirus
> at last it all has
> at least some explanation[86]

Whatever new forms the Russian artistic left evolves after the years of pandemic and war, Pavel Arseniev is sure to be part of the story.

3

Language Poetry Is Leftist

THE LONG DURÉE OF ALEKSANDR SKIDAN

*M*ORE THAN ANY OTHER FIGURE in Russian poetry, Aleksandr Skidan (born in Leningrad, 1965) serves as a living link between the new Russian left and the unexpectedly glamor-tinged last days of the Soviet underground. He is, by far, the most senior and storied member of the *[Translit]* circle. As a founding member of the art collective Chto Delat; poetry editor of the prestigious *New Literary Review;* and the poet of his generation most identified as Dragomoshchenko's heir, Skidan is a St. Petersburg cultural institution in his own right. As he often reminds interviewers, Skidan never received a formal higher education: in that sense, he belongs less to the ranks of post-Soviet academe-adjacent intellectuals than to the last generation of Soviet autodidacts. Skidan even worked as a Leningrad stoker—the profession romantically associated with Soviet-era poets, musicians, and artists (not least among them Joseph Brodsky and rock star legend Viktor Tsoi of the group Kino)—to free up time for totally independent literary pursuits.[1] By age and experience, Skidan belongs to an entirely different generation than Medvedev and Arseniev—which makes all the more remarkable his choice to throw his considerable talents and reputation in with a circle of younger, decidedly post- (or even post-post-) Soviet and politically radical poets.

And yet Skidan has purposefully linked his name to those of Medvedev, Arseniev, and other *[Translit]* figures, through shared publication venues, public events, collaborations, and professed politics. The move has not been without its dangers or detractors: for example, in a highly critical opinion piece for Colta.ru, "The Megaphone as a Tool of Production," Russian literary scholar Aleksandr Zhitenev dismisses all this "new social poetry" as a "grand fake."[2] Ascribing the rise of left-leaning poetry in Russia to cynical careerists, Zhitenev lists as the most prominent examples none other than Skidan, Medvedev, Arseniev, and Osminkin. But if the youngest writers on that list could be suspected (at least conceivably) of trying to make their name on the leftward wave, Skidan certainly needed none of it. Instead, he chose to potentially jeopardize his already considerable prestige to legitimize the efforts of younger comrades: penning reviews and contributing introductions to their works, publishing in their samizdat venues, and participating in countless readings and performances (including of other poets' work, such as Keti Chukhrov's verse dramas).[3] The task of this chapter is to understand what, aesthetically and politically, Skidan and the younger post-Soviet avant-garde poets have meant for each other. The publication of new work from Skidan—the cycle *The Works and Days of Daniil Ivanovich* in 2018 and the collection *Contamination* in 2020 in particular—reveals a writer ablaze, arguably more prolific and consumed by a guiding vision than at any other stage of his career. If Arseniev and the younger generation of *[Translit]* poets learned much of what they know from studying Skidan, we now see that for the past twenty years Skidan has also been studying them.

Skidan's take on leftist Russian poetry resembles more the erudite experimental verse of Dragomoshchenko and global language poetry than the relatively accessible work of Medvedev (whom Skidan nevertheless championed early and often in essays, reviews, and introductions). Forged in the tradition of Aesopian language designed to slip past Soviet censors and resistant to a false candor he associates with systemic violence, Skidan looks to the relatively autonomous sphere of art for emancipation—Marxism à la Adorno rather than Lukács.[4] A direct disciple of Dragomoshchenko, Skidan was a witness to and active participant in the early exchanges with Hejinian and other American $L=A=N=G=U=A=G=E$ poets.[5] Indeed, as a bridge between the once dissident or performatively apolitical Leningrad underground and the new Russian left, Skidan challenges narratives that might cast the *[Translit]* constellation as a faddish Western derivative. From Skidan's perspective, Arseniev and company aren't imitating Brooklyn or Philadelphia (as in a common rebuke from critics who prefer their Russian poetry "authentic" and "national") but are doing what St. Petersburg's bohemians have always done: challenging authority and opening a window to the world.

In the context of Putin's Russia and catastrophe capitalism, that includes re-habilitating a rich and complex global canon of Marxist thought.

Dragomoshchenko represented a similarly radical reopening of borders for Russian poetry in the late Soviet period. In the 1970s and early 1980s, a number of Russian artists and writers began to closely follow recent trends in international arts and literatures hitherto rarely accessible in the Soviet Union. Jacob Edmond writes that the vanguard of the time

> adapted Conceptualism and poststructuralism to the radically dif-ferent Russian context. . . . Their dialogue with the West took on re-newed urgency in the late 1980s when the literary field was transformed through the collapse of strict censorship and the institutions of Soviet samizdat culture, the move to a free market economy, and new possi-bilities for emigration and travel. In response, Prigov and Dragomosh-chenko in particular (and in their wake younger poets such as Aleksandr Skidan and Dmitri Golynko-Vol'fson) came to rethink their national literature and avant-garde practices in relation to a new, more global context.[6]

Skidan's contemporary, the Russian civic poet Elena Fanailova has put it, "The task of our generation was to become citizens of the world."[7] Dragomosh-chenko indicated a way forward that put poetry, rather than performance, at the vanguard's edge. For Skidan, that move was already inherently political, signaling a steadfast rejection of entertainment (and by extension, a rapidly transforming late- to post-Soviet culture industry). As Stephanie Sandler points out, Dragomoshchenko also exemplified a key turn in Russian verse toward critical theory: like Hejinian ("who produced remarkable versions of his poetry in English"), Dragomoshchenko wrote poetry to "register thought in process, turning the poetic text away from its legacy of perfectly achieved linguistic virtuosity toward a more open-ended form of verbal provocation."[8] Edmond, Sandler, and Fanailova all recognize Skidan as Dragomoshchen-ko's most influential successor. Skidan in turn considers his encounter with Dragomoshchenko's poetry and their subsequent friendship as among the main events of his life. He describes that initial encounter as a veritable rev-elation: he came across Dragomoshchenko's poetry reading the Riga journal *Rodnik* in the subway, and it "hit me like an electric shock: you can write this

way in Russian—this wasn't a translation."[9] From there—from Dragomoshchenko's overcoat—an entire generation of Russian poets was born.[10]

   Skidan has many marvelous genealogies to offer on the topic of his literary
origins. He reports beginning to write at eleven or twelve, inspired by a book
about the young Pushkin and his rowdy "post-Lycée years in St. Petersburg,"
in particular the "friendship(s) with the future Decembrists, and anti-
government poems. . . . I started imitating Pushkin."[11] From there it was
Mikhail Lermontov, Sergei Esenin, Vladimir Mayakovsky, Alexander Blok,
Boris Pasternak, and Osip Mandelstam, until

> I stumbled on Apollinaire, and it made me absolutely high. This "he-
> retical" vers libre line continued later, when I discovered Robert Lowell
> and Tadeusz Różewicz. Under the influence of Lowell, as well as experi-
> mental jazz (the trio Ganelina, Chekasin, Tarasova), I came to experi-
> ment with free verse. . . . Through Dragomoshchenko with whom I
> became friends in 1992, I learned about the language school. . . . The last
> poetic shock was Alexander Vvedenski. It was a shock, after which I
> could not recover or return to myself. And now I do not know whether
> I'll ever recover. He is the most radical poet of the 20th century.[12]

While he defines his poetics as the continuation of a century of experimental,
mostly free, verse, Skidan also posits a steady distance from a mainstream
in Russian poetry—less a matter of prosody than intellectual aims and discursive context. He has even described his oeuvre as "not so much on the horizon of Russian poetic canon" but akin to theoretical work by "Bataille, Benjamin, Agamben, the Russian Formalists and Bakhtin / Voloshinov . . . not
the Silver Age."[13] If Medvedev found his hero and archetype in Serge, and
Arseniev in Tretyakov, for Skidan, the paradigmatic representative of the historical Russian avant-garde with the most to offer the twenty-first century is
decidedly Vvedensky. Each contemporary avant-gardist must also navigate
between the Scylla and Charybdis of Dragomoshchenko and Prigov, their
most recent predecessors: Medvedev, while admiring Prigov, veers away from
both; Arseniev follows the former more in verse, the latter in performance; and
Skidan has moved from close adherence to his former mentor Dragomoshchenko to, most recently, a fierce hilarity that at least superficially resembles
Prigov but ultimately reads as entirely Skidan's own.

A rare bird as a Marxist virtuoso poet in the early years of the new century, prior to *[Translit]* Skidan found his people in the world of contemporary art instead—specifically, in the other members of the art collective Chto Delat. Founded in 2003, Chto Delat are now by far the most internationally visible and influential representatives of contemporary Russian leftist art. A group of artists and philosophers (including Dmitry Vilensky, Olga "Tsaplya" Egerova, and Nikolay Oleynikov; academically luminous names such as Oxana Timofeeva, Nina Gasteva, Artemy Magun, Alexei Penzin, and Ilya Budraitskis; as well as Skidan and fellow *[Translit]* poet Keti Chukhrov), they produce a newspaper but also performances, installations, videos, and philosophical texts crossing historical avant-gardes with contemporary art and theory from around the world, with a strong foundation in Western Marxism. The group, which defines itself as a "self-organized platform . . . intent on politicizing knowledge production through redefinitions of an engaged autonomy for cultural practice today," shares its name with Nikolai Chernyshevsky's 1863 novel and Lenin's 1902 tract (*Chto Delat'*). Likewise, the group's central activities (the publication of an international leftist newspaper; see also onetime member and frequent collaborator Natalia "Gluklya" Pershina's seamstress art praxis) serve to recall the first collectively organized socialist projects in Russia. Their manifesto proclaims:

> At this reactionary historical moment . . . we have to move away from the frustrations occasioned by the historical failures to advance leftist ideas and discover anew their emancipatory potential. . . . We stand for a distribution of the wealth produced by human labor and all natural resources that is just and directed towards the welfare of everyone. We are internationalists: we demand the recognition of the equality of all people, no matter where they live or where they come from. We are feminists: we are against all forms of patriarchy, homophobia, and gender inequality.[14]

Two decades after their first ventures, the core membership of Chto Delat remains surprisingly stable and the group continues to find ways of producing challenging, politically relevant art. Through their choices of performance setting (frequently streets, squares, and other public spaces) and of forms (choruses, multiple subjects, experimentation with speaking as an all-encompassing "we"), the collective reanimates artistic engagement with the public for a post-Soviet age. Their educational endeavor, the unofficial street

FIGURE 3.1 Aleksandr Skidan reading at a gathering of Chto Delat's School of Engaged Art, June 3, 2016. NEPROTV.BLOGSPOT.COM.

"School of Engaged Art," meanwhile serves as a crucible for emerging artists across Russia year after year.

Chto Delat witnessed literature fade from relevance and contemporary art become a tool to "legitimize the capital and status" of Russia's new ruling class. As Skidan explains in more than one interview, they refused to either participate or stand by: "We do not only criticize but also identify alternatives. We make less noise than 'Voina,' but we offer real solutions."[15] For Skidan, being part of Chto Delat appears to have offered the embodied, collective modes of aesthetic production not afforded by writing alone: just as Medvedev turned to music and Arseniev to performative actions, so too did Skidan find in contemporary art the fuel to sustain more solitary poetic pursuits.

From Trans-formation to [Translit]

Skidan is as voracious a curator of Russian poetry as he is of international critical theory—as the title of his volume of collected essays on poetry,

Summa Poeticae (*Summa poetiki*), suggests. The central text of the collection, "Trans-formation: The Poetic Machines of Alexander Vvedensky," is dedicated to the memory of Dragomoshchenko and has in turn been translated into English by Lyn Hejinian and Lucas Stratton.[16] In this evident manifesto, Skidan outlines the underlying principles that make Vvedensky's work not only vital for the "later emergence of an independent cultural movement in Leningrad, including the phenomenon of samizdat" but also "acutely contemporary."[17] Setting aside the usual categories of the absurd, irrational, and so forth that often delimit studies of OBERIU poetics, Skidan focuses on form. He identifies six principles as constitutive of Russian experimental poetry: heteromorphousness; heteroglossia; desubjectification; the use of poetic machines; metapoetic functions; and "trans-formation." With each category and each description, he outlines his own program as well:

1. *Heteromorphousness:* Vvedensky's verse is programmatically heterogeneous, or heteromorphous, which is to say that it is constructed by means of constant alternations and sequences of replacements, so that within the confines of a single poem, there's a great diversity of structure-creating elements, such as lineation, type of verse, stanza structure, meter, catalexis, rhyme.

2. *Heteroglossia:* the explosive dramatization and hybridization of forms and genres, the incorporation of "conceptual" personae, and the strong "specific gravity"—given the historical background of a homogeneous, primarily traditional, and monological lyric—of impersonation and indirect speech.

3. *Desubjectification:* the dispersal of the speaking subject into a multitude of "voices"; its decentralization, additionally accentuating the suspension, displacement, or misidentification of the "I" (or authorial agency).

4. *Poetic machines:* use of recurrent folkloric models, with their "chirring rhythms" and "circus-booth rhyme schemes," as a generative model; use of vulgar punning and other wordplay, which undermines habitual and axiomatic verse-writing.

5. The *metapoetic function:* criticism of the poetic mode of expression from within and by way of poetry itself—that which, elsewhere,

paraphrasing Vvedensky (who was paraphrasing Kant), I propose we
call the "critique of poetic reason."

6. *Trans-formation:* Vvedensky's poetic machines are configured in
such a way that they accelerate progress vertiginously, forcing language to act deliriously and to approach its very limits (producing
asyntactical, agrammatical, asemantic enunciations).[18]

While Skidan notes the use of similar techniques in the work of other
twentieth-century poets, including Blok, Khlebnikov, Mayakovsky, and Vaginov, he argues that only in Vvedensky's case do they unite into a coherent
metapoetic critique. Moving forward a century, the same six principles
shape Skidan's own experiments and to a large extent the contemporary
poetry that he identifies as kindred—the work of select members of the
[Translit] kruzhok.

For Skidan, Vvedensky's texts embody Bakhtinian heteroglossia in unexpected verse form. Principles one, two, and three all touch on ways in which
a multitude of voices and formal techniques take the place of the missing subject.[19] The remaining principles all have to do with undermining poetic
habit: defamiliarizing the poetic function, as it were, with an eye to moving
beyond what is already graspable by "poetic reason." All six formal principles, but perhaps especially desubjectification, are readily identifiable in Skidan's own work: despite moments of seemingly shared biography, his "I" is
not the lyric persona of late modernism, but defracted, revealed as a floating
shifter pointing only to the slippages of identity inherent in life and language.
It is only through "radical disbelief" in the self that the poet finds "ways to
verbalize his experience, to represent it in a textual form that can shatter the
unconscious axioms and expectations of cultural consciousness."[20] Hence the
emphasis on interruption, swerve, shock—"no, this is not possible but it is
here and hence possible"—precisely the experience Skidan describes when
first encountering Dragomoshchenko's poetry. A poet's poet, but a politically
leftist one, Skidan narrows his focus on a short list of fellow virtuosos that to
him represent the most genuinely radical strains of Russian poetry and
thought. The last principle, "trans-formation," proves especially elusive to
identify—much less to achieve—but to my mind has the strongest futurist
political implications.[21] It is trans-formation that Skidan has been studying

throughout his lengthy career, and it is trans-formation that Skidan is ultimately after.

   Alongside defamiliarizing, desubjectifying, and destabilizing poetic techniques, Skidan seizes on the terminology of machinery so common in the
writings of the OBERIU: "Daniil Kharms generalizes from the insight of
many of his predecessors, including Edgar Allen Poe, Baudelaire, Gerard
Manley Hopkins, as well as the Dadaists (viz. Schwitters' Mertz-machines or
Duchamp's assemblages) and Surrealists (viz. automatic writing and the 'exquisite corpse' games), when he writes in his journal: 'For now I know four
types of verbal machines: poems, prayers, songs, and spells.'"[22] The OBERIU
were adepts of poetry as a "machine of punning permutations—phonetic,
syntactic, phraseological, grammatical, and semantic"; or as Skidan writes
elsewhere, Vvedensky's "*word* machines are also *worm* machines—they consume the carrion of dead devices and techniques."[23] Word / worm machines
offer a way to revivify metapoetic function without betraying principles of
poetic experimentation; without acquiescing to clichés of self and other; and
without falling prey to the aesthetic, intellectual, and ultimately political failures of imagination that lead us to accept (as in Badiou's formulation) the "inevitable and 'natural' character of the most monstrous inequalities."[24] What
Skidan terms revivifying metapoetic function is the same force that I identify
throughout this book as the resumed modality of the Russian avant-garde.

   Vvedensky matters even today because he does not merely critique common
practice, or even language, rhetoric, and discourse, but the apparatus itself:
"Vvedensky questions poetry . . . poetry's limited means for producing
meaning, its problematic aesthetic conventions and norms, and their bankruptcy."[25] Skidan concludes the piece with an overview of Vvedensky's legacy
for contemporary Russian poetry, closely matching his own poetic genealogy
in the process: "Vvedensky's interest in subversive combinatorial possibilities
is continued in the works of Dmitry Prigov; Prigov's poetic machines construct
a logic for utterances of different types, from the artistic to the ideological,
from the religious to the scientific, while still keeping the critical function
in the foreground. Desubjectification and / or the problematization of the
subject's position is most vividly expressed in Arkadii Dragomoshchenko's
work and in that of those young poets who emerged in the second half of the
2000s."[26] All the young heirs of Vvedensky whom Skidan goes on to name
are poets associated with *[Translit]*, in whom Skidan recognized the next

wave of OBERIU and Conceptualist energies, recast in twenty-first-century form. All challenge the institution of Russian poetry (trademark, as it were) while continuing to practice at its margins.

When pressed by interviewers to specify his own poetic agenda (which he prefers to do obliquely, through literary critical essays on his heroes and protégés), Skidan points to the short speech he delivered upon receiving the Andrei Bely Prize in 2006 as his most relevant poetic statement of method. In that speech, "Protocol on Negative Poetics," Skidan identified the collection *Red Shifting* as the heart to his body of work:

> Linguistics, psychoanalysis, political economy, and other disciplines act in *Red Shifting* as a repressive discursive regime, leaving no space for traditional lyricism, displacing it to the outskirts of the dispersing galaxy of cultural meanings of the universe—to archaic, pre-industrial production. But, at the same time, this strict regime is colonized and undermined from within, becoming the battleground for a new lyrical subject. . . . Another important motif in *Red Shifting* is a critique of commodity fetishism in its aesthetic appearance. . . . Hence the resistance to the work of art, the resistance to art as the temptation to become established in a number of other fetishes of the culture industry.[27]

The political intention behind Skidan's formal experimentation is laid out quite explicitly in this speech: he means for his texts to critique literature from within; to resist ossification into lyric subjecthood; and to refuse, by any means necessary, assimilation into the market economy. Formally, this kind of struggle entails a poetics of hybridization—of poetry and "ugly" prose, as in the long discursive forms Skidan generally favors—and more specifically, of poetry and critical theory. Lyric virtuosity that remains within the "framework of conventional metrical verse," by contrast, not only does not extend past "the limits of what can be called the Russian cultural matrix," but according to Skidan, "feeds" on it. When asked (often) in interviews if he considers himself a Russian poet at all, given the international influences evident in his works, Skidan responds: "I could say I'm a universal writer—in the sense of Dostoevsky's 'Pushkin Speech.' . . . This notion of being Russian-as-Universal, without nationalism, is close to me. I see Mandelstam as the second revelation of such a personality—absolutely Russian but at the same time Jewish, and Hellenic, and universal."[28] He then continues, adding political edge to the previous examples: "In political terms, the only solution is a new International(ism)."[29]

The 1999 poem "Scholia" serves as an eloquent introduction to Skidan's signature style. Composed of fragments (scholia are typically grammatical, critical, or explanatory comments) presented as if collected from the margins of a missing original text, the poem pulls together Skidan's key intellectual sources and characteristic formal devices. Written just as Putin was coming to power (in the same year as Viktor Pelevin released his postmodernist classic *Generation P*), "Scholia" shows Skidan picking up the loose and trailing threads of a tormented century in literature and philosophy. Skidan's calling card on Vavilon.ru, "Scholia" is true to its name and glides from allusion to allusion: Immanuel Kant, Martin Heidegger, Hannah Arendt, Walter Benjamin, René Magritte, and Gertrude Stein, among many others.[30] The ten stanzas—or more properly, notes—are each set off by an opening asterisk and footnote missing source texts. One missing original is Heidegger: one scholia opens, "in Being and Time—(page / 163) H. asserts." Without the (translated) text in front of us, however, we have only Skidan's not-quite-legible notes, as if working from memory in the face of an absent or destroyed library of world culture. Even so, the ruins of world culture, curated by Skidan, offer more to contemporary Russian poetry than imitations of the dominant strain that he refers to vaguely as "Silver Age."

The opening stanza (so to speak, or some such unit of text) serves as an establishing shot, estranging us out of one mind frame while presenting a semifamiliar whirlwind of impressions and cacophony of voices. We are tempted to read for recognizable bits of narrating voice amid the multimedia noise of the surrounding shifting world:

всё что связано с подлинностью
мыльный привкус

техномузыка из дверей кафе
пролегомены

ко всякой будущей метафизике
воображаемые решения

катакомбы
"никогда не говори со мной таким тоном"

красно-коричневая чума
новый порядок означающих

the sun is going so fast

берёзки
полупроводники

everything having to do with authenticity
taste of soap

techno coming out of the café doors
prolegomena

imaginary solutions
to any future metaphysics

catacombs

"never speak to me in that tone of voice"
. a red-brown plague
a new order of signifiers

the sun is going so fast

birches
semi-conductors[31]

Despite the evident emphasis of the words on the page as just words on a page, and despite the list structure reinforced by the title, readerly habit is overwhelmingly strong. If we want to read for Joycean stream of consciousness and psychological realism, we might imagine the poet reading (Kant,

Prolegomena) and struggling to concentrate while the distractions of the day pour in: ambient techno; overheard snippets of rudeness; political fears of a red-brown alliance between communists and fascists; an English phrase; the clichéd birch trees of nationalist visual culture; the rapidly digitizing post-Fordian world. That reading nearly holds: hence the tension around subject formation in these long, turn-of-the-century works by Skidan. But where another poet might begin scattered but (even inadvertently) gradually cohere around an inevitably unifying worldview and sense of self, Skidan maintains dispersion through length, repetition, and emptiness—his word and worm machines. As one repeating fragment puts it, "a headless man walks lives / for four hours" (obezglavlennyi / khodit eshche chetyre chasa). What we instinctively try to piece back together isn't the poet's shadow double: it's a moving corpse.

Even in translation, international reviewers report that Skidan's poetry feels like "a recording of experienced language, from theoretical quotes to overheard banter and impersonal signs / instructions, written without concern for the author's role as the origin of the language presented."[32] We recognize a kindred style to that of Arseniev—who learned so much of form and content from Skidan, and from Dragomoshchenko behind him—but with a different urgency and temporality to the collecting project. Arseniev's assemblages are self-ironic and postdystopian, winking at the pairings of Wittgenstein and Vimeo; but Skidan imbues similar forms with the edge of imminent apocalypse.

> реклама volvo и вульвы
> нила и сены отца и сына
>
> (параллелизм
> аллюзии
>
> пустые места
>
> теодицея
>
> для пассажиров с детьми
>
> паронимическая аттракция

<это не стихотворение>

это теологические ухищренья товара

самореклама (откровение

святого духа
в абсолютной разорванности

advertising of volvo and vulva
nile and seine father and son

(parallelism
allusions
vacant seats

theodicy

for passengers with children

paronymic attraction

<this is not a poem>
this is the theological dodge of commodity
self-advertising (the revelation

of the holy spirit
in absolute rupture

The stanza's first line swerves into the realm of commodity fetish, where the foreign car brand is as desirable as the female organ it aurally echoes: in some post-Lacanian reading, Volvo and vulva might as well be the same thing. More of the same follows: what were once likely the most romantic river names to a Soviet child now serve to move product. The desecration of desire is unmissable when the onslaught of advertisements expands to include "father and son." Theodicy, the theological tangle of thorns that explains the presence of evil in a world made by divine goodwill, has no convincing words to explain late capitalism. But we cannot trust any of the words on the page to mean what they say anyway, for the author (function) is a known victim of paronymic attraction, the distorting effect on a word by one of its more familiar paronyms. The quoted aside "<this is not a poem>" in turn mimics Magritte's half provocation and half truism: for the cultural artifact is never its missing original, but a signifier divorced from the signified, read as the loss of the divine (of meaning) in the stanza's opening and closing lines.

What is the poetic text in the twenty-first century, if not a

первобытный идол
фетиш или Грааль

[. . .]

опредмечивания
превращения в вещь

пройти через отчуждение
развоплотиться

<эстетический опыт>

превратить себя в изысканный труп
surplus value

primitive idol
fetish or Grail
. . .
turning into objects
transforming into things

to pass through alienation
to become disembodied

\<aesthetic experience\>

to transform yourself into an exquisite corpse
surplus value

Skidan appears to be clawing toward a formulation very close to Sianne Ngai's insight, that the only power poetry retains under late capitalism is a unique ability to theorize powerlessness. If words can expose—not merely reinforce, obfuscate, or prettify—the processes of contemporary alienation and the transformation of vitality into surplus value, they can offer a starting point for imagining something other. But there is a price for breaking the peace and dedicating your writing to the metapoetic function, a price Skidan describes in odd imperatives in interviews: "Write in the absence of a response, but for the sake of acquiring it. To appeal to the people in the absence of people, but for the sake of its formation. And this can only be achieved as follows: becoming a stranger to yourself, your language and your country."[33] Unlike some of the younger poets in the *[Translit]* circle who seem to accept this precondition a priori, Skidan's poetry shows the scars left by the process of estrangement. Relinquishing the subject is painful; abandoning the poetic function maybe even more so. Texts like "Scholia" hardly read as cute or playful, but rather openly ascetic and even just barely keeping nihilism at bay.

Yet amid the wreckage of language, Skidan manages to lay out his aesthetic and political mission in plain poetry, echoing his words in "Protocol on Negative Poetics":

если искусство хочет выжить
в условиях промышленной цивилизации
художник должен научиться воссоздавать
в своих произведениях разрыв
между потребительской стоимостью
и традиционной понятностью

if art wants to survive
in the conditions of industrial civilization
in his works the artist must learn

to reproduce the rupture
between use value
and traditional intelligibility

He repeats "<the rupture>," visually demarcated as such, in the next line, and suggests that it is "in essence / the experience of shock." The closing stanzas run through a blur of literary and philosophical references central to Skidan's understanding of ethics and aesthetics alike: "a poem in prose / about tender buttons" (Stein); "the angel of history with a swastika" (Benjamin); "aleatorics / clynamen" (Lucretius); "elective affinities" (Goethe); "the aestheticization of politics" (Benjamin again); and that only scratches the surface allusions. Politics advance on eros and vice versa: Heidegger flirts with Arendt, and terrible questions whirl about the lot of them, including the wherefore of poetry after the unimaginable. Ultimately Skidan refuses to write verse at all but documents instead a series of ruptures: "Scholia" imagines Russian poetics as a series of critical commentaries on world thought, revealing and perhaps reveling in a second-order relationship to the word. The enemy is always fascism in its legion of forms—including, and above all, its internalized forms—while many of Skidan's heroes form an Internationale of resisting, not uncommonly Jewish, intellectuals.

Writing between Language

Noting the challenge of writing about contemporary poets who themselves so "comfortably cross the theory / poetry divide," Stephanie Sandler remarks that even linguistic boundaries fail in the case of Russian poets who have made such thorough studies of American poetry and critical theory.[34] Skidan is the paradigmatic case study, as a poet whose original work has been profoundly shaped by translating others.[35] Translation might even be more fundamental to Skidan than to Medvedev, for whom it also serves as a recurrent source of inspiration: Skidan's poetry in some integral way reads *as* translation (and perhaps as *tamizdat,* or literature from "over there"). If Medvedev studies a concept or form and then pulls it into his own project, reinventing Bukowski or Serge for a tormented twenty-first-century Russia, for Skidan there is no "own" style, only a bricolage of linguistic insights scavenged from the junkyards. Skidan is a brilliant translator of extremely difficult English-language poetry: the uncanny

FIGURE 3.2 Skidan at the Kelly Writers House in Philadelphia, February 27, 2016.
CHARLES BERNSTEIN / PENNSOUND.

speed and agility with which he renders American experimental poetry into erudite, obscene, or colloquial Russian can only be explained by the fact that he has been doing so his entire life.[36] Skidan emphasizes the centrality of borrowed words to his own texts, which not only translate foreign experiments to Russian terrain but actively retain the alienating sense of cultural foreignness. In interviews, Skidan insists that the intellectual detachment necessary for the work of translation is also needed to produce decent originals.[37]

Nearly all of Skidan's critics, translators, and contemporaries stress the worldliness of his poetry. Dmitry Golynko sees his friend and collaborator as the best example of a nearly forgotten Soviet phenomenon: many talented young writers in the late Soviet period were "enormously well educated" in world literature, the only autonomy afforded to them in a corrupt social order determined by "senile" ideology.[38] Autodidact translators like Skidan, according to Golynko, made remarkable strides and over time produced a veritable library of brilliant "transposition[s] of world poetry into Russian."[39] Their astonishing erudition not only covered classics and modernist canons but stretched into remarkably thorough and up-to-date knowledge of contemporary literature—and proved to be not long for the world (in the "new capitalist and

glamorous Russia such cultural utopia is totally gone away").[40] Today's writers
have to work furiously just to survive, and have no time to read, much less
follow foreign literatures; today's stokers could never survive on one day job
alone. Golynko sees his and Skidan's shared mission as (anachronistically)
resisting Russia's speedy submersion into chauvinistic provincialism and
struggling—against the tragic incursion of late capitalism into all realms of
work and life—to remain in dialogue with world poetry: "For the most advanced contemporary Russian poets such as Arkadii Dragomoshchenko, Alexander Skidan, Kirill Medvedev or Elena Fanailova (all of whom [have been]
widely translated into English) the act of translation or the reading of translated verses means the intense training and broadening of the poetic vision.
Furthermore, the process of translation could be interpreted as the furious
competition with your rivals in other languages, in which you are always belated in comparison with the strongest figure, but this belatedness guarantees
for you the accumulation of your own creative efforts."[41] Golynko's list of
Russian-language poets best able to convert belatedness into furious futurism
begins with Dragomoshchenko and Skidan. Skidan, as Golynko sees him, is a
master of a "dispersed aleatoric" language "depicting the contemporary human
being through the broken glass of twentieth-century infinite thought."[42]

Skidan's 2001 poem "The Big Glass" ("Bol'shoe steklo") reads as a striking illustration of Golynko's point. The piece is composed of ten sections offset by
asterisks, with single lines like clipped snippets of language pulled from the air
(à la Bakhtin, à la Kristeva). The extra spacing allows Skidan to resist, even visually, integration into some semblance of narrative flow or false coherence. Lines
are separated from other lines; quotations, foreign languages, and brackets suggesting stage directions or asides abound. As if taking Roman Jakobson's poetic
function (the key linguistic function oriented toward the message itself; the op-
erative function in poetry, slogans, and other verbiage meant to be striking) to
self-destructive logical extremes, Skidan's lines of text appear to be only about
the failures of lines of text. This, I propose, is what Skidan terms the metapoetic
function, or critique of poetic reason: he uses every technique available to highlight the aesthetic and intellectual incoherence of what he's gathered. Skeptics
(Zhitenev and others) might view such word and worm machines as inflicting
violence on the Russian language, but Skidan actually suggests the reverse: he
refuses and reveals the systemic violence hidden by illusions of unity.

"я-люблю-тебя"
—логические предложения
не могут быть ни подтверждены
ни опровергнуты опытом

"I love you"
—logical propositions
can neither be proven
nor refuted by experience

Often in Skidan's work, the familiar outlines of an erotic fabula (narrator, woman, desire) serve as an excuse for an abstract meditation on language. But it is not only "she" that is always changing in these works: Skidan's style is easily misread as modernist fragmentation but in my reading is too thoroughly poststructuralist, post-Fordist. The poem opens with intimations of a romantic rendezvous but utilizes the uncomfortable familiarity of cliché to dwell on form instead of content, questioning the stability of each linguistic unit—not only "love" in that first simple sentence, but "you," "I," and the spaces in between words. Dmitry Kuzmin, who has likened Skidan's shattered signature style to Russian "fragging" ("the dispersion of discursive cohesiveness that scholars in the United States have attributed to American poetry in the Vietnam War era"), recognizes the extreme citation practice and inclusion of foreign languages as linked to Skidan's poststructuralist understanding of subjectivity.[43]

есть речи
значенье
прагматика
синтаксис
указательное местоимение
согласование огласовка
ни одно слово не лучше другого
<цитата—это способ прервать контекст>
тысячелетнее царство
let it come down

there are languages
there is the meaning of speech
pragmatics
syntax
demonstrative pronoun
concord pronouncing
no one word is better than another
<citation is a means to interrupt context>
thousand-year empire
let it come down

The unexpected line in English echoes the title of Paul Bowles's 1952 novel
(another classic Bowles tale of an American's existential crisis abroad),
swiped in turn from *Macbeth*. The last spoken line before Banquo's murder,
the phrase refers to rain but takes on the ominous undertones of premedi-
tated crime and preordained destiny. *Macbeth* serves as a particularly apt
intertext for the intersections of erotics and politics in Skidan's reflective
verse, which tend so much toward horror, self-reference, and a deep invest-
ment in exposing the "prison-house of language."[44] But Shakespeare—like
Heidegger, like Marx—is only available in the form of reflection and shattered glass.

письменный проект революции
страница изъеденная червями
четвёртая власть
конь блед

чёрная фигура на чёрном
угрызенья террора
первый фильм братьев Маркс
антропологический эксперимент
с двух шагов
расскажите нам как всё происходило

the written project of revolution
page eaten away by worms

> the fourth power
> pale horse
>
> black figure on black
> pangs of terror
> the first film of the Marx brothers
> anthropological experiment
> from two steps away
> tell us how it all took place

Turning over various clichés of rhetoric about the revolution, Skidan tries on one apocalyptic image after the other: the pale horse; the black figure on black; the archaic "pangs" (*ugryzen'ia*) of terror. But the rising sense of fear or revulsion isn't about some nearly unbelievable past *then,* but an eventless flattened *now.* When the allusion to Marx finally comes, it is to the wrong one, or the wrong ones: the Marx brothers (first comes tragedy, then farce). The last few lines, meanwhile, suggest the (post-)Soviet citizen as native informant, mined for information about the greatest anthropological experiment of the twentieth century.

> мутноглазое бешенство телевизоров
> солярный цикл
> будто вступаешь внезапно в свою же мысль
> soleil levant cou tranché
> **твои волосы темнее каштанов**
> слова услышанные в тот день
> утверждать обратное
>
> the murky-eyed fury of televisions
> solar cycle
> as though you are stepping suddenly into your own thought
> *soleil levant cou tranché*
> **your hair is darker than chestnuts**
> words heard on that day
> to assert the reverse

Two forms of typographical marker compete for the reader's attention: the standout line is either the French in the Latin alphabet or the Cyrillic in bold immediately after. "Rising sun sliced neck" is from Guillaume Apollinaire's 1913 "Zone," arguably the central poem of his career (prefacing the collection *Alcools*).[45] The bolded line in turn is a Russian translation of Paul Celan's 1943 "Your hand."[46] Skidan's heroes collide here as overheard and disembodied voices, some in translation and some not, with no explanation offered for either their inclusion or presentation. When every line begins to read as haphazard citation, we are no longer able to read (normally) at all. If we try to control the text through intertextual analysis (the "stock-in-trade of Russian modernist studies"), we fare even worse.[47] The mode of reading Skidan's text imposes instead forces us to read badly and with no semblance of control.

Elsewhere Skidan inserts a line from Dante's *Divine Comedy* ("as experience and art show"; *Purgatorio*): "sì come mostra esperienza e arte." This particular citation might explain Skidan's title: "As when from water or mirror the beam leaps the opposite way, rising at the same angle as it descends, and at an equal length departs as much from the fall of the stone, *as is shown by science [art] and experiment,* so it seemed to me I was struck by light reflected there before me, so that my sight was quick to flee" (canto 15).[48] I have written elsewhere about contemporary writers "reflecting" the iconic mirror imagery of Russian poetry from the previous century.[49] Skidan's contemporary, the metarealist poet Olga Sedakova, for example, mirrors manifesto poems by the two precursors she most directly invokes to motivate her own practice, each of whom used reflective glass as a multilayered metaphor for poetry itself: Pasternak and Brodsky.[50] But Skidan's "mirror of poetry" fails to reflect at all, offering only ontological paradox in the last line, "the transparent non-being of glass" (prozrachnoe bebytie stekla).

три типа эзотерических слов
число необходимых условий
и он вошёл в дом и записал
секс—легален
смерть—порнографична
серебро—то из чего изготовлена серебряная чаша
открывающаяся здесь перспектива
все предложения нашего повседневного языка
в нереализованной форме

поэзия как истребление ценности
нейтральность смысла
и потом
никаких изображений действительности
одна пустыня

three types of esoteric words
number of necessary conditions
and he entered the house and jotted down
sex is legal
death is pornographic
silver is that from which the silver bowl is made
the perspective which opens here
all the propositions of our daily language
in an unrealized form
poetry as extermination of value
neutrality of sense
and later
no representations of reality
only desert

Bringing together (as equivalent?) Judaic esoteric knowledge and postmodernist theory, Skidan adds to his personal canon Celan, Benjamin, Jacques Derrida, but also French Egyptian Edmond Jabès. (In an interview with *The Forward,* Skidan named all the above as sources.) Here too Skidan flirts with a mystical-Jewish-socialist worldview: for while Skidan does not entirely identify as a Jewish poet (his mother is half-Jewish), as he puts it: "On a more metaphysical level, what Jewishness is for me is an experience of going astray, of being lost in the desert, and also the endless experience of finding a way, of finding a thread, to escape."[51] The sense of difference from his surroundings, the desire to be read out of context, comes through in everything he does: Dragomoshchenko's introduction to a bilingual edition of *Red Shifting* casts Skidan as a "Backwards Mirror" himself—a man out of time, reflecting an alternative past.[52] "The Big Glass" rests on foreign languages and incomplete translation to refract Skidan's Russian, and on the extreme use of citation ("<citation is a means to interrupt context>") to break down speech into that of many others. Like the language poets he so admires, Skidan picks out consumer-era clichés to *detourn*—but he cites equally endlessly from his favorite literary and philosophical sources, pitting against the present the very words that taught him to think. Benjamin Paloff argues that Skidan's poems are hardly removed from a "concrete and accessible reality" but indeed "preoccupied with the language and imagery of mundane experience, even as that experience is abstracted by concepts or obscured by cognitive static."[53] The misplaced Soviet flâneur and his reader are left at an intersection of realms: neither inferno nor paradiso, this.

Paloff reads Skidan as a poststructuralist who "lost faith in the signifying function of language" (the title of Skidan's central collection is, after all, *Red Shifting*), and moreover one who has taken a step beyond that "axiom of postmodern thought" that we cannot communicate our experiences accurately to others: "A translator of Slavoj Žižek and Jean-Luc Nancy into Russian, Skidan echoes their fundamental doubt in the individuality of the individual. His work suggests instead that the individual self is also a construct or empty signifier, a bewildering, constantly shifting confluence of impressions, voices, and impulses."[54] If we are inclined to view Skidan through lenses of modernism and postmodernism, we make sense of his shifting dreamscapes exclusively as landscapes of loss. Such readings are not unconvincing, but push, in my view, Skidan's politics and collective work with Chto Delat and younger radical poets to the side. The loss of faith narrative does not explain Skidan's prolific output, continued experimentation, nor the way he is careful to turn his back on nostalgia in his own essays and interviews. When Skidan writes—in lines often cited from "The Big Glass"—"three or four inches from the groin / to specify is to ruin poetry" (v dvukh-trekh diumakh ot pakha / utochnit'—znachit isportit' poeziiu), his next move is not entirely clear: Is he going to do exactly that? Sometimes, ruining poetry is the best plan. The lyric subject may be bewildered to discover that "he" does not exist: the political thinker is not.

Shifting Red

Skidan's understanding of avant-garde poetry emphasizes "shock" over "new," for he harbors a suspicion of the market logic of novelty and of art that lends itself to commodity forms:

I am haunted by the feeling that there is actually an immanent logic of art itself, an artistic development that picked up speed . . . somewhere in the mid-nineteenth century. According to this logic, each next step must be a break with earlier rules and norms. We can see that artistic ideas that were full of political meaning soon become products that write themselves into the frame of an immanent aesthetic logic, which has no relation to the transformation of the existing order of things. . . . As a result, aesthetics takes on the role of a double agent.[55]

In the essay "The Resistance of / to Poetry," Skidan writes that resistance should not be confused with new names, or "novelty for the sake of novelty (novelty caters only to the consumer value of a product)."[56] Instead, and by means of the clashing prepositions in his essay's title and central insight, he means to describe an "insolvable dual meaning" that promises "a more demanding and possibly a more real failure."[57] Avant-garde poetry as practiced by Vvedensky, Dragomoshchenko, and the small handful of Skidan's most consistent international inspirations carves out an alternative space not only against the unpoetic world but against dominant poetic institutions: against all practices that in some way, by means of literature, nevertheless support and interdepend with the status quo. By virtue of the relative autonomy of poetry as an aesthetic linguistic practice—and by virtue of double marginalization as avant-garde and poetry—such praxes have the potential to slip, if perhaps just for a moment, past the iron grip of the present.

A defining poem of Skidan's career and arguably his most sustained early attempt at embodying the resistance of / to poetry, the 2002–2003 "Red Shifting," anchors his collection with the same name. The title comes from physics: red shift, or redshift, refers to a phenomenon whereby light or other electromagnetic radiation is shifted to the red end of the spectrum. An increase in the wavelength of electromagnetic radiation results in a corresponding decrease in frequency, as in the Doppler effect (the frequency of a wave changes in relation to the motion of the observer; named after Austrian physicist Christian Doppler). Skidan of course chose the title for the political pun: "The title, the science aside, is an indirect reference to my personal background. In recent years, in Russia we have witnessed the rare appearance of what might be called leftist grass-roots politics."[58] Skidan's red shift is his attempted escape from the solipsism of becoming a sort of Brodsky 2.0, and an alternative to leaving Russia for abroad—to name the obvious trajectory he could have easily adopted. The lengthy, distinctively fragmented (or more accurately, shattered) manifesto-monument opens with a disorienting gaze at St. Petersburg's facades—and at the ruins of Leningrad, discernible through layers of visible history in a walkable palimpsest. The city and the eye adjoin and seep past the limits of discrete units.

> Эти парадные выглядят как разграбленные гробницы.
>
> Склепы, подвергшиеся нашествию и поруганию с чёрного входа истории—в эпоху, что сама давно уже отошла в область преданий.
>
> Иные производят впечатление лабиринтов, уводящих в толщу воспоминаний о ледниковом периоде.
>
> Двойная экспозиция позволяет обнаружить призрачную, галлюцинаторную природу этих последних.
>
> Они отслаиваются от сетчатки под стать ветшающей, облезающей штукатурке, за которой проступают всё новые и новые геологические слои.
> . . .
> И вместе с медленным просачиванием его вязкой, тягучей субстанции в зрачок история совпадает с собственным истоком: насилием.

> These entranceways look like plundered tombs.
>
> Crypts, subjected to invasion and desecration through the back door of history—during an epoch which itself has long ago departed into the realm of legend.
>
> Others produce the impression of labyrinths, withdrawing into the thick of recollections of the ice age.

Double exposure allows one to discover the ghostly, hallucinatory nature
of these latter.

They flake away from the retina, as though decaying, peeling plaster,
under which emerge ever-new geological layers.
. . .
And together with the slow seepage of its viscous, glutinous
substance into the point of the pupil, history coincides with its
own origin: violence.

Even without the place markers that occur later in the text (Uprising Square,
Nevsky, Kazan Cathedral, Pushkinskaya), there is no missing the location:
St. Petersburg, Petrograd, Leningrad, St. Petersburg, where "history coincides
with its own origin: violence." Architecture, the roving eye(s), photography
and film interpenetrate, making it hard to distinguish the subject and object
of observation. Here again is Skidan's characteristic chain of signifiers, in
place of more stable metaphor, in action: entranceways look like tombs, like
crypts, like labyrinths, like glaciers, like double-exposed photographs, like
the damaged eye, like architectural plaster, like layers of the earth. The signature device is thus a kind of extreme metonymy. The oozing eye (sliced à
la Luis Buñuel and Salvador Dali's 1929 *Un Chien Andalou*? Kino-Eye à la
Vertov?) leaks into the pupil; the origin of violence is violence. The abandoned
palaces of a vanished empire invaded through the "black," or service, entrance
(s chernogo vkhoda) during the equally vanished Soviet era continue their
decay under new, mostly invisible, management. Skidan's eye scrapes familiar
locations as if adding a post-Soviet postscript to Walter Benjamin's *Arcades*.

After this establishing shot, the erotic leitmotif enters, linked to the
English language.

Когда G. переходит на английский язык, она словно бы отсл-
аивается, как переводная картинка, от расплывающегося образа
себя же самой, с которым, казалось бы, породнилась.

Речь преображается, становится неуступчивей, суше; в ней про-
буждаются властные нотки неуёмности, силы влекущие и отталк-
ивающие, вытесняющие в какой-то вакуум.

. . .

Она доставляет мне удовольствие—языком, на котором я едва успеваю за ней угнаться, чувствуя, как сам превращаюсь в чужестранца себе самому.

Переведи.

When G. moves into the English language, it's as if she peels away, like a transfer sheet, from the blurring image of herself, with which, it would seem, she had become related.

The language is transforming, becoming unyielding, drier; commanding little notes of irrepressibility are awakening in it, and forces, attracting and repelling, squeezing into some sort of vacuum.
. . .

She gives me pleasure—with her tongue, in which I barely manage to keep up with her, feeling as if I am turning into a foreigner to my very self.

Translate.

The text is littered with figures indicated only by first letter (enticing G.; nearly as enticing A.; tipsy V.) along with well-known St. Petersburg characters and institutions (Tsaplya, another founding member of Chto Delat; the *Moscow Art Magazine,* where Chto Delat and allies often publish). Margarita Shalina writes of *Red Shifting* that "characters from mythology, critical theory and literature coexist with Skidan's intimates from contemporary St. Petersburg."[59] It is tempting—voyeuristically pleasurable—to read for incorporated fragments of confession, to unpack autobiography through gossip's cross-reference to Skidan's purported lives and loves. But the dramatic degree of zoom-out is ultimately as destabilizing as any of the other machines Skidan puts to use for and against poetry: in other words, yes, but so. Rather than romance between S. and G., we recognize the literary patterns of male-narrated desire; we think of the origins of patterns of speech and their transformations through translation. G. isn't a woman at all but a letter from the Latin alphabet, blurred in Russian translation as if by transfer sheet (in Russian quite literally *perevodnaia kartinka,* or "translating picture").

The narrator's rival for G.'s affections is not only a foreigner but metonymically linked to the rival media haunting "Red Shifting" from the opening lines:

За эспрессо с мороженым в "Сладкоежке" спрашиваю, насколько серьёзен её роман с К. (Две его фотографии из альбома вперемежку с городскими пейзажами и моими портретами, сделанными в предыдущий приезд, из-за которых я наговорил в гостинице кучу глупостей.)
. . .
(Я достаю сигареты, перед глазами—две этих фотографии; я хочу их забыть, хочу их видеть, но чтобы забыть, нужно о них написать, а чтобы видеть—наоборот, нужно быть с G.)
. . .
(Ведь фотографию невозможно уничтожить, невозможно порвать; это многоголовая гидра имени рождённого под знаком Сатурна Б., близорукого, страдающего одышкой еврея, эякулирующего в гроте на Капри в ладошку Аси Лацис.)

Over an espresso with ice cream in "Sweet Tooth" I ask how serious is her love affair with K. (Two of his photos from the portfolio alternate with urban scenes, and portraits of me, taken during her last trip here, about which I blathered a bunch of stupid nonsense in the hotel.)
. . .
(I take out a cigarette, and, before my eyes are these two photographs; I want to forget them, I want to see them, but in order to forget them, I need to write about them, and in order to see them—I need the opposite: to be with G.)
. . .
(In fact it's impossible to destroy a photograph, impossible to tear it up; this many-headed Hydra named in honor of the one born under the sign of Saturn B., the myopic, short-winded Jew, who ejaculated in a grotto on Capri into the little palm of Asya Latsis.)

If Mikhail Bulgakov's Woland falsely promised a generation that "manuscripts don't burn," Skidan suggests the opposite: all paper burns as quickly as cigarettes, but photographic negatives last forever, asexually reproducing their endless doubles. As in the poem's title, the technological or scientific reference always gives way to politics, which is in turn the same thing as erotics. For Skidan, photography—art as mechanical reproduction—immediately conjures one of his early idols: Benjamin, the "myopic, short-winded Jew" who also shifted red and traveled to Soviet Russia for the love of Latvian Bolshevik Asya Latsis. Benjamin understood the cognitive and political potential of photography: to show what is not visible to the human eye; to reveal complex formations of past and present; and, in the hands of photographer-writers, to politically transform the world.[60]

Skidan reverses Benjamin's trajectory to Russia in pursuit of Latsis, and in turn recollects the journey westward of another (imagined) Russian:

Свидригайлов уезжает в Америку.

Об этом его "отъезде" я делал доклад в 1994 году в университете Айовы.
. . .
Эй, вы, Svidrigaylov.
Что вы думаете об удовольствии?
. . .
Когда я фотографирую себя одного на вокзалах или в аэропортах, я выбрасываю или разрываю фотографию на маленькие кусочки, которые я позволяю себе выбросить через окно, если это поезд, или оставляю их в пепельнице или журнале, если это самолёт.
. . .
Присутствовала ли на этом докладе Г.? Не помню.

В любом случае, она отредактировала мой текст, более того, переписала его набело. Мне хватило бесстыдства сделать это её руками (рукой).

Svidrigaylov is leaving for America.

About this "departure" of his I have a talk at the University of Iowa in 1994.

. . .

Hey, you, *Svidrigaylov.*

What do you think of pleasure?

. . .

When I photograph myself alone at train stations or airports I throw away or tear up the photograph into little pieces, which I allow myself to throw out through the window if it's a train or leave in an ashtray or inside a magazine if it's an airplane.

. . .

Was G. present at this talk? I don't remember.

In any case, she edited my text, more than that, made a fair copy of it. I had shamelessness enough to do this with her hands (hand).

Going to America stands in for suicide in Dostoevsky's book: indeed, the New World might as well have been the underworld for centuries of Russian writers to whom it represented an unreachable realm, an impossible utopia / dystopia of mythical freedoms or alien ideologies. Skidan, lecturing on Svidrigaylov at the Iowa Writers' Workshop, might as well be sending home postcards from the house of the dead. Shredding and discarding photographs of himself (alone) is a controlled form of self-destruction, and those photos again stand in stark contrast with the fair copy—a form of sexual reproduction?— made of the narrator's text by G., by hand. The rivalry between media is savage here, as is the (probably shameful, probably exploitative) longing to reconstitute a self *with* the other, by means of the other. The aim is subjectivization rather than false self; politics rather than police.[61] Whether *this* narrator can get there—whether he can break out of the ranks of the already dead—is less clear, first and foremost to him.

 In interviews and critical essays, Skidan consistently links the polyphony of his forms to his politics, mediated by way of an understanding of the self and other. (He reports, "From the early 1990s, itself a time of breaches, I began to question the idea of authorship," experiencing himself as "a person writing who consists of other voices, of an endless dialogue of voices . . . there is no rigid or stable 'I' who writes, but instead a constant process of sharing, of addressing and hearing."[62]) However, Skidan writes politics very differently than do either Medvedev or Arseniev—despite the fact that the latter has been thoroughly influenced by Skidan. Skidan aims, as he puts it, to "follow Go-dard's dictate—not to shoot political film, but to shoot film politically."[63] Moreover, he sees in poetry a lingering (perhaps resurrected) power to slip outside the existing order of things in an era dominated by visual forms. For Skidan, part of the inherent politics of poetry is as *pharmakon*—the remedy / poison—to visual culture.

An earlier era rebelled against language in favor of multimedia and vi-sual thinking: Rudolf Arnheim, a pioneer of film theory, posited in his 1969 treatise *Visual Thinking* that the linear sequence of language expressed only a fraction of the workings of the mind and argued for the primacy of the visual.[64] In the same decade, Marshall McLuhan—credited by some for predicting the World Wide Web thirty years in advance—published his *Gutenberg Galaxy* (1962) and *Understanding Media* (1964). Marie-Laure Ryan summarizes the key insight from McLuhan that helped to shaped decades of media theory: medium affects the message, and "print culture favors logical, abstract, and controlled thought, at the expense of spatial perception and of the artistic, holistic, metaphorical, or musical types of imagination."[65] And in those same years, Guy Debord published *The Society of Spectacle* (1967), with the primary thesis that capitalism reduces society to spectacle, the "autocratic reign of the market economy."[66] For Skidan, finding his footing in Russia in the 1990s, Debord seemed like the prophet to follow.

Skidan describes the new Russia as an even more bankrupt incarnation of Soviet-style ideological control: "The 'soft' terror of the mass media and the cult of consumerism have replaced ideological control in the post-Soviet space. . . . The speed with which information is transmitted via electronic and wireless networks has increased so exponentially that our customary (bookish) skills for reading and making sense of it malfunction. . . . Televi-sion, the Internet, mobile telephones, computing, and all the other forms of instantaneous recording and communication form a market of synthetic, si-multaneous perception that deepens its industrialization and automation."[67] In the brave new world of the twenty-first century (in Russia and in the United States alike this time), Benjamin's photographs have multiplied and come to life, and they bombard would-be subjects from every angle through the visual culture of late capitalism, an anthropological experiment without a trace of utopian illusions. Poetry, the weapon of the weak—unspectacular, unpopular, monochrome, boring, slow, of little to no market value—has some small chance to stand outside a totalizing media economy busily forging the new man in all-encompassing laboratories. However, despite or because of a to-the-death competition with rival media, a number of Skidan's most iconic poems are about the visual arts. (As one reviewer puts it, Skidan's journey into the psyche "passes through" cinema and anticinema.[68]) Memory, in particular, is mediated by photographs and movies: "Red Shifting" oddly echoes, even as it rejects, the lyrical autobiographism of Andrei Tarkovsky's 1975 masterpiece *The Mirror*. To write politically is to follow and transubstantiate Godard.

In 2015, I had the opportunity to work closely with Skidan on translations of his works for a University of Pennsylvania collective translation workshop. Skidan chose to return to several of his shorter "film poems" from the end of the 1990s, rewriting them in real time with the help of new readers and writers.[69] I translated two with his feedback and input: "A Short Tango" and "Kino Eye." Both read as deceptively simple on the surface, with which they are very much concerned. Originally written a decade or so before "Red Shifting," they show a dramatically different side of Skidan's style and broaden our understanding of his range, prefiguring in some ways the striking new poetry he has published in the years since.

> Марлон Брандо говорит по-французски,
> и ничего не говорит. Грохот
> сабвея, моста медленное сверло.

> Ласка, кремирующая ответный
> безблагодатный жест. Она
> состригает ноготь на пальце,
> входящем позднее в его промежность.
> [. . .]
> Танго с голой
> задницей, танго.

> Marlon Brando speaks in French,
> and doesn't say a thing. The noise
> of the subway, the slow drill of the bridge.

The caress incinerating the responding
grateless gesture. She
clips short the nail on her finger
later to enter his rectum.
[. . .]
Tango with a naked
bottom, tango.

From the first line, we know we are in Bernardo Bertolucci's *Last Tango in Paris,* the scandal of 1972 that paired an aging Marlon Brando with newcomer Maria Schneider (so traumatized by her experiences on set that she swore never to film another sex scene again). Skidan's poem summarizes the film with terse verbal elegance yet reveals nothing beyond what we already know: sound as noise, surface erotics, bodies, scenes. We watch Skidan recall a canonical film from Europe's richest decade of political and cultural foment, but it is as if the poem repeats as well as retells the gesture of the film's central conceit: the damaged protagonists launch into a physical relationship without sharing anything else. To my ear there is an echo of Vasily Kamensky's 1914 "ferroconcrete" poem *Tango with Cows* here as well—even when aiming for minimalism, Skidan loves cross-cultural montage.

[. . .]Условие
принято: никаких имен, никаких
дат, историй из детства. Разве что
танец,—и рикошет

пули,
обрывающей никчемный экстаз

[. . .]The conditions
have been accepted: no names, no
dates, no childhood stories. Only
the dance,—and the ricochet

of the bullet,
cutting short the useless ecstasy

Brando (or "Brando"—actor, character, and visual image) fades into a reminder of the medium's mortality and the passage of time: "a pitiful / pale spot, / gleaming in the darkness of the final frame" (zhal'kaia / belesaia tochka, / mertsaiushchaia v temnote final'nogo kadra). Skidan allows us no glimpse of a lyric subject watching or remembering these films, no portrait of the poet as a young man, nor even a single word of meditation on what these shared ekphrastic memories might signify. In interview, he clarifies that he also didn't allow himself to rewatch the films he wrote about for this cycle: "It was something like an experiment on myself, an attempt to carry out a phenomenological reduction."[70] The fabula of Bertolucci's film offers a near allegory of Skidan's poetic experiment: reduction, strict rules, refusal to share.

Written for the same early cinematic cycle, "Kino Eye" in turn allows for slightly more lyricism, toying with repetitions of Romantic imagery, but it too relies on the reader / viewer's memory of the film to come to life. The Romantic allure is borrowed and bracketed, as it were. Would there be pleasure in the text at all without the sense of recognition and shared memory—and perhaps for some reader-voyeurs, the shared memory of (shameful) desire? Again, unmistakably from the first line, this time we are in Werner Herzog's *Aguirre, the Wrath of God* (also 1972). A volatile Klaus Kinski mimes madness too believably in the jungle, under the camera-eye of his "best fiend" director.

Агирре, гнев Божий, поет
индейскую песню. В скважины перуанской флейты
хлещет христианская кровь.

Листва. Солнце.
Бесшумно
за борт падает часовой.

Беглец никуда, ниоткуда, Кински,
помутившийся кинокамеры глаз
трахает невинную дщерь.

[. . .]

Агирре, гнев Божий, поет
индейскую песню. В скважины перуанской флейты
хлещет христианская кровь.

Листва. Солнце. Медлительный
свинец реки.
Отравленная стрела

в шейных позвонках командора
вращает непотопляемый плот,
Ноев обезьяний ковчег.
В мертвой точке вращенья пейзажа.

Aguirre, the wrath of God, sings
an Indian song. In the shaft of the Peruvian flute
spurts Christian blood.

Foliage. Sun.
Inaudibly
the sentry falls overboard.

A fugitive to nowhere, from nowhere, Kinski,
the camera eye clouding
fucks his virgin child.

[. . .]

Aguirre, the wrath of God, sings
an Indian song. In the shaft of the Peruvian flute
spurts Christian blood.

Foliage. Sun. The slow
lead of the river.
The poison arrow

in the cervical vertebrae of the commander
rotates the insubmersible raft,
Noah's simian ark.
In the blind spot of the rotating landscape.

Skidan singles out both of these ekphrastic poems in interview and cites precisely this cycle—written at the end of a century—as the moment of his attempted break from lyrical subjectivity. This may also explain the Dziga Vertov title: as Skidan puts it, "I needed to grab hold of something material, subject to physical sensation—something that would allow me to take the position of an external, detached observer and therefore to escape 'direct' lyric confessional writing. And that's what brought me to cinema."[71] This fabula is a feint: we are looking at another poem about the rivalry of arts.

Cinema affected all other media in the twentieth century: with the introduction of film, in a matter of decades, literary forms were displaced "from the position of unquestioned dominance which they enjoyed for four centuries in the West."[72] Building on Fredric Jameson, Julian Murphet argues in *Multimedia Modernism* that media ecologies display "savage competition for resources, sudden mutations, survival of the fittest, extinction of unsuccessful species."[73] Competition with other media forces literature especially into self-consciousness and a quest for meaningful materiality.[74] This is what Skidan seems to be after in the cinema poems, ultimately: to steal for poetry the detached, mechanical eye that he felt it needed but also to rewrite his favorite films after 1968 without the spectacle.

Skidan proved a prescient observer of the rapidly transforming media ecology and its political implications in Russia of the 1990s. In the essay "Poetry in the Age of Total Communication," he examines poetry's attempts to survive, including the use of electronic music and video / slide projections (e.g., by the Riga-based group Orbita). "The premise," he writes, "is that the word as such has become devalued and ineffective and, therefore, needs to be compensated by an energetic audiovisual supplement."[75] To stay afloat, poets now also aim for spectacle, for audience interaction; in the most ambitious cases, for Total Art. When given the option, writers abandon the word for newer media, seduced by the siren call of contemporary art. For Skidan, as for his close friend and contemporary Golynko, such poetics articulate a radical mistrust of text as such, "unprofitable and useless . . . without audiovisual vaccinations and injections."[76]

Ultimately, Skidan sees fresh hell in poetry's most recent inclusive shift:

> The center of creative work has shifted to the visual arts because (1) they immediately reflect, and partly coincide with, the new technogenic

environment, (2) which mobilizes the cerebral and sensorimotor resources of human beings along with the earth's natural resources and outer space. (3) The visual arts correspond to the dominant regime of temporality and synthetic perception established by the mass media. (4) They are inscribed in the culture industry and, consequently, (5) in the capitalist machine, which deterritorializes any form of identity based on linguistic competency. This competency has been replaced by (6) an expanded (re)production and consumption of audiovisual images, (7) which now form the primary zone for experiments with the collective unconscious. This unconscious is nowadays not structured like a language (per Lacan), but like an exteriorized sensorium, a screen-projected ectoplasm whose center is nowhere, but whose affects are everywhere.[77]

Skidan sympathizes with Orbita and supports with enthusiasm the leftist experiments of his *[Translit]* comrades, but in his own poetic practice Skidan neither adds AV nor sings. He prefers to remain unprofitable and useless.

Coda: Contamination

For years after his monumental political poems of the 2000s, Skidan was everywhere as a critic, an essayist, an editor, collaborator, and political thinker—but less so as a poet. Without an outright gesture of refusal like Medvedev's, he seemed to have hit an impasse in terms of his own publishing. And then something shifted, again. In 2018 Skidan released as if out of nowhere a novel, *A Guide to N (Putoveoditel' po N)*, an extraordinary pseudoautobiography of Friedrich Nietzsche as schizophrenic text–cum–gravestone to continental philosophy. While responses to the work are still coming in, the novel promises to cement Skidan's status as one of the major Russian writers of our time even well outside of leftist or poetic circles. Moreover, the novel was accompanied by an expansive new cycle of poems published in the same year; two years later, midpandemic, Skidan released an entirely new book of poetry.

Matvei Yankelevich, introducing translations from the 2018 cycle *The Works and Days of Daniil Ivanovich*, notes that "over the last few years, the poems Skidan posts sporadically on his Facebook account had been brief and dense, sometimes just a quatrain or two, chock full of what cannot be called allusions in the traditional sense (as in his work in the 1990s and 2000s), but rather of something one might liken to broken hypertext links."[78] As the title suggests, the 2018 cycle is about a parodic version of Kharms—written in a version of Kharms's signature "anegdote" form, accessed by way of Prigov and the decades of experiment since. Yankelevich calls Skidan's versions "little pressure cookers" that *detourn* but also "zombify a dead literary language"— zombie-poems.[79] To a certain extent Skidan's prevalent tactic, of mixing the mundane with literary references, is consistent with his earlier work; and yet the poems read as fundamentally different in tone. Rather than an attack on the previous century's avant-garde (a mockery of Kharms's pretensions, as the cycle could easily be read), the cycle in my view works to reanimate Kharms's signature form, simultaneously lifting it into contemporary context and paying the most appropriate homage to the OBERIU master: reductio ad absurdum.

What strikes me most about Skidan's poetry of the past few years— including *The Works and Days of Daniil Ivanovich* and the (well-titled) 2020 collection *Contamination* in particular—is a fierce and prolific new vitality. Working in sharp, short forms and in hilarious, on the surface at least accessible (radically democratic?) language, Skidan no longer seems to be referencing the avant-garde and studying OBERIU trans-formation from across the abyss of the twentieth century. He appears to be reliving it in real time: mocking, synthesizing, and churning out word / worm machines that chew through our own moment without distance or pause:

папа умер мама умер
умер я и сам
а потом я вызвал убер
убер убер убещур
приезжай-ка насовсем
будем резать будем пить
на фонтанке водку
все равно тебе возить
харонову лодку
ах в краях далеких тех

люди люди люди
кто-то должен продолжать за них
а не то чтоб бляди

papa died mama died
I died myself
and then I called an uber
uber uber ubeshchur
come on here for good
we're gonna cut we're gonna drink
vodka on Fontanka
anyway you've got to carry
Charon's ferry
ah in those far-off lands
there are people people people
someone's got to go on for them
not whores

Uber, Uber, ubeshchur—from the ride-sharing technology's name Skidan extracts the arguably most famous lines of Russian avant-garde poetry: Kruchenykh's "Dyr bul schyl / ubeshchur." Kruchenykh infamously claimed that there was more Russian literature in those nonsense (trans-sense) lines than in all of Pushkin's *Onegin:* so too, Skidan mercilessly implies, "uber uber" in Cyrillic profoundly encapsulates contemporary Russian culture. A language of literature and street violence emerges as a mix without contradiction, without the strong sense of register-clash such lines might have invoked mere decades ago: all is ridiculous, all is poetic, and it burns with an irrepressible, merry rage that bodes ill for the institutions it means to topple.

The fathers are dead, the mothers are dead, "I" is dead. But somewhere beyond the waters there are "people people people" worth living for. It is in such texts that we can discern what I suggest is a reverse influence from the younger poets (Medvedev, Arseniev, and to my ear, perhaps especially the contagiously fun Osminkin) whom Skidan has mentored over the years, and whose energy and output evidently inspire the older poet with hope for the future. It is as if what Skidan and others ultimately tried to conjure since the turn of the twenty-first century was a new kind of Russian poet—and it worked. From 2003 to 2022, the Russian poetic left has spread, diversified, grown in readership and influence: Skidan's *Contamination* came out in October 2020, undeterred by even the peak of the global pandemic. His publishing house, the independent St. Petersburg institution *Poriadok slov,* celebrated the event with a dual reading, on Zoom for virtual audiences and on the Fontanka canal for those in person.

As Skidan put it in an interview a few years back, when faced with the recurrent critique that difficult poetry, small journals, and minoritarian practices cannot change a thing, and hence might as well not exist (a curious ontology): "Yesterday I flew to Khrabrovo and on the road there in the taxi saw a huge number of caterpillars that had crawled out to bask in the sun—and, maybe, no one else saw them, but does that mean they were never there? And today's downpour probably made them return to their wormy apples. So it is with modern poetry."[80] Skidan imagines the outburst of leftist political poetry emerging from Russia over the past twenty years in similar terms. Red shift. Today's downpour may well have driven the caterpillars underground, but that doesn't mean they were never there—or that they might not return, in greater numbers, at the next slightest break in the clouds.

4

Dmitry Golynko

WRITING POETRY FOR ZOMBIES

*N*OT UNLIKE ALEKSANDR SKIDAN, his friend and frequent collaborator Dmitry Golynko (né Golynko-Vol'fson) pushed the boundaries of Russian poetry from a perspective informed by critical theory and global art practice. Golynko (born in Leningrad in 1969, died in 2023 in the same city by another name) was also on the older edge of the spectrum of poets associated with *[Translit]* and the new Russian left. But unlike Skidan, Golynko was a formally trained academic, with a PhD and a specialization in media studies: for a while, he was among the few in the group to successfully retain a precarious position in Russian academia.[1] I argue in this chapter that Golynko pioneered the by now prevalent understanding of Russian poetry as a form of global and contemporary art, informed by and in dialogue with critical theory. In that sense, Golynko followed Dmitry Prigov in the metamorphosis of the Russian poet into an art world figure. However, Golynko was less performative trickster than erudite theorist: his contribution lay in absorbing and synthesizing swaths of political and aesthetic theory and teaching it to whomever will listen. A number of the younger *[Translit]* poets studied with Golynko, formally and informally. Many more have been deeply influenced by his lectures and texts on new materialism, affect and ecology, accelerationism, and posthumanism—informed by conceptual frames and case studies from around the world as well as near neighbors (Slovenian psychoanalytic circles; Polish left intelligentsia), students, and friends.[2] In this chapter I argue that Golynko, still relatively understudied or read outside of his collective context by many scholars, was in many ways the key media theorist of *[Translit]*.[3]

Golynko's poetry of the past two decades appears coconstitutive with his research and reads as less in dialogue with Pushkin than with Warhol. Praxes like Skidan's and Golynko's adjoin in many respects, while remaining distinctive stylistically; and the two are often linked by critics and scholars. But the resemblance is perhaps best thought of as a case study in convergent evolution: two perceptive language artists, having survived the transmutation of late Soviet into contemporary Russia, both arrive at a leftist political orientation and renewed interest in poetry as a medium for political aesthetic expression. If Skidan's shattered monuments reveal many archeological layers of modernity and the traumas of their passage, however, Golynko's signature style (long combinatorial poetic cycles alongside polemical essays) reads as if written long after subjectivity, long after the death of the last lyric hero, even long after the last human.

In a review of one of several bilingual English and Russian editions of Golynko's poetry, Eireene Nealand summarizes his career path as follows: "Golynko came of age as a writer during Russia's Perestroika period in the mid-1980's and 1990's when an almost chance meeting between Arkadii Dragomoshchenko and Lyn Hejinian resulted in the exposure of the young poet to work by American writers such as Lyn Hejinian, Susan Howe, Charles Olsen, Michael Palmer, Robert Duncan and John Ashbery."[4] Jacob Edmond and Cilla McQueen likewise consider Golynko, alongside Skidan, as one of a small group of St. Petersburg poets profoundly shaped by Dragomoshchenko (and American language poetry, again by way of Dragomoshchenko and Hejinian).[5] However, as Ilya Kukulin notes, Golynko is an especially tricky poet / writer / thinker to pin down, and his origin story is hard to trace: his output is wildly prolific but also diverse, consisting of varied experimental texts and essays in several languages, alongside academic genres. Golynko's writing also took a radical turn around 2001–2002 (by no coincidence, as I argue, the same years as Medvedev began publishing his first books of politically charged poetry, and a year before Chto Delat came into existence—the end of the cease-fire). Before all that, Kukulin describes a younger Golynko as seemingly another "exaggerated-Petersburg author, complicated and mannered," although he adds that, with the wisdom of hindsight, careful readers might now find even in Golynko's early texts less a recycling of the St. Petersburg myth than something "quite modern."[6] Dmitrii Bak likewise notes Golynko's dramatic shift at the turn of the century away from the "corroded theme of St. Petersburg's carnival buffoonery—to a strict poetic political economy of meanings, to deliberate series of variations on given topics."[7]

Still other factors make categorizing Golynko's poetic oeuvre seem like a losing proposition. Kevin Platt points out that, though nearly of the same generation as now canonical post-Soviet postmodernists (Pelevin et al.), Golynko doesn't read that way. Unlike the majority of writers who made their names in the literary underground before or just after the fall of the Soviet Union, Golynko had the late bloomer's advantage: while belated dissidents were still lowering lances against Soviet memories, Golynko had moved on to "new fights, both aesthetic and political."[8] Just as the new era was beginning to show its second set of teeth, Golynko found his voice in a productive, recursive minimalism.

By the 2000s, Golynko had already evolved his most distinctive form: "In the place of poem-like twisting and whimsical narratives appear unique cycles of stanzas, serially developing one main theme. In the place of a linear (sometimes—complicatedly multi-linear!) narrative—musical variations of leitmotifs embodied in crisp series of stanzas, clear to the point of transparency; and at the same time [we encounter] punctuation marks inside the individual poems consistently challenging the boundaries of lines and stanzas."[9] Pressed to describe this new style, critics wax metaphorical, comparing Golynko's poems to "scalpels sharpened by years of linguistic oversimplification at the postmodernist scab that formed after the Soviet Union's dissolution in 1991," or to "serial music, slender and demonstratively cold verbal aleatorics."[10] Indeed, his best-known cycle of poems, "Elementary Things," resembles precisely computer-generated text, as if some posthuman intelligence had been set the task of relentlessly trying out variations on a given theme. More playfully, we might consider Golynko's forms as akin to Andrei Bely's lined and numbered—and I would argue, wildly avant-garde—symphonies, equally disparaged by contemporaries as overambitious and mostly unreadable. Fittingly, Golynko has been a longtime member of the Bely Prize jury, and his breakthrough 2002 cycles were written exactly one hundred years after the *Dramatic Symphony*.

"Lots of Different Things" ("Mnogo raznogo," 2003) serves as a relatively approachable introduction to Golynko's poetry, revealing what I would con-

FIGURE 4.1 Dmitry Golynko contemplates media spectacle after history.
JACKET2 MAGAZINE.

sider his signature techniques in a nearly straightforward if detached meditation on reading, memory, and emotion:

1

читатель разглядывает гору книг
много разного он из них разузнал когда-то
много сведений, толковых теорий, больших идиом
много точных и правильных наблюдений
теперь эти источники сомнения и тревог
пылятся, свалены в груду в углу, на стуле
читатель себе удивляется, вот книгожор
сколько ему довелось перечитать, чихая

the reader scrutinizes a pile of books
he found out lots of different things from them once
lots of information, many sensible theories, big idioms
lots of correct and precise observations

now these springs of doubt and anxiety
gather dust, piled up in the corner, on a chair
the reader is surprised at himself, what a bookhead
how many of them he managed to read through, sneezing

2
. . . теперь книга ценна ему
не тем, что вложили в нее ум
честолюбие автора, его гений

. . . now he values a book
not because of what the mind, the vanity of the author,
his genius had put into it

3
совсем иным—тем состояньем
или той ситуацией, когда эта книга лежала
у него, читателя, на коленях
иль перед ним на столе; книга в его
памяти вызывает ассоциации с моментом
прошлого, отведенным ее чтению
внимательному, урывками
взахлеб или по диагонали

but for something else entirely, the condition
or the situation when the book lay
on his, the reader's, knees
or in front of him on the table, the book triggers
associations in his memory of the moment
in the past allotted to reading it
carefully, in snatches
unable to put it down, aslant[11]

The stanzas that follow reveal each book's associative memory of a moment
preceding a rupture; a snatch of emotionally tagged memories punctuating
a continuum of dusty texts and pressing engagements. In the hands of an-

other poet—even in the hands of politically kindred and thoroughly theorized poets like Medvedev, Arseniev, or Skidan—such stanzas would likely still begin with the semblance of autobiography, or with the "I" at least as a point of departure. But Golynko's "reader" is as distant to the author as to anyone else, regardless of whose story is being told. Golynko states in one of many manifestos that in his view, private history, including the poet's biography, "can be retold only in terms of social experience, more often negative than positive, the experience of habitual disorder and class inequality."[12] Distance is, and enables, the plot: the understanding that there is nothing outside the social allows the poet to "carry out a severe political diagnosis of contemporary man," including "his longing for social justice and simultaneous lack of faith in the possibility of its realization, his syndromes of melancholy and existential reverie, his atrophied desires and total deficit of futurity."[13] Golynko's characteristic move is to coolly observe his own life and mind (or someone else's; we can't tell, and it doesn't matter) as of interest only because entirely symptomatic. The degree to which Golynko appears to have internalized this fundamentally anti-Romantic, antilyric stance is what sets his work apart, and allows him to use language to think, to do things with words instead. The lingering romance with world culture (albeit leftist, emancipatory world culture) still evident in Skidan's assemblages shades for Golynko into an analytic interest in the use value of deconstructive tools that are as quickly left behind when they grow stale—as is any form, or poetry itself.

Everything is just as it appears: all is surface, (*nouveau-*)*nouveau roman*, poetry of postinteriority. Golynko summarizes even the story of his personal aesthetic / political evolution by listing the names of the publishing houses behind his key publications: the means of production are the story. In 1994, the small and bohemian independent publisher Borey-Art released his early collection *Homo scribens*. In 2001, *Directory* came out with Argo-Risk ("thanks to the enormous efforts of Dmitry Kuzmin, the most advanced content-provider and promoter of contemporary Russian poetry").[14] Golynko suggests that it was in this second book that his literary technique evolved toward long, narrative "novels-in-verse" dedicated to the "ludic chaos and anxiety" of Russia post-perestroika.[15] By 2003, New Literary Review, the most prestigious publishing house in Russia, picked up Golynko's most celebrated collection, *Concrete*. That third book is divided into two parts, consisting of poems written before 2002 and those after; and it is this second section that marks the start of a distinctively radicalized phase for Golynko.[16] The Golynko of *[Translit]* burst into view with ready Russian examples of a new left poetics— and soon enough he began publishing in his own *kruzhok*'s journal.

Golynko's stylistic change to serial forms ("decontextualized fragments of alienated expressions without any subject") was inspired too by the dramatically changed status and conditions for writers in post-Soviet Russia. If Soviet artists and intellectuals once took up menial jobs (Skidan as stoker) to free up maximal amounts of time for reading world literature, Golynko experienced firsthand the radical change in the cultural and actual capital afforded literature in the new Russia. The "sacral metaphysical status of literary language" gave way to "everyday electronic chatter" under the looming shadow of "notorious Putinesque affluence," as he puts it in interviews.[17] Poetry's devalued status brought practical concerns as well: Golynko, who has spent time at the Iowa Writers' Workshop as well as other writing residencies in the United States and Europe, reminds international readers that Russian poetry is not supported by a well-developed academic creative writing infrastructure, and that moreover "the number of the literary magazines (and the printing runs) decreased catastrophically" in the post-Soviet period.[18] In the United States, by contrast, MFA programs blur institutional boundaries between creative and scholarly writing, and in the process afford economic as well as social support entirely absent in Russia, where writers experienced the horrors of privatization and resource redistribution from the trenches rather than at a safe remove. A diminishing number continued to look for new language and forms to describe the banal collective tragedies of the everyday: most moved abroad and / or looked for other lines of work. It is in no small part due to the relative lack of institutional allies within Russian academe that the remaining experimental writers find themselves in dialogue with international interlocutors.

In a manifesto for *[Translit]* issue 8, "Untimely Notes on the Status of Literary Work," Golynko generalizes his experiences and observations into a call to action: "Whatever model of literary work a writer has chosen for himself, sacral or profane, archaic or innovative, diverse or self-absorbed, it is crucial that this work remain not entirely adequate to the present moment; that it deviate from its time in one direction or another, toward cruel criticism or total disregard."[19] Like Skidan, Golynko finds promise in poetry's cognitive dissonance from the contemporary, whether it be achieved by mining the past or anticipating the future, or both. As a scholar of Russian literature (among other global and interesting forms) he finds it particularly productive to reanimate the old ghosts of St. Petersburg / Petrograd / Leningrad / St. Petersburg. Of course, it was Petersburg, ever the metropolis of "idle dandies unladen with families, social status or [other] liabilities," that sparked the newest Russian avant-garde. For so Golynko describes the seemingly inexhaustible subversive potential of his city: "It was the Ghost-city, the Demonic mirage, mass scale dreaming. Petersburg perfectly pictured the idea of Bohemia. . . . [And once again] the late Soviet period and early stage of wild Russian capitalism . . . created the most suitable circumstances for bohemian identity and bohemian communities."[20] One hundred years after Bely and company did much the same, twenty-first-century Petersburg bohemians continue to view their city as an "infinite cultural archive" that they treat with continuous irony and cheerful sarcasm, all the more so as this archive famously consists of "clichés and secondary copies of European culture."[21] Like Marshall Berman, Golynko views St. Petersburg's crooked mirror to the (former) West as an aesthetic and intellectual asset, allowing for some recurrent version of the "modernism of underdevelopment" to spring early from its haunted streets.[22] So it was in the nineteenth century, at the turn of the twentieth, and so it could be today—if any writers survive cognitive and disaster capitalism.

Now as in the past, Golynko writes, St. Petersburg's youthful bohemian subjectivity lingers between that of bourgeois and revolutionary, serving as a stage in the transition from rebel to radical. Moreover, he argues that while such bohemia might seem to have no past or future, "that's not true at all": the lived present of St. Petersburg's bohemia is indeed a kind of "imaginary future zone that already exists today. . . . It may be a little naive and simple-minded, but certainly full of creative potential."[23] Golynko's work after 2002, then, should be understood as emerging out of transitional bohemia and taking full advantage of his city's strange temporalities. For Golynko, it was predetermined that a project like *[Translit]* would appear precisely in St. Petersburg, city-archive of world culture, in poor copy. His mission has been to guide himself and others along the road of intellectual emancipation, speeding the transition.

Socially Applied Poetry

One of Golynko's most overtly programmatic essays, "Applied Social Poetry: Inventing the Political Subject," was written in response to the political events in Moscow of December 2011. Golynko explains that his inspiration came partly from events in the streets and partly from reading at the right moment the internationally renowned Polish artist Artur Żmijewski (a founding member of *Krytyka polityczna*). In a comparable manifesto from 2007, "Applied Social Art," Żmijewski argues that art can again be used "for the most diverse goals: as an instrument of receiving and disseminating knowledge, as a factory of cognitive procedures, based on intuition and imagination, as an occasion for learning and for political action."[24] Following Prigov's insight that what is possible for global art should be possible for Russian poetry, Golynko extends these goals to certain kinds of poetic practice. However, the translation, as it were—from Polish to Russian, from art to poetry—leaves remainders and plenty of room for anxiety, not least over the difference in reception. A visual work of art (an installation, or a performance especially) has the advantage of physically gathering an audience, and hence maintains a potential for direct and fluid relationships between performers and audiences very different from the ways in which we typically consume poetry. But perhaps that distinction held only in the last two centuries: part of the *[Translit]* constellation's resistance of / to Web 2.0 (to borrow and slightly skew Skidan's words) lies in the different way poetry is experienced if encountered "collectively" in off- and online platforms. So it was before solitary reading culture emerged in bourgeois Europe; and so, in different incarnations, it is again across the world.

Still, in contemporary Russia, the call for a socially applied poetry, Golynko acknowledges, "may appear questionable and somewhat paradoxical, given that in the second half of the twentieth century poetry has become a marginal and practically unfinanced occupation."[25] Today's poet is thus typically stuck oscillating between several bad choices: mimicking pathetically the "romantic myth of the solitary genius" even if professing progressive politics; haughtily asserting "aesthetic autonomy and the hermetic closedness of his creations" à la Vladimir Nabokov in perpetuity; or chasing recognition and sustenance via the available apparatus of literary and educational institutions (the elite literary mainstream). What slim chance, then, does a leftist poet today have to produce "an instrument for the practical transformation of society and the correction of social troubles?" In what turns out, retroactively, to have been an uncharacteristically optimistic piece (Golynko witnessed firsthand and suffered personally the waves of repression and mood of defeat that followed the jubilation of the 2011–2012 protests and stopped publishing poetry for many years), he dares imagine how such a slim chance might look:

> The poet with a radical gesture renounces the principle of aesthetic autonomy, as well as the use of the stereotypical (Romantic and modernist) postures of the poet-prophet, demon or eccentric. At the same time, he is compelled to free himself from the illusion of artistic independence and to admit his absolute dependence on antagonistic social codes. . . . Applied social poetry arises in that moment when the poet delegates his unique authorial voice to that mass of the disenfranchised and the oppressed, which has been stripped of the possibility to speak in the field of the contemporary culture industry.[26]

Renouncing performative and narcissistic self-fashioning as an irrelevant and damaging distraction from the pursuit of knowledge, a politically engaged poet can aim instead to produce texts that "distinctly express that ethico-political measure of the current day . . . in the language of direct and immediate intervention in current events."[27] If Skidan's take on contemporary Russian avant-garde poetry abjures or brackets the subject, Golynko tries to delegate the poetic voice to disenfranchised collectives. He doesn't try to imagine and ventriloquize subaltern subjectivities: he works on the level of language as a sort of collective unconscious.

Not unlike the Polish Żmijewski, Golynko sees clearly the direct line of influence from his childhood and education in the Soviet Union to a renewed interest in political art and poetry. Every poem, back then, was potentially dangerous and thus significant, a potentially transformative social act: this was true not only of unofficial culture (for example, "the literary flank of Moscow Conceptualism with its imitations of down-to-earth, quasi-middle-brow speech, riddled with ideological clichés") but also of official Soviet poetry, which constantly signaled its intention to improve social reality. Today, a post-Soviet poet can do many things that were impossible then, with one brutal exception:

> The poet can reproduce nationwide resentment in response to inflation, poverty, and catastrophic social inequality; he can give voice to collective

traumas tied to the loss of the imperial historical perspective; he can adopt a civic pose, bursting out with angry sarcastic attacks or even extremist appeals. At the same time, he has the option of reacting to current events, to pass moral or legal judgment on them, to expose them to severe criticism, etc. What he categorically does *not* possess any more is that function of active and effective social intervention in which both official and unofficial Soviet poets once took such pride.[28]

If authoritarian political regimes tend to take the written word seriously, as presenting a legitimate danger to ideological stability, liberal governments declaw and "equate the written word with private self-expression, granting ideological power to commercially profitable media culture" instead.[29] It is no wonder that international trends in politically engaged poetry coincide so closely with times of global financial crisis and resulting social volatility: the open question is whether poetry can escape the mode of private self-expression without jumping over to the side of profit, as Skidan debated in his critique of poetry's multimedia flirtations.

In the most lucid summary of his aesthetic and political stance at the time, Golynko argues that applied social poetry (his precise and detached language for what I call the revived Russian avant-garde) must aim higher than civic poetry clichés: even when it necessarily includes "two-dimensional poster truths," these must always be accompanied by "attentive intellectual reflection, taking into account historical genesis, class identity, and [one's] role in the system of social differentiation."[30] Whereas postmodernism sought to and occasionally succeeded in making poetry into an entertaining vaudeville variety show, applied social poetry "translates the utopian drives and liberating tendencies of the revolutionary avant-garde into the language of the epoch of failing cognitive capitalism."[31] Like other poets of the *[Translit]* circle, Golynko recognizes that he must not only write about politics but invent a new way to write politically, and he tries to do so methodically and systematically rather than intuitively. To participate in the radical project of subjectivization and in the cocreation of new collectivities, the socially applied poet must accept his (her, their—for Golynko begins to pull gender as well as class to the foreground of emancipatory critique) full immersion in the system, develop detached but analytic connections to the disenfranchised and oppressed, and sharpen any available stolen tools in preparation for futurity. Russian leftist poetry, like other would-be radical forms of knowledge production, must cultivate new and revolutionary subjectivities from the wreckage of the former bourgeois(ish) subject. That insight, and his model, is Golynko's ultimate contribution to the new Russian left: indeed, I suspect that the unassuming poet-scholar was patient zero for many Russian poets of his and subsequent generations, infecting the new era with a reimagined theorization of political poetry.

Golynko's rejection of the Russian lyric hero echoes other critiques of the poetic subject in the global traditions related to language and conceptual poetries (and in which he is well read). For example, as Walt Hunter highlights in his study of contemporary emancipatory poetry as a world form, Saidiya Hartman's work shows that "the very premise, the very idea, of a bourgeois lyric subject is made possible by the existence of a (lyric) object: the commodified human, the Atlantic slave trade, and the ongoing racialized violence necessary for the continuation of capitalism."[32] We might flip this insight from very different but no less violent or racialized spaces to comprehend Golynko's strange denizen of contemporary Russia in the poetic cycles—here a reader, there a man in a black coat, or a faun, or an elementary thing—as a local variant of *lyric object*: a commodified human or no-longer-human actant. More radically postsubject than even Arseniev and Skidan, Golynko probes the varieties of lyric object by submerging fully into the language of the world around him. The effect is different too from the more familiar strategy of overidentification with the language of the enemy to highlight internal contradictions and thus undermine from within (as Žižek theorizes, or as Alexei Yurchak writes similarly of late Soviet *stiob*). Although there is that too, Golynko resembles more Prigov at his most austere, when critique passes from the critique of police, authorities, power, or even art to a critique of grammar, of vision, of structure as such. Where Golynko differs from Prigov, in my view, is in a more contemporary and all-encompassing understanding of the political. He names and catalogues the damage / potential of a postapocalyptic world.

Golynko's 2003 poem "Whip It Out" emerges out of the same protofascist linguistic effluvia that filled Medvedev with horror when that younger poet witnessed it sharing shelf space with his own literary efforts. Finding distance through forms born of combinatorial technique and social vision, Golynko decides to dive straight in.

1

вынь да положь, да зажуй
человек в черном плаще
смотрит, на лестничной клетке
разминулись ребенок

паралитик, в коляске
и террорист чеченский
кто они, жертвы системы
или части ее, вот вам встряска

2

вынь да положь, да зажми
человек в черном плаще
смотрит, где бы подрочить
ты же солдат, говорит себе

но солдат, замыкающий
ряд, и выламывающийся
из ряда солдат, суть одно
и то же, супчик говяжий

1

whip it out, yeah, eat it up
a man in a black raincoat
sees, in the stairwell
they cross paths, a child-

paralytic in wheelchair
and a Chechen terrorist.
what are they, victims of the system
or a part of it, there's a shock for you

2

whip it out, yeah, get a grip
a man in a black raincoat

looks around, where to jerk off,
you're a soldier, he tells himself,

but a soldier bringing up
the rear and a soldier breaking
rank, are in essence
the same: beef soup

The comic-book central figure serves in place of a narrator, a participant-voyeur of the various horrors of the system. If "Lots of Different Things" featured an opaque and distant "reader" as the focalizing agent of action, here Golynko goes further. The man in the black coat is not only a lyric object but an antilyric object: an unpoetic and indeed mostly visual nonentity that provides Golynko's form with its point of eternal return and roving, unpleasant eye. (Social poetry, Golynko writes, "forces the poet to be a bit of an anthropologist, an ethnographer, a political thinker, to conduct journalistic investigations, and, if need be, to become a fighter on the barricades, whether imaginary or real."[33]) The man in the black coat *looks*, that much can be said of him: for example, "at the undeveloped / ribcage, belonging to / an unknown" (smotrit na slaborazvituiu / grudnuiu kletku, prinadlezhashchuiu / neizvestnomu); at other suspected victim-perpetrators of the system, like the strangely paired Chechen terrorist and paralyzed child; or for a place to masturbate in peace. The man in the black coat even speaks to himself, but he does not think; he has no interiority. When Golynko wants to be particularly unpleasant, his nonentity voyeur is most often a "he."

Bits and pieces of language collide like "little bricks out of which a new explosive and unpredictable social reality is amassed," but Golynko's language couldn't differ more from Skidan's citations and Arseniev's philosophical borrowings.[34] If Skidan challenges the present with an agonized archive that reads like shredded notes of citations from an alternate past, Golynko forces us to examine our flattened eternal present cruelly reflected in our once most Romantic form: lyric without depth, past, or future. Golynko not only consigns his voice to the other(s), but, as Kevin Platt notes, "resolutely refuses to offer poetic beauty as a justification or legitimization" of social ills, in what is less a rejection than an attempt to resuscitate the aesthetic as a "socially potent instrument."[35] One of Golynko's translators, Rebecca

Bella, explains her understanding of his project as follows: "By producing *in poetry* the cheapest, emptiest, most jarring, strung out, amped-up picture of capitalism, [Golynko's] sharply-focused jump-cut images elicit protest."[36] Disgust may be the first step to emancipation.

9

вынь да положь, да прикуси

[. . .]

строящего рынок, на булку, крошенную
голубям, набухший сосок
прижимает губами, переваривает
узнанное, не сказать, чтобы вкусно

whip it out, yeah, take a bite

[. . .]

organizing the market, white bread,
crumbled for pigeons, lips pressed
to the swollen nipple, digests
the recognized, can't say it's tasty

For Golynko, his era, unlike that of illustrious dissident precursors Mandelstam and Brodsky, tastes exactly like free market white bread. Blood or earth would be a dramatic improvement.

Emancipatory Graphomania

If Skidan links the younger generation of *[Translit]* poets with Dragomoshchenko, the Leningrad underground, and the global legacies of *L=A=N=G=U=A=G=E*; and if Arseniev is best contextualized as continuing in that tradition, learning from Skidan in turn; then Golynko (and Roman Osminkin in his wake, as I argue in Chapter 5) belongs to the Prigov line. For an academic specializing in media studies, Prigov makes an especially tantalizing precursor—as the figure who did the most to merge Russian poetry and Conceptualist art, and to expose the always already performative identity of "Russian poet" by taking text-worshipping and logocentric tendencies to hilarious or offensive extremes.[37] Golynko, like his former student Osminkin, but unlike nearly any of the other case studies explored in this book, is moreover specifically interested in graphomania as a defining tactic of Prigov's enormous poetic output, which through its very bulk makes a mockery of close reading.

According to the late poet Aleksei Parshchikov, Golynko's poems resemble Prigov's in that they "lead us from stanza to stanza, switching from one emotional / informational node to another, unfolding, continuing and weaving, like an ornament of vocabulary formations, masses, closed clusters, each of which gives the impression of being a complete form, having a beginning and an end, while we weigh the adequacy of any statement, choosing it, say, for a citation. . . . It is like we click the computer mouse and move from one site to another. This principle of nested dolls on the Internet."[38] Parshchikov's insight, that Golynko's unpoetic poetic forms probe and unfold in a way that feels computational, echoes too what Hillel Schwartz has called the culture of the copy: modernity's fear / desire of the duplicate, the double, the decoy, the backup copy, reproduction in its many messy forms.[39] Golynko uses copy culture to take an odd, alienated turn out of the possibilities afforded to language poetry in the Russian context. What is striking is that Golynko's carefully handcrafted cycles actually read as more computational than Arseniev's digitally crafted but evocative experiments. But of course, Golynko might say: under the conditions of catastrophe capitalism, computer poetry reads as richer and more lyrical than human-generated text.

Golynko's most famous serial form or cycle of poems (it has been called both, highlighting the collapse of the individual unit of text into the collective), "Elementary Things," also from the breakthrough 2003 collection, illuminates the full potential of his unforgiving combinatorial deluge.[40] Here, moreover, the new Russian lyric object no longer resembles a human at all. Many critics, translators, and perceptive readers have tried their hand at guessing what Golynko's eponymous "thing" might be. Bak writes that the elementary thing "corresponds with the concept of elementary particles: the impersonal, smallest bricks of existence, that at the beginning of the last century took the place of atoms, which for thousands of years seemed indivisible"; the elementary thing is "more fractional than the human personality: alive, animated, personified, more like an atom."[41] Ilya Kukulin points to the resulting reading of human behavior as mechanized, and to the implication that the recurrent pronoun "she" for thing (*veshch'* in Russian) may be some kind of sexual robot (à la Keti Chukhrov's love machines, explored in Chapter 6). Female-gendered elementary things, the second poem or stanza states, "don't get periods."[42] Whatever these shape-shifters are, such particles are the only actants left in the postapocalyptic eternal present.

Each of twenty-five subpoems in the cycle (or as Golynko put it, again echoing Bely, multiline and narrative novel-in-verse) is branded with the letters *ET* and the stanza / fragment's number. The opening suggests a philosophical treatise will follow, something of a postmodern *De rerum natura* by Lucretius, before proceeding directly to the absurd.

ЭВ 1

элементарные вещи
много места не занимают
видно, это формула современности
занимать места немного
если место причинное оно
соприкоснется с чем-нибудь посторонним
если место задымлено без огня без причины
ему сподручней с ничем соприкоснуться
потому-то элементарная вещь такая дурында
будто ее полжизни держали в дурдоме
окончательно сбили с панталыку
но элементарные вещи не так-то просто
сбагрить с рук и упечь в кутузку
они меняют места проживанья
прежде, чем место себя заметает
подобно гаметам они

ЭВ 2

к элементарной вещи подбирается тузик
чтоб помочиться, иль просто обнюхать, облаять
но элементарная вещь не протестует

[...]
элементарные вещи всегда на службе
у самих себя, и капля
крови, темнеющая на элементарной вещи
не ее проблема—месячных у них не бывает

ET 1
elementary things
don't take up a lot of space
that must be the formula of modernity
not to take up a lot of space
if the place is procreative it
will come into contact with something foreign
if the place spews smoke without fire or cause
it's handier for it to come into contact with nothing
that's why the elementary thing is such a ninny
as if it had got kept half its life in the nuthouse
discombobulated completely
though with elementary things it's not so easy to
send 'em packing, lock 'em up in the slammer
they change their places of residence
before the places manage to cover over
like gametes they are

ET 2
spot steals up to an elementary thing
to pee on it, sniff it out, bark at it
but the elementary thing doesn't protest
[...]
elementary things are always on duty
toward themselves, and the droplet
of blood showing on an elementary thing
isn't its problem—they don't get periods

The first four lines read nearly with a straight face (the formula of contemporaneity is to take up minimal space) but then quickly spin out of control.

The elementary thing is a particle, a part of speech, but also a she, a *durynda* or moron, possibly a robot or an animal, a force, a substance, an inescapable thing. On the level of poetic function, elementary things are clearly broken signifiers. Golynko goes a step further here than Arseniev, who borrowed Chomsky's phrase, "colorless green ideas sleep furiously," an example of a perfectly grammatical sentence that nevertheless means nothing, for the title of his Kraft chapbook. Golynko writes his entire cycle of poems as if in that same Chomskian mode: his Russian is simultaneously hilarious to Russophone audiences and disquieting, for all this "unmotivated vomit" seems to signify an unpleasant deeper truth beneath surface-level incoherence. When we cling, nostalgic, to older forms of poetry and art, our longing or *algea* is to return to the comforting illusion of a whole ego, of the well-defined human, of discrete units and boundaries (or political borders!) that hold. But the individual or human is no longer a unit in this vision of the contemporary world, but akin to a territory under constant imperial incursion, with violently changing borderlines and place names; a vessel or host for more powerful agencies that pour through our bounding membranes, showing the lie to any remaining posited difference between persons and things.

Of course, "the poet" vanishes entirely in such work, becoming an amplifier for the psychic and linguistic waste produced by the Russian language (people? nation?) in a given moment in time. Digging through the garbage with him, we find fresh hell at every corner:

ЭВ 4
элементарная вещь отправляется на рынок
уцененной белиберды, покупает
на распродаже что-нибудь приятное и полезное
анафему или любовь
товар беспрецедентно быстро приедается
он подвергнут обструкции, закинут
в корзину из низкопробного пластика
элементарная вещь что-то ломает
наверное, руку помощи свыше
элементарные вещи всегда одиноки
хотя и прикованы все к одной точке
то попарно, то поочередно

одиночество, одиночество—это что
осведомляется элементарная вещь у
это знакомо, отвечает
подкатывая немотивированной рвотой

ЭВ 11
элементарная вещь денежку копит
приумножает по зернышку сбереженья
естественно, в евро, не в национальной валюте [. . .]

ET 4
the elementary thing heads for the market
of discounted trash, purchases
something pleasant and practical at a sale
anathema or love
the goods satiate with unprecedented speed
are subjected to obviation, flung into
basket of inferior plastic
the elementary thing breaks something
must be the arm of help from on high
elementary things are always lonely
although all chained to the same point
either by turn or in pairs
loneliness, loneliness, what's that
an elementary thing addresses
that's familiar, answers
rolling out unmotivated vomit

ET 11
the elementary thing saves moolah
stores up savings grain after grain
obviously in euros not in national currency [. . .]

Golynko thus opens with a feint—we are momentarily thrown by the elementary things, like red shifters, and imagine ourselves in the realm of physics rather than politics—but in no time we understand that, yet again, this is a

poem about late capitalism and what the era of total market has done to
people, to language, to land and weather and water, to things. The posthuman
particle seems at times to share agency and family resemblances with the
human—we recognize "her" as possessed of a body, sexualized and reproduc-
ible—but all pretense of psychology, of inner life or subjectivity, has vanished
into thin air and been revealed as meaningless, an error of our continued
projection. The elementary thing is so small as to be only surface.

ЭВ 21

[. . .] все, что следует знать об элементарной вещи
у нее нетварная, морбидная, неживая природа
элементарная вещь всегда имитирует что-то
реже себя, чаще папского нунция, сатрапа
старика-настоятеля или мачеху-маньячку
по обычаю, нелюдей иль культурных героев
иногда подражает обездвиженному истукану
в рядно обряженному кадавру
лектору в аудиторном почете
иногда гусарит, обмахивается доломаном
носит чекмень, на ободе водоема
она—кувшинка, лилия, цветочки святого
элементарная вещь ведет образ жизни приятный
чисто контемплятивный

ЭВ 25

элементарная вещь сама себе табулятор
сама устанавливает пробелы, разграниченья
итерации [. . .]

ET 21

[. . .] what should be known about the elementary thing
it has an increate, morbid, inanimate nature
the elementary thing is always mimicking something
rarely itself, more often the papal nuncio, satrap
old father superior or stepmother maniac
usually monsters or cultural figures

it sometimes imitates an immobilized idol
cadaver tricked out in sackcloth
professor basking in auditoria
at times struts like a hussar, fans itself with a dolman
wears a cossack coat, on the rim of the reservoir
it's a water lily, madonna lily, the little flowers of a saint
the elementary thing leads a pleasant kind of life
purely contemplative

ET 25
the elementary thing is its own tab key
sets spaces by itself, and borders
iterations [. . .]

Is she the symptom of a twenty-first-century horror, a monster born after the nuclear age?[43] Technology (or *techne,* or knowledge production in its material forms) is certainly to blame for the elementary thing coming into view—including the urban culture that Golynko so loves and that can, on occasion and perhaps by mistake, produce transitional spaces and cultures that in turn allow beings like the poet to survive in the rubble. The elementary thing lives in the nightmare megacities of the future that have already arrived, coming into being before our unseeing eyes: metametropoli never designed with human beings in mind, but composed of screens, digital currencies, copies of copies, penetrating light and noise, and biopolitical self-monitoring to make Foucault shudder. The post–Cold War posthuman presents a porous mesh through which something else (currency? mysterious base economies? elementary things?) pulses, moves, acts, but again by definition never reaches consciousness or self-determination. Golynko's vision here echoes Viktor Pelevin's viciously parodic speech on oral and anal wow impulses to earn or spend, and on *Homo zapiens* (the new man) in *Generation P* (published in the year of sea change, 1999): "Comrades in the struggle! The position of modern man is not merely lamentable; one might even say there is no condition, because man hardly exists. . . . HZ is simply the residual luminescence of a soul fallen asleep."[44] Golynko, however, doesn't seem to be kidding. More than that, he suspects that the only way forward, again, is through: it is not so bad, perhaps, to be a monster.

Monstrology and the Zombie Proletariat

One of Golynko's most imaginative essays, "Democracy and the Monster: Several Theses about Visual Monstrology," was published in the 2005–2007 issue of *Moscow Art Journal* (also featuring Chukhrov, Oxana Timofeeva, and several other Chto Delat associates).[45] Drawing on a characteristic array of sources, Golynko defines what he terms "monstrology" as a key analytic practice of our age. Indeed, he argues, monster studies of various forms coincide with such cultural theory as is concerned with the human and its symbolic signs and limits.[46] Golynko runs through a series of foundational critical monuments of the early twenty-first century and finds them again and again to deploy or study the monster as a constitutive category: in the work of Badiou, Negri and Hardt, Gerald Raunig and Stefan Nowotny, Žižek and the Slovenian school associated with the journal *Rearticulation,* and others. Indeed, monstrousness turns out to be "an immanent feature of modern 'necrocapitalism': the vampiric exhaustion of living labor of workers described by Marx turns into an uninterrupted process of inexhaustible enrichment. Super popular in cultural theory, the monster's figure gradually ceases to be an abstract political metaphor. The monster becomes an indication of the coexistence of a dangerous, indomitable and difficultly predictable Other, supporting and at the same time undermining the symbolic order of global capitalism."[47]

Through a variety of forms and topics, monster studies preoccupy themselves with an other who threatens to undermine the foundations of the dominant symbolic order. If in film or popular culture, for example, we think we (should) identify with those who survive—or want to survive—the encounter with the monster, cultural monstrology encourages us to question who or what is being represented as the threat and what political purpose that representation serves. The very body of the monster terrifies because it is "derived from the displacement, shift or decomposition of traditional high meanings or stable ideological codes"; but it also "denotes class, gender and racial differentiations, the foundations of the European civilization model and contributes to their continuous renewal."[48] In visual culture especially, the monster resides at the limits of what can be depicted, the limits of representation as such: every culture has them, but the most terrifying monsters never fully

ХУДОЖЕСТВЕННЫЙ ЖУРНАЛ
MOSCOW ART MAGAZINE 77/78

Дмитрий Голынко-Вольфсон. Демократия и чудовище. Несколько тезисов о визуальной монстрологии

Дмитрий Голынко-Вольфсон

Монстр в роли агента культурного знания

В эпоху позднего капитализма всестороннее осмысление монстра, изучение его исторических ипостасей и социокультурной среды обитания стало опознавательным знаком той части культурной теории, которая задается вопросом, что такое человеческое и каковы его символические признаки и пределы. Достаточно упомянуть несколько фундаментальных сочинений, задавших важнейшие траектории мысли в 2000-е годы и обозначивших фигуру монстра в качестве одной из главных мыслительных категорий. Это "Век" Алена Бадью, где катастрофы XX столетия прочитываются как неизбывное столкновение с Веком-Зверем, персонажем стихотворения Мандельштама "Век" (1922). Именно способность заглянуть в зрачки чудовища позволяет соприкоснуться с истиной События и понять жесткую логическую связь политических решений и поворотов, характеризующих этот отрезок времени.

Это и книга "Монструозность Христа" или очерк "Соседи и другие монстры: призыв к этическому насилию" Славоя Жижека: евангельская метафора ближнего своего, которого положено возлюбить, как самого себя, истолкована им подобно угрозе вторжения (или прямой интервенции) безликого монстра, воплощения неистребимого Другого. Это и трехтомник Негри и Хардта "Империя" (2000), "Множество" (2004) и "Commonwealth" (2009),

Материал проиллюстрирован работами Патриции Пиччинини разных лет

FIGURE 4.2 Golynko, "Democracy and the Monster: Several Theses about Visual Monstrology."   *MOSCOW ART MAGAZINE.*

come into view. (The monster presents the "most serious challenge to the entire traditional system of representation, to all the usual visual codes and techniques associated with depicting the social reality of the late capitalism era."[49]) The monster resides beyond the boundaries of the possible and permissible, thereby continually constituting them—but also awakens alongside an insurmountable fear of its monstrous form "an undeniable desire," which, as Golynko reminds us, "Kristeva equates to disgust, attraction through fear and repulsion."[50]

The thrilling conclusion of Golynko's whirlwind theoretical overview (which reads as a veritable who's who of contemporary leftist thought, with a particular interest in the Slovenian psychoanalytic school) calls for a reverse identification that reveals the emancipatory potential of the modern monster. If monsters are used to imagine and police the borders of identity (of race and nation, gender and sexuality, economics and class, as well as human and nonhuman), then the monster also captures "the emancipatory politics of spontaneous rebellion against the neoliberal system of soft coercion and all controlling bi-power":

> A modern monster can be drawn in the form of a declassed proletarian of intangible labor huddling in slums, preserving the traits of a tame neighbor for the time being, but full of desire to rebel against the rules and prohibitions imputed to him by neoliberal governance structures. His revolutionary impetus is predetermined by his own deep alienation, an insurmountable monstrosity that is practically impossible to pacify and utilize, that is, to put into service the dominant social institutions. . . . In addition, monsters are inclined to unite together, into maneuverable political economic communities that are not engaged in the production of values, but in the reproduction of horror, delight, desire, and pleasure, and therefore resemble the utopian models of the indescribable and idle community proposed by Maurice Blanchot and Jean-Luc Nancy. Forming a collective body, united by the principle of group solidarity, the monsters crowd and fall upon the symbolic citadels of neoliberal capitalism.[51]

Rather than fear the encounter with the monster (and the deformations wreaked on our minds and bodies by the post-postmodern world), we should embrace our own monstrous potential and in so doing recognize that the monster *is* the revolution, the monster *is* the avant-garde. Chto Delat's breakout philosopher, Oxana Timofeeva (known internationally for her treatise *The History of Animals: A Philosophy,* translated in 2018 with a foreword by Žižek) arrived at a similar conclusion in the years following the 2013 and 2014 waves of repression and imperial expansion in Putin's Russia. In an essay for *e-flux,* Timofeeva suggests that we have nothing to fear from the end of the world, and that we need only break past catastrophe capitalism into a "catastrophic communism": "It will not get worse, it's already worse. . . . Wars, repression, butchery, and so forth—are really visions of our present zombie apocalypse." Hope, she suggests, is what keeps us back, dreaming that we are still alive in the old way, that we have a future as liberal subjects: "Only when already dead, and facing no future, do we really have nothing to lose."[52] The zombie proletariat know how to enjoy a revolution.

What Golynko has been trying to do all these years, beginning with his sudden dramatic break with poetic subjectivity in 2002, is to imagine a poetry that engages with the monstrous *as* the political: never visible and obvious but hidden and unknown, emergent and ever shocking. Golynko offers a powerful rejoinder to those critics who find nothing but monstrous forms in his poetry: he writes poetry for zombies.

In "The Faun and the Few," also from 2002, Golynko toys with the combinatorial possibilities enclosed in the title to explore principles of radical negation and the limits of the human. Each poem is titled "the faun and un-," using the prefix *ne* (*favn i ne-*) to generate an alternative mythology for the Anthropocene from the (always already borrowed and foreign) Russian language.

Фавн и нежный
если фавн—женщина, знающая
живая привязанность, глубинное чувство
душевная близь, tutti frutti
втемяшится, пыжится, пырхает
и никнет в полное оледененье
вакханка обмахивается тирсом
при перезагрузке скрипты полетели
нежный высвобождается от поножей
в житницу сыплется

the faun and the unfeigned
the faun—perhaps a woman, who knows
true attachment, inner feeling
nearness in the soul, tutti frutti
takes hold in the mind, chirps, spurts,
bows toward absolute freeze
Bacchante fans herself with her thyrsus
the fonts freaked during reinstallation
the unfeigned steps from her greaves
pours to the granary pours

Фавн и неприкасаемый

фавн—женщина, но не каждая
неприкасаемый—тоже не всяк мужчина
хлюпик, рохля и мачок отметаются сразу
равно неженка, трудоголик
или мямля, с места в карьер приставала
у неприкасаемого и фавна ничего
не получится—это издалека видно
тут не нужен экстраординарный опыт
херачить им незачем вместе

the faun and the untouchable

the faun—a woman, but not everywoman
the untouchable—likewise not everyman
wimp, runt, macho are brushed off at once
also the sissy, workaholic
mumbler, and right-off-the-bat harasser
between untouchable and faun
it can't work out, that's clear enough
takes no great insight
they've no reason to hack it together

Again we begin with gender. The word faun is grammatically gendered male in Russian but is "perhaps a woman," though perhaps "not everywoman." We begin with blurred binaries and boundaries amid ruins; so too are figure and foreground, actant and environment, signifier and signified confounded. The bourgeois(ish, in the Russian context) male lyric subject (we may as well call him "Pushkin" for the sake of convenience) is the first thing to throw off the spaceship of post-postmodernity.

The postapocalyptic, arcadian setting of "The Faun and the Few" is oddly even harder to parse than that of the grimmer "Elementary Things." Critics, reviewers, and even his translators haven't known entirely what to make of this particular cycle, and fewer try to offer coherent readings. Nealand notes the gender play and suggests that Golynko's fauns "find themselves *behaving in a manner traditionally allotted to the degraded female.*"[53] Eric Dickey speculates that perhaps "Golynko suggests that nature is capable of undermining authority when a resource is overtapped, [as] when a woman has reached the end of her rope, she can stop providing."[54] Associations of nature and the feminine aside, the interpretability of such work falls into question. But so too neither party in the "faun and un-" pairings knows how to break past the conjunction, nor the space of difference between them.

Фавн и неумека
фавн умеет заботиться о
приободрять, казаны драить
нужные бланки заполнять
изменять кому-то, когда невмоготу
сосать карамельки и барбариски
грызть косхалву, перебирать щавель
кэш изымать из хлипенького банкомата
неумека тоже совсем приобвыкся
разевает варежку когда надо

the faun and the unskilled
the faun knows how to look after
cheer up, scrub a pot
fill out the necessary forms
betray someone, when it's unbearable
suck caramels and cherry drops
nibble on halvah, clean fennel
get cash from the beat-up bankomat
the unskilled is also completely used to
breaking it down, when necessary

Фавн и неказистый
фавн—женщина только-только
молодая, уже страшится старенья
боится—морщинками пойдет, обрюзгнет
сплошные болячки, клиника всякая
воз и ныне там, ни одной бороздки

неказистый позволяет фавну себя
поцеловать, нахмурив лобешник
если бы все тогда состоялось
сколько такому цена

the faun and the unendowed
the faun—a woman, ever so
young, already scared of getting old
she fears, wrinkles will come, and flab
sores everywhere, everything clinical
the cart is still there, not one furrow
the unendowed allows the faun
a kiss, on crumpled brow
if all this were to happen
what would be the price

I read Golynko's faun as a perfect monster, a lyric borrowing from antiquity used here to attack the limits of the lyric from every angle, just like the categories of comprehensible personhood. Part human part animal, part subject part object, born of language but a foreign borrowing Cyrillicized at the dawn of Russian Romantic poetry (see for example Pushkin's "The Fawn and the Shepherdess," written when he was sixteen), the monster has always been there.

A comparable moment in American poetry after $L=A=N=G=U=A=G=E$, to my mind, is Anne Boyer's extraordinary English-language poem / essay (it also has been called both) "The Animal Model of Inescapable Shock" (2012). Boyer, a contemporary verbal artist politically and aesthetically kindred to the *[Translit]* school, gives us eerily familiar combinatorial horror and inhuman humanoids:

If an animal has previously suffered escapable shock, and then she suffers inescapable shock, she will be happier than if she has previously not suffered escapable shock—for if she hasn't, she will only know about being shocked inescapably.

But if she has been inescapably shocked before, and she is put in the conditions where she was inescapably shocked before, she will behave as if being shocked, mostly. Her misery doesn't require acts. Her misery requires conditions.

If an animal is inescapably shocked once, and then the second time she is dragged across the electrified grid to some non-shocking space, she will be happier than if she isn't dragged across the electrified grid. The next time she is shocked, she will be happier because she will know there is a place that isn't an electrified grid. She will be happier because rather than just being dragged onto an electrified grid by a human who then hurts her, the human can then drag her off of it.

If an animal is shocked, escapably or inescapably, she will manifest deep reactions of attachment for whoever has shocked her. If she has manifested deep reactions of attachment for whoever has shocked her, she will manifest deeper reactions of attachment for whoever has shocked her and then dragged her off the electrified grid. Perhaps she will de- velop deep feelings of attachment for electrified grids. Perhaps she will develop deep feelings of attachment for what is not the electrified grid. Perhaps she will develop deep feelings of attachment for dragging. She may also develop deep feelings of attachment for science, laboratories, experimentation, electricity, and informative forms of torture.[55]

Boyer's humanoid animals, like Golynko's fauns and elementary things, give the lie to illusions of selfhood in the twenty-first century, and remind us of the costs and usual victims of those illusions. Golynko's monsters have a more specific geopolitical locus. The monster born of ecological catastrophe serves the same function as the communist other of the Cold War: the con- venient object against which the "Western" subject can be defined. The two figures come together in the zombie proletariat; and so too the Soviet Union, in video games and recurrent Cold War rhetorics, remains the spectral zombie state par excellence. Accepting the charge, Golynko writes poetry for and about the zombie proletariat. As coming chapters will show, that move proves especially fruitful for socialist feminist philosophers and poets: Chukhrov too picks up on the political potential of the already dead; and Rymbu on the ecological dread implicit in Golynko's irradiated texts through her own passionate visions of a landscape as monstrous as its surviving creatures.

Russia after the Rain

After the rise and fall of the years of international protest, socially applied poetry, along with other forms of newly energized and optimistic political art, suffered a near-mortal blow and faced a new crisis of cultural repression from the state and internal disappointment and splintering.[56] In an English-language essay (shared with me in draft form) titled "'New Thingness' and the Materiality of Trauma in Contemporary Art," Golynko contemplates where we are now, after the revanchists won in Russia—and in the United States, much of Europe, Turkey, Hungary, and in more and more nations across the world: "Questioning its own economical market foundation, social values, ideological vehemence and institutional transformations, the system of contemporary art detects itself in an unsteady postcapitalist phase (schematically outlined in the prominent book written by two British left accelerationists Nick Srnicek and Alex Williams). . . . The planetary fiasco and defeat of the horizontal protest movement in 2011–2012, which arose on a global scale from Syntagma Square to Occupy Wall Street, have enforced contemporary art to rethink and revise its political role and assignment in the context of the aesthetic regime (Jacques Rancière)."[57] The corresponding transformation of art practices in recent years "from activist participatory art to post-activist strategies" is echoed in detached critical practices and the gloomy observation of "contemporary postcapitalist turmoil from the point of view of speculative materialism and depressive pessimistic realism."[58] The avant-garde moment of 2011–2012 flared with political potential and enthusiastic artistic involvement, and just as quickly died back down to a simmer. What Golynko calls the "deliberately inhuman art of new thingness" took its place, present in critical tendencies ranging from speculative realism, object-oriented ontology, to politico-economic accelerationism (from which Golynko maintains a distance). The question remains whether such strategies have sufficient—or any—amounts of revolutionary potential.

Golynko wonders whether contemporary engaged art is indeed again already over, "ceasing to be an integral part of planetary informational and communicative networking" and once more just a "ruined pile-up of the broken 'dark' or 'dead' media, signaling the eternal end of communicative resources and the emergence of the era of total excommunication."[59] The flip side to weaponizing poetry's lack of power to theorize powerlessness is ultimately a nihilist celebration of powerlessness as such: "Controversial and disputable in the sense of their political engagement, ethical commitment and critical omnipotence, the poetics of 'new thingness' and the methods of speculative realism still might reveal and detect the most anxious and traumatic moments of the contemporary, postcapitalist or postcommunist stages in the development of global civilization."[60] By no coincidence, from the collapse of the Russian and global political protests to the years of pandemic (a global shut-down so nightmarish as to belong better to Golynko's serial poems than our lived experience), Golynko confined himself mainly to reading and writing essays rather than to new poetic experiments. Characteristically, he included his own work and recent interests in the defeatist turn he describes. He continued his international collaborations and returns through translations to earlier work: new poetry, however, seemed to be on pause, waiting for the next historical moment, a new interstice to open.

In "Keys to Yonder" ("Kliuchi ot kraia"), published in Kevin Platt's translation in *Jacket2* in 2014, we might glimpse one quiet echo of earlier moments of hope.[61] We can only imagine what else might have come, in time, perhaps after a long time, time he should have had.

1

ключи от края оброблены на
пространство посередине, покрытое лохматой
волосиной, иль слитого грина
откатом, или выделенной смазки
хлюпаньем, всем, к чему нужен ключ
особенный, обнадежив близкого обещаньем
близости, его подводят туда, где плюнь
и разотри, тут не до пощады

1

the keys to yonder have been dropped off in
the midst of space covered over by a greasy
hair, or by a kickback of laundered dough,
or by a slurp of excreted mucus—
covered by everything that requires a special key,

granting hope to thy neighbor with the promise
of closeness, they bring him to the place where, cut the
crap: there's no mercy here

This particular piece of combinatorial spinning in place ritualistically returns
to the phrase "keys to yonder," contrasting the desire for transcendence with
the understanding that that very desire is expressed through "a pastiche of
borrowed phrases" that refract "a world of violence, depravity, isolation, alienation, and hopelessness."[62] The war isn't over—it never is—but: "whoever
was sent for the keys to yonder / is in no hurry, knows that time runs
slowly / ahead."

*   *   *

This chapter is dedicated to the memory of Dmitry Golynko.

5

Poetry in the Age of Digital Reproduction

ROMAN OSMINKIN

*I*N 2015, New York's New Museum published *The Animated Reader,* an anthology of contemporary poetry released in conjunction with the *Surround Audience* triennial.[1] In a review of the collection, "Let's Take a Very Fucking Poetry Lesson: Art's Crush on Poetry," Tracy Jeanne Rosenthal identifies one voice in particular as defining the existential pulse of the anthology and its rekindling of the love affair between contemporary art and poetry: *[Translit]* cofounder and former student of Dmitry Golynko, Roman Osminkin. The way Rosenthal phrases her admiration is also striking: "Roman Jakobson, one of Russian Formalism's central antecedents, once described poetry as 'organized violence committed on ordinary speech.' In *The Reader,* contemporary Russian poet Roman Osminkin (whom *The Reader* introduced me to), appropriates Jakobson to *reductio ad absurdum.*"[2] Multiple critics follow Osminkin's own suggestion that he's engaging in a kind of Russian Formalist practice 2.0: from the vantage point of New York, the slide from one "Roman" to another, across a century of Russian thought, looks smooth. If "Jakobson's Formalist maxim is often read as an oxymoron: what can poetry actually *do*?" Rosenthal writes, then Osminkin speaks for his generation when he accepts that poetry's "lack of social agency strengthens its capacity for social diagnosis" but moves on to call for direct action as well: "Osminkin's 'Poems and Fuckery' closes with the appeal, 'so hurry up and write / . . . and finish your poem already / maybe / you / can still / save someone.'"[3]

Tom Healy of the *Miami Rail* likewise ends his review of *The Animated Reader* with Osminkin, zeroing in on the same lines as best capturing the global zeitgeist of young radical verbal artists: "There's a thrill to be found in the urgent demands [these poets] put on themselves to say something, anything that might (not?) be poetry now. Here's how Roman Osminkin puts it: 'abbreviate, use acronyms / be lucid and convincing / and finish your poem already / maybe / you / can still / save someone.'"[4] The list goes on. Scott Indrisek singles out Osminkin in his questions for editor Brian Droitcour; and Droitcour obliges with the following explanation:

> Osminkin uses Jakobson's quote as the first line of a Facebook status update that goes on to transform it through a daisy chain of substitutions ("language is organized violence against society / society is organized violence against nature / nature is organized violence against all existence" etc.). . . . If I remember correctly, that Jakobson quote is from his early wild years in Moscow or Prague, but later, when he settled down at MIT, he realized that there's nothing that boring or blasé about ordinary speech, and he came up with a model of communication that identified six functions of language. . . . Jakobson developed that model to add complexity to cybernetic models of language that came out in the 1940s and '50s.[5]

Editor and reviewers alike seize on Osminkin's contributions as central to *The Animated Reader*'s larger project (clearly, of repoliticizing experimental poetry) and key to its continuity with twentieth-century intellectual revolutions and avant-gardes. What catches their eye in Osminkin's unexpectedly fun and vital work is the Marxist relationship to art; the simultaneous interest in direct action and digital remediation; and the evident reimagining of earlier Russian art and theory—even the Formalist echo of his name.[6]

Osminkin (born in Leningrad, 1979) appears increasingly in international media and scholarly work as the next Russian poet to watch, most often in the same breath as Kirill Medvedev and Pavel Arseniev. Press coverage of the 2014 Manifesta scandal in St. Petersburg lists Osminkin, Arseniev, and others as the instigator-curators of *"Apartment Art as Domestic Resistance,"* a parallel public program developed by Polish curator Joanna Warsza in response to the Chto Delat–led protest of the biennial (which, again, took place in the Winter Palace, symbol of empire, shortly after Russia's annexation of Crimea).[7] Elena Fanailova has commented that "contemporary political and social po-

FIGURE 5.1
Roman Osminkin
and Nikita Safonov
in the curated
"apartment-
exhibit" of several
of the poets' living
space in St. Peters-
burg. Image used
for the cover of
[*Translit*] issue
15 / 16. [*TRANSLIT*].

etry began developing in Russia about eight years ago. . . . The young, edu-cated audience loves Kirill Medvedev, Roman Osminkin, and Andrei Rodi-onov."[8] In the introduction to *Not a Word about Politics!,* a bilingual Russian and English collection of Osminkin's poetry and essays put forth by the New York–based independent Cicada Press (2016), Joan Brooks describes Osminkin as

> a central figure in the vibrant, if for the moment depressingly marginal, Russian community of leftist artists, writers, activists, and intellec-tuals. . . . He is a regular contributor to *Translit,* the most influential leftist journal of poetry and poetics in Russia. He frequently collaborates with the Chto Delat group and other artistic collectives. His musical project, Texno-Poetry, performs regularly at festivals, art openings, and benefit concerts, often alongside Kirill Medvedev's Arkady Kots band. He lived in the famous commune on Kuznechnyi Lane in St. Petersburg, a buzzing hive of avant-garde antics and meta-political conspiracy. He is a member of the Russian Socialist Movement and a Ph.D. student at the Russian Institute of Art History, writing a dissertation on partici-patory art and its popular manifestations beyond the art world.[9]

Brooks stresses the importance of Osminkin's physicality to his readings, perfor-mances, and actions, calling him "utterly unique in his body, his movements" and noting the calculated clash between an at times "brash masculinity" and "the falsetto of heights of his gender-ambiguous voice and the bony frame protruding from underneath his muscles—he is quite emaciated in fact, maybe even malnourished."[10] Physical presence and performance is so cen-tral to Osminkin's poetics that his printed texts alone serve as but a partial introduction to the larger project. Those who have attended Osminkin's events and observed his interactions with audiences can attest to the contra-dictory simultaneous desire his performances provoke—to respond with knowing laughter, and to stop laughing and "get political."[11]

*   *   *

IN THIS CHAPTER, I highlight the centrality of performance to Russian po-litical poetry through a study of the most digitally remediated poet of

[Translit]. It is striking that nearly half the protagonists of this book (Medvedev, Osminkin, and Chukhrov) quite literally sing their work, if only Chukhrov does so with professional ease. The inimitably charismatic Osminkin follows in the Prigov school of Conceptualist play but takes the performance of Russian poetry to newly politicized heights through musical collaborations, parodic videos, and graphomaniacal output online via social media. More than any other poet in this study, Osminkin consistently uses digital technology to draft, edit, and disseminate his poetic texts. At the same time, he insists more than others on the importance of the bodily presence of the poet at events, moving through multiple ironized roles and onstage costume changes (from St. Petersburg poet to street thug to self-conscious political activist). Such art practices rely on audience presence and participation, as well as on shared and site-specific experiences. Moreover, Osminkin's work foregrounds the influence of feminist art on his practice, eschewing the masculinism and aggression of earlier Russian avant-gardes to explore instead the subversive power of what Sianne Ngai has referred to as the "cuteness" of the avant-garde. Unlike some of the other left feminist poets in this book, Osminkin can readily poke fun at the masculine cult of the Russian avant-garde poet (among other things) by over-embodying that role as well.

If some of the aesthetic practices explored earlier in this volume seem to long for or conjure future poetries, Osminkin appears to fully inhabit Futurism in the present. He is as interested in earlier avant-gardes as the other poets of the *[Translit]* constellation, but his work presents as too contemporary to read as citational. Indeed, his practice illustrates many of the central claims of this book: that Russian leftist poetry rekindles itself in dialogue with the world of contemporary art; that avant-garde marginality affords a space for institutional critique that coexists with the direct action of activism; and that not only Russian but international audiences are hungry for a post-Soviet literary left to redeem (or rescue) the aesthetic and political legacies of socialism for the twenty-first century. And it is in Osminkin's work—alongside that of the fiercely talented women of the final chapter and conclusion, Keti Chukhrov and Galina Rymbu—that the growing theme of gender politics begins to reach a crescendo.

Below is a still of Osminkin performing "Why do you poets . . ." (Chto zhe vy poety) from a video clip recorded by his frequent collaborator Sergei Iugov and edited and published by Osminkin on YouTube along with the accompanying

FIGURE 5.2 Roman Osminkin performs "Why do you poets . . ." among train station workers.   ROMAN OSMINKIN, "WHY DO YOU POETS . . . ," YOUTUBE.

text in 2013. The clip—one of nearly a hundred such clips of recorded performances or performative lectures by Osminkin available via YouTube or Vimeo and other video-sharing platforms—sets a poetry recital against the unlikely backdrop of a busy train station. Slightly amused but mostly stony-faced workers go about their business as Osminkin seeks out an appropriate location for a comically ironic avant-garde manifesto (initially available only online, but since released in the 2015 collected volume *Texts with External Objectives* by the publishing house of the prestigious *New Literary Review;* and then in bilingual edition—the publishing history again telling the story of a star on the rise).[12]

After the subheading online, which clarifies that this piece is "about the reasons for the early departure of some and unwillingness to depart of other poets" (O prichinakh rannego ukhoda odnikh i nezhelaniia ukhodit' drugikh poetov), the text opens with a demand for "you poets" (presumably the current reigning literary mainstream) to make way already and get dead, following the brilliant example offered by the Romantic duelists of Russian poetry, Pushkin and Lermontov.[13]

Что же вы, поэты
поздно так уходите

вроде не шахтеры
на забой не ходите

посмотрите, пушкин
лермонтов от пули
пали на дуэли
вы не мрёте хули?

why do you poets
leave so late
you're not miners, you know
going to the coal face

take a look at pushkin
lermontov—from a bullet
they fell in duels
why the fuck are you still here?

We could trace the waves of Russian avant-gardes across the twentieth century solely through a survey of texts about Pushkin. The 1912 manifesto *Slap in the Face of Public Taste* declared it time to jettison Pushkin from the ship of modernity, but, like a guilty memory in Andrei Tarkovsky's 1972 film *Solaris*, Pushkin returns eternally to Russian poetry, provoking subsequent generations to keep throwing him off the ship. When Osminkin cheekily calls for contemporary poets to "be like Pushkin" and a host of other Romantic or neo-Romantic poets, he invites them to die early (and thus on time), not to write like Pushkin. Thus Osminkin, too, participates in what we might call an absurdist tradition of *imitatio Pushkini*.[14] The comparison with coal miners and other workers laboring for a living may motivate the choice of setting and highlights the contrasting comfort that "you poets" have been enjoying at the workers' expense. (Readers will recall the mission statement printed on the back of all Kraft books: "The paper on which this text is printed is called 'Kraft' by the printing industry. The same kind is used by post office workers and in many other technical enterprises . . . which corresponds to the vision of the authors whose texts are printed on this page and in this series.")[15] People who labor for a living are one thing, but poets (or "poets") should not try public patience by surviving past their sell-by date. So Osminkin declaims, swaying and gesticulating, while his orange-vested accidental "extras" try not to look at him, or the camera, or laugh.

The stanzas that follow run through selections from the cherished classical Russian poetic canon of the nineteenth and twentieth centuries, focusing exclusively on the gruesome deaths of poets such as Gumilev, Blok, Esenin, Khlebnikov, Mayakovsky, Mandelstam, Pasternak, Kharms, Vvedensky, and so forth. Osminkin delivers his squandered poets in list form and folksy accentual verse, with comically unexpected rhymes ("bullet / scum" in Russian: ot puli / khuli), wild register mixing ("mandelstam, too, fuck," mandel'shtam i tot blip), and sly repetitions. For example, "the whirlwind of the revolution" (vikhr' revoliutsii) is antirhymed with the same phrase, inviting laughter at the cliché and implying that the improvising, arm-waving declaimer could think of nothing else on the spot. The repetition is all the more eye-catching in a stanza so short that the only new information it allows are the poets' names and the word "tozhe" (or "too") in the original:

гляньте гумилева
вихрь революций
гляньте блока тоже
вихрь революций

look there's Gumilev
whirlwind of the revolution
just look at Blok
the whirlwind of the revolution

The unceasing feminine endings—common enough in Russian modernist poetry but striking for a contemporary experimental poet who keeps company mostly with free verse-ifiers—add to the impression of listening to darkly but pleasurably comic verse.

Yet the humor is really quite black, given the rapid accumulation of bodies and the suggestion that today's poets follow in the footsteps of their martyred heroes. When Mayakovsky became "incomprehensible to the masses / he spoke, the floor is yours / comrade Mauzer" (neponiatten massam / molvil vashe slovo / tovarishch mauzer). The rhythm breaks on the last line; in the video, Osminkin delivers the line with a militant fist raised and the footage breaks off, with the recital resuming in a slightly different location after the cut.

> жизнь в абсурде
> хармсу расшатала нервы
> а введенский сразу
> на смерть держал равненье

> life in the absurd shattered
> kharms's nerves
> while from the get-go vvedensky
> followed death's example

What began as generational conflict, a demand that the old make way for the new, and as a list of permutations running through the early deaths of Russian poetry, blends into a statement of lineage with Old Testament echoes as well as an unexpected textual graveyard: the folk song version of Jakobson's 1930 essay "On a Generation That Squandered Its Poets."[16]

The question that Osminkin knows will be on the mind of older generations in Russia at least, is: What new terrors might a new militancy bring? Is it really time once again for a neo-avant-garde to throw the literary establishment (such as remains of it) off the high-speed train of (post)modernity?[17] While there are no contemporaries mentioned in his litany, it does not take much guesswork to imagine the intended audience of his admonitions or threats: the same dated, liberal, elite intelligentsia whom Medvedev critiques so devastatingly for their convenient worship of luminaries past, even as they remain unquestioningly entangled and complicit in the institutionalized fascisms of the present. Osminkin probes at this earlier generation's fears of a new left throughout his oeuvre—quite explicitly in this piece:

> я шучу конечно
> вы живите дольше
> ну не то чтоб вечно
> все же неприлично

[. . .]

все равно туманны
наши для них книги
хватит с этих хамов
и в кармане фиги

I'm joking of course
go on and live long
well not eternally of course
that would be indecent

[. . .]

our books will still be murky
to these vulgar boors
to hell with them, it's enough just
flipping them off behind their backs

In his video performance of the poem, Osminkin laughs with theatrical om-
inousness after the (hardly threatening, thoroughly self-mocking, politically impotent) final lines and storms off, stumbling slightly—presumably
into the future; perhaps into the past. The joke is on the would-be avant-
gardist, but not solely; and the humor does not preclude other action.

Performing Russian Poet, Politically

Essentially all of the poets associated with [Translit] take strategic advantage,
in some way, of the space that Prigov opened up in Russian poetry. Osminkin
arguably tries to do so the most overtly: he even worked, with Golynko as
his supervisor, on a dissertation exploring Prigov's contributions to contemporary art. But why is Prigov ultimately so important to this overtly
leftist group of contemporary poets and activists?
    Prigov brought Russian poetry into the space of contemporary art: specifi-
cally, into the space of Conceptualism and performance art. More a poet in

quotation marks than a poet, Prigov was a performance artist playing "great Russian poet," undermining the logocentric tendencies of Russian culture by taking it to an extreme. Slavoj Žižek has argued that "overidentifying with the explicit power discourse . . . taking the power discourse at its (public) word, acting as if it really means what it explicitly says (and promises)—can be the most effective way of disturbing its smooth functioning."[18] Alexei Yurchak defines late-Soviet parody, or *stiob,* similarly.[19] Through such actions as his notorious performance of the opening of Pushkin's *Evgenii Onegin* as a faux Buddhist mantra and then faux Muslim prayer, Prigov disturbs the mystified function of the text in Russian culture precisely by exposing it as sacred. The graphomania of Prigov's poetic output (estimated at around forty thousand poems) in turn disrupts a privileged mode of reading: of exegesis, the close reading of the text for its hidden worth and difficulty, the Romantic mode as well as the Soviet / dissident preoccupation with Aesopian language that could slip subversive meanings past censors. Through its very bulk, Prigov's oeuvre forces us into a kind of distant reading *avant la lettre,* reading practices that move rapidly across many poems in search of sense and metanarratives.[20]

The younger generation of performing poets, following Golynko's model and including Osminkin, Medvedev, and Arseniev, takes strategic advantage of the space opened up by Prigov. In an interview with me in August 2013, Medvedev suggests the following line of descent:

> What was Prigov's accomplishment, in large part? In that he learned each time, with a mass of the most diverse methods, to confront the reader with that serious, that modernist approach to art, to the poetic subject, to language in general. That is, you begin reading [Prigov's work] as verse, and then you understand that it is impossible to read it that way, as verse; but as that frame of mind persists inside you, it creates a conflict. And on that, it seems to me, it all rests. Each time, some kind of neat creation of the unified, logocentric subject falls apart. And it falls apart namely through an impulse from below . . . a kind of direct and immediate and unpoetic discourse. And in that, it seems to me, Roma [Osminkin] has glimpsed some kind of potential for a new democratic approach in Prigov's poetics. And he decided to develop it in a more engaged direction.[21]

Osminkin uses a line from Prigov as the epigraph to an essay ("On Method") describing his own poetic practice: "I think that the most democratic literature

FIGURE 5.3 Dmitry Prigov reads Pushkin's *Evgenii Onegin* as a Buddhist chant and Muslim prayer. "ART VIA VIDEO" STUDIO OF THE ARTS PROJECT FOUNDATION, FILMED BY YULIA OVCHINNIKOVA, YOUTUBE.

is not one that is comprehensible to everyone, but one that pays attention to all conventional linguistic gesture."[22] In the context of Osminkin's art and activism, the emphasis on democratic literature reads very differently and implies concrete political goals. In essence, the poetic praxes of the [*Translit*] school are post-Conceptualist in their political directness, yet reluctant to cede the sophistication and wit of Russian and international postmodernism.

The paradox, of course, is that Prigov (still) speaks to incomparably wider audiences precisely because he was never specific in his deconstruction; because his critique extends as if in every direction, leaving no ground stable enough to stand on, much less take an earnest political stance. And indeed, Mark Lipovetsky identifies a persistent and unresolvable contradiction between the two aesthetic approaches he finds in Osminkin's work—between politically engaged and deconstructive Conceptualist poetry.[23] He identifies both tendencies with earlier but ultimately ideologically incompatible Russian avant-gardes: one the world-building, earnest left avant-garde of

Tretyakov and *LEF* (Arseniev's heroes) and the other the supremely ironic postmodern avant-garde (as it were) of Prigov and Conceptualism. I see the point but argue that the relationship between avant-garde waves can be read as more dialectical than contradictory, and that Osminkin finds mutually corrective potential in their clash. Osminkin finds a defense against nihilism in the overt politics so many of his heroes espouse and another against the creep of revanchism that too readily follows in the footsteps of (what Hal Foster terms "reactionary") postmodernism.[24] As he points out in his own critical essays and poetic texts alike, Osminkin locates the shared root of both aesthetic tendencies in the early decades of the twentieth century, among the artistic and scholarly discoveries of early Russian avant-gardes and Formalists. It is those years of intellectual and aesthetic acceleration, as well as the twilight years of the Soviet Union (which he, coming of age in the reckless 1990s, mostly missed) that seem to make the most sense to Osminkin, offering an alternative temporality that he can re-create and call home.

For Osminkin as for Medvedev, another productive tension lies in the imperfect equation between his written poetry and musical performances. Practices of performing poetry—more than that, of performing Russian poet in a new cultural-historical moment—merge into protest rock, folk, and synth-pop with musical group projects like Tekhnopoeziia and Arkady Kots. While musical performances reach a broader audience and are often held in support of political causes, written poetry allows for sustained attention and experimentation. Yet the two clearly bleed into and influence each other. As Brian Massumi writes in *Semblance and Event: Activist Philosophy and the Occurrent Arts,* "Art claims the right to have no manifest utility, no use-value, and in many cases even no exchange value. At its best, it has event value."[25] Aesthetic experiment models what unalienated labor might look like even as it opens a space for critique, aiding in the emergence of political subjectification and of new collectivities. If we consider aesthetic productions primarily as relational events, the borders between poetry and protest and rock break down entirely, reflecting the poets' actual practice. In Osminkin's presence in particular, those borders prove so porous as to be nearly invisible.

Osminkin's poetic experiments, like those of his *[Translit]* collaborators and friends, make free use of his biography as well as of regional current events, referring to incidents and situations all too familiar to his audiences and communities, witnesses and coconspirators. One of Osminkin's best-known

FIGURE 5.4 Roman Osminkin performs "Jesus Saves Pussy Riot." ANDREY KUZMIN, YOUTUBE.

songs, most often paired with Medvedev's "The Walls," is an original composition written in response to the jailing of Pussy Riot in 2012: "Jesus Saves
Pussy Riot" (Iisus spasaet Pussy Riot). Several versions and performances
can be found on YouTube and by now in print form. In the video from which
the still below is taken, the cameraman angles down from Osminkin onstage to show a young woman dancing with a toddler to the synth-pop musical accompaniment.[26] Youth, humor, play, innuendo, and a kind of paradoxical innocence set the tone, despite the political fury equally evident in
the words. Osminkin includes the lyrics to his song in his Kraft book of
poems and manifestos Comrade Word (Tovarishch Slovo, 2012). On the page
he introduces the text as "a song written in support of the feminist group
Pussy Riot on March 8, 2012, which they spent in jail," thus emphasizing his
contribution as a tribute (ironic? serious? both!) in honor of International
Women's Day, dedicated to the jailed artists.

The song is very much of its moment as an occasional work of protest
culture, even while it recasts the story of Pussy Riot into a kind of timeless
Russian fairy tale—a familiar and folksy iteration of the Romantic podvig, or
feat. The tune is catchy, rousing, and meant to move audience bodies (joyfully,
despite the topic):

меж казацкой нагайкой
и чекистским наганом
вьются девичьи стайки
боевым авангардом

и на лобное место
и в сакральный собор
льётся девичья песня
панк-молебна хор

between the whip of the cossacks
and the chekists' revolver
flock maidens armed
with militant avant-gardism

and on the place of skulls
and in the sacred cathedral
rings the song of the maidens
and a punk-prayer choir

Osminkin's identification and alliances are overt. The actions of the young women or "maidens" (inverting the smear campaign run against the young women by Russian media, which predictably stigmatized them as sexually promiscuous and bad mothers) are recognized as militant avant-gardism. Like the poet, and like the rest of their generation, Pussy Riot must find a way to navigate between the Cossack far Right and the Chekist false Left; they too fight by means of song.

The opening stanzas launch into the more jagged rhythms of the contagious chorus:

Иисус спасает
Патриарх карает!
Он, осведомлённый, прекрасно знает:
Надо двух невинных бросить на костёр
И тогда заткнётся всякий на язык остёр
[...]

Надо двух невинных
посадить на кол
И тогда заткнётся каждый, каждый пиздабол!

Jesus saves
the patriarch punishes
he's enlightened and well knows
the two innocents must be
thrown in the fire
and that will trip every other sharp tongue—
[. . .]
the two innocents must be
impaled on the stake
and that will shut up all this pain-in-the-cuntery

Registers mix in shocking, if hilarious, rhymes: the sexual violence of "impaled on the stake" (posadit' na kol) leads to the untranslatable yet related expletive "pizdabol" (pussy pain, as it were). Pussy Riot are first maidens, then "innocents" or Christian martyrs, consumed by the passion of the rekindled avant-garde. The most satisfying lines expose the ideological distance between any recognizable form of Christianity and the "enlightened" patriarch's violence as the Prigovian (but also Žižekian) slide into the discourse of the other side in Osminkin's hands turns into over-the-top overidentification. Osminkin plays something of a Sacha Baron Cohen–as-Borat role in such poems and performances, enthusiastically calling for Pussy Riot to be burned at the stake or impaled (or elsewhere, composing damning faux folk songs of praise for Crimea's annexation). Through ironic overembodiment, he mocks not only the politics but the aesthetics and paranoiac heteronormativity of the Putin regime.

Osminkin's attack grows personal from there: the patriarch, initially called by his title, is named and thereby exposed as a man; and moreover, one who serves two masters:

Как удобно решать
от имени Бога
Кому жировать
а кому в тюрьму дорога

Кирилл Гундяев
не гоже как бы
Служить и Господу
и кагэбэ

it's so nice to decide
in the name of the lord
who gets fattened up
and who's en route to jail

Kirill Gundiaev
it doesn't do
to serve both the lord
and the KGB

The unexpected invocation of the former name of the secret police serves as the song's climactic *j'accuse* indictment—of the Putin regime and its political-historical hypocrisies, and of the church's transparent, unapologetic complicity. Osminkin's song in short tries to repeat and amplify Pussy Riot's *podvig,* less blaspheming than cursing this particular state church and its criminal hypocrisies. Osminkin presents himself as a "Russian poet" just as much as the Pussy Riot performance in the Church of Christ the Savior was a "prayer": the appellation creates an internal contradiction before some audiences conclude, indeed, why not? Moreover, by conspicuously baring his body in performances of "Jesus Saves Pussy Riot," Osminkin draws our attention to the eroticized nature of the spectacle presented by Russian mainstream and oppositional "Western" media depictions alike of the group's members (Nadezhda Tolokonnikova and Maria Alyokhina in particular). Again, overidentifying with the systemic violence of a voyeuristic but punishing gaze, Osminkin appears to enthusiastically invite spectators to objectify him, too. The humor that ensues, however, feels more edgily hysterical than the wry ironies of Conceptualism. The sense of collective camaraderie, of "getting the joke"—and sharing the political ire, and punk rock burn-it-down energy—that his performances inspire likewise marks a departure from mere confirmation of shared intellectual sophistication. Osminkin invites us to listen to his voice and to look at him—at his body, movements, setting, as well as at the words once the text appears in print—and pulls our looking into the orbit of his aesthetic and political praxis.

Brooks describes Osminkin as "an adept of dialectical anticipation, preserving the communist horizon as something we can only approach obliquely, not as an abstract ideal, but as a vibrant presence in our daily life," concluding that "such practices of de- and re-subjectivization are essential as we prepare for the renewal of militant struggle."[27] Somewhere there lies the resolution to Osminkin's seeming contradiction: he is playing at Russian poet for laughs, and he frequently mocks his own activism, yet he is as serious about both as he is about the emancipatory power of laughter. Just as Keti Chukhrov declares, in the next chapter, that all art is communist, so too Osminkin sees a rich tradition of emancipatory linguistic insubordination as the best of what Russian poetry has to offer world culture, Pushkin included. That tradition only grows stronger with our laughter.

The Limits of Digital Emancipation

If Osminkin's humor and physicality are central to his poetic performances, then he is forced more than most to rely on digital remediation and dissemination to share the spirit of his work with a wider community than can be present at each event. In the new poetics, as in the lived experience of Osminkin's generation, virtual and tangible worlds merge; in this fluid on- and offline existence, [Translit] resembles a number of left-leaning journals proliferating around the globe. In schematic terms, it seems fair to summarize the political unconscious of earlier Russian online poetry projects like Vavilon. ru and LitKarta as reflecting the hope for a liberal public sphere. On the right side of the political spectrum, sites like Traditsia.ru tried to tame and render politically useful its eponymous tradition through conclusive lists of the acceptable Russian literary canon. More radical experimental practices on the political left end of the spectrum, finally, seek to draw attention to the media and online platforms themselves—and to the way that they shape us. I therefore find myself returning to the offline-online dichotomy investigated in Chapter 2 as fundamental to the practice as well as the dissemination of politically engaged poetry in the twenty-first century, in

Russia and elsewhere. The limitations of the digital in part explain why so much of contemporary engaged poetry insists on physical performance: on the presence of the poet's body; on physical and ethical risk; and on breaking down the walls between performer and spectator. Readings, concerts, festivals, performances, actions, sit-ins, protests, and encampments like Occupy Abai demand and build the "strong ties" required for collective action—in Malcolm Gladwell's words.[28] The remediations of political art online in turn seek to both represent these experiences and to push against the common uses of digital technologies in ever more creative and politically charged ways.

Prominent techno-pessimists have argued against the collectivity-building potential of digital technologies, admitting few or no exceptions. Gladwell claims that social media create weak ties at best: pithily phrased, "the revolution will not be tweeted." Evgenii Morozov in particular has denounced "slacktivism," which he defines as "feel-good activism that has zero political or social impact but creates an illusion of having a meaningful impact on the world without demanding anything more than joining a Facebook group."[29] Instead, Morozov warns, what social media can actually do is "create serious risks for activists, given the increased possibilities for monitoring by state security apparatus."[30] Meanwhile, Zygmunt Bauman's broader diagnosis is that "contemporary hardships and sufferings are dispersed and scattered; and so is the dissent that they spawn."[31] Such critiques have posed crucial interventions in what a decade ago seemed unbounded popular techno-optimism, based on the presumption that faster communication inevitably leads to the increased potential for collective action (for the good). Such early warnings that the most recent technological revolution was less revolution and more coup—ushering in a new reigning corporate oligarchy—seem particularly prescient a decade later and offer at least a partial explanation for the seeming global failure of the international protests that had fueled much of the optimism.

But many scholars, artists, and activists look for middle ground, and reject the rigid online-offline dichotomy.[32] In *Tweets and the Streets: Social Media and Contemporary Activism,* Paolo Gerbaudo suggests that "social media use must be understood as complementing existing forms of face-to-face gatherings (rather than substituting for them), but also as a vehicle for the creation of new forms of proximity and face-to-face interaction."[33] Gerbaudo speaks of "choreography" and the "symbolic construction of public space" online and offline, witnessed during the organization and implementation of varied global protest events. Gerbaudo's observations stand particularly well when it comes to explaining the success of Osminkin's fluid but always politically aimed practices. No other poet in the *[Translit]* circle is quite so prolific and active across social media platforms (Osminkin can be found on Facebook, YouTube, and Vimeo, as well as a growing number of others); few seem as precisely focused on the specific problems and dangers inherent in each new online genre or remediated form.

How then can leftist poetry make use of tempting but utterly complicit Web 2.0 platforms, moving beyond utilitarian dissemination or the simplest forms of remediation?[34] To make sense of digital genres, we are called on alternatively to zoom in, to the close reading of more familiar literary analysis, and to zoom out, to more distanced approaches that take into account platform, popular practices, and digital and other anthropologies. The digital is not itself a medium: to paraphrase Lev Manovich, we would do better to think in terms of metamedia; in Massumi's phrasing, "Digital technology is an expanding network of connective and fusional potentials. . . . You can take any existing genre of artistic practice and fuse it with any other."[35] The exploration of practices rather than textual units leads us to ask the questions how, where, when—as much as what—of a text. For Osminkin, digitally remediated avant-garde poetry must attack not only the institutions of art and poetry but also the institutions of digital remediation (while, naturally, taking maximal advantage of both).

Many Russian poets post their new work (along with rediscovered favorites by others) on Facebook, but Osminkin does so with graphomaniacal frequency and invites a different degree of participation and collaboration from his "friends." Alongside other playful posts, such as one in which he calls himself the "master of the meme," he posts a draft of the untitled piece "a little class warfare" (nemnogo klassovoi bor'by) on August 2, 2013.

Later that day, he adds several more lines through Facebook's comment function before returning to the poem on August 5 to add the chorus—and to post a YouTube clip of himself singing the piece (accompanied by Medvedev on guitar) and walking the streets of St. Petersburg. The clip was shot on August 4, the previous day, and the words appear at least partly improvised. The next day, Osminkin adds them to the original posting. The final version (if it makes sense at all to think in such terms; more precisely put,

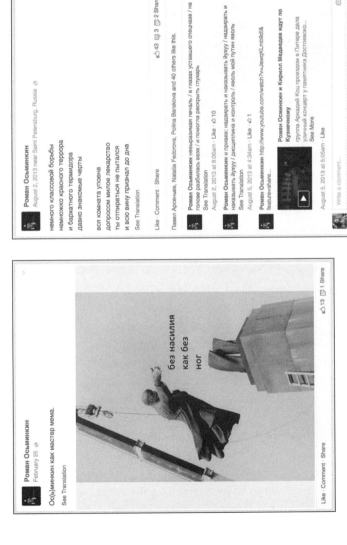

FIGURE 5.5 Screen captures from Roman Osminkin's Facebook page, accessed June 9, 2014. ROMAN OSMINKIN / FACEBOOK.

the version he later performs and sends on for translation) includes all the
lines, with a few minor textual and formatting changes.

немного классовой борьбы
немного красного террора
и бархатного термидора
давно знакомые черты

a little bit of class war
a little bit of red terror
and the features loved to tears
of a velvet thermidor

I give an overview of such practices in Chapter 2, but here want to address a
question frequently raised by international readers of the *[Translit]* group: Why
are artists such as Kirill Medvedev, who stopped publishing to distance himself from corrupt and complicit institutions, willing to have anything to do
with Facebook—surely the embodiment of corporate "evil media"—at all?

Each of the *[Translit]* poets ultimately answers that question in a slightly different way, while the family resemblances remain strong. For some the question of
pragmatism and use value outweighs the risks (as I suspect is the case for Medvedev); or is so secondary to aesthetic practices to serve primarily personal, organizational, or advertising roles. For others, the global reach of Facebook stands in
contrast to the Russian VKontakte, suggesting there are Westernizer and Slavo-
phile factions of social media users, so incarnated for the twenty-first century.
Local activists should pick local foes, or so the implication goes. For yet others,
the digital is a space both like and unlike many others to occupy and in which
to create instances of opposition. I place Osminkin in the last category and
link his general subversively humorous practice of overidentification with the
enemy to his social media usage as well. When Osminkin uses Facebook,
he abuses it: through a Prigovian graphomaniacal overproduction of poetic
posts, he reveals the absurdity of posting at all and makes the Facebook feed
experience, through the process of contagion, all read as absurdist theater, a
total art avant-garde. While Osminkin's is far from the only subversive aesthetic
practice to occupy its social medium, as the international interest in his work
shows, it is a powerfully articulated and directly political one.

Adding political poetry to discussions of the efficacy of protest culture off- and online pushes us to reexamine the relationship between rhetoric and aesthetic, relatively autonomous uses of language and visual media. The avant-garde mode, moreover, challenges experimental poetry to turn against these new institutions, alongside more familiar attacks on literary publishers, reviewers, and prizes as explored in Chapter 1 and Medvedev's communiqué of refusal. Again, as Skidan devastatingly described the politics of the visual turn in contemporary Russian culture: "The center of creative work has shifted to the visual arts because (1) they immediately reflect, and partly coincide with, the new technogenic environment, (2) which mobilizes the cerebral and sensorimotor resources of human beings along with the earth's natural resources and outer space. (3) The visual arts correspond to the dominant regime of temporality and synthetic perception established by the mass media. (4) They are inscribed in the culture industry and, consequently, (5) in the capitalist machine, which deterritorializes any form of identity based on linguistic competency."[36] Faced with this machine, poetry "must still invent means for dwelling in the heart of this absolute rupture, for delivering and enduring it as an openness to the future. And, perhaps, as an openness to future (absolutely real) collective actions."[37] As reviewers of Osminkin's poetry have been quick to pick up, Osminkin more than most thinks that there may be time still, after the most recent poem has been finished, to stop scribbling and "save someone."

Ultimately, what the work of Osminkin and his *[Translit]* comrades throw back into broader discussions of leftist protest culture is the presence of self-conscious aesthetic production, re-created for the digital age: this poetry, despite all acrobatic genre-bending and interdisciplinary experimentation, still insists that it is poetry. More provocatively put, such work cannibalizes other forms and media and claims for an all-encompassing vision of contemporary Russian poetry a special and lasting ability to imagine, and participate in, the processes of potentially emancipatory subjectivization and collectivity building.

Poetic Embodiment

In the manifesto that prefaces his Kraft chapbook *Comrade Word,* Osminkin tries to explain his generation's seemingly paradoxical need to combine poetry with direct action:

To take the poetic word out of an indifferent mode of existence, and to rescue the poet from the pose of alienated prophet, poetry must be made material in a concrete moment in time and space, the poet turning to face unfolding history.

In the moment of the public speech act, the poet takes responsibility for his own voice, and thereby accomplishes a socially responsible act. . . . The main thing happens: the word is pronounced (materialized) and the act accomplished, which means that thought does not remain starry-eyed inspiration, but "performs itself" into the socium.[38]

While Osminkin has been a dedicated presence at protests and meetings of the RSD, the emphasis throughout this essay is on materializing poetic language through voice and presence. Osminkin believes that a poet can accept responsibility and face history through the tangible risk of performance: that the word is made flesh by "performing itself" into the body politic.

While all the poets of the [Translit] circle read or perform their work (and that of others, as singers, in the case of Medvedev and Chukhrov; or participate in collective performances like Arseniev with the Laboratory of Poetic Actionism or Skidan with Chto Delat), Osminkin marks the extreme case here too. The text-only versions of his work read as scripts, secondary to the in-person performances: hence his heavy reliance on countless video clips and social media dissemination to reach "as if" in person such audiences as haven't encountered him directly first. He relies on voice, posture, costume, setting, and other aspects of performance to add layers of ambiguity or irony as he needs them, allowing him to write, declaim, or sing language clearly not his as if at arm's length. What Skidan does through citation and Golynko through seriality, in other words, Osminkin accomplishes by means of body and voice. This is also Osminkin's way of injecting a kind of direct politics into his poetic work—through presence, risk, and a fluid, dialectic relationship with other participants, who in turn he never sees as just audience or public but instead as equally present actants and political agents. Indeed, a reverse logic seems to hold as well: it is because of the limitations of digital reproduction that legitimizing and bond-forming performances require the poet to be bodily present at protests, arrests, or other charged events, and to be willing to be identified as the person doing these actions. While other [Translit] poets are also memorable performers and savvy users / critics of digital media, Osminkin's practice is arguably the most committed to the clashes and convergences of performance and remediation. Osminkin responds to critiques of the apparent contradictions of his politics and aesthetics by stressing that the contradiction that interests him the most in his work is that between "performative presence—the body of the performer—and the mediatic flows into which such linguistic play is constantly subsumed."[39] If the body is all earnest risk, remediation envelops it in ironic flow.

Osminkin's extreme practice can shine a light on more common iterations of the same instinct; for online dissemination is frequently offset by a strong emphasis on performance. Poetry readings maintain a particular aura in Russia, as Stephanie Sandler writes: "The fascination with poetry readings has its own history, one that is specific to a cultural moment or a national tradition. . . . Poets in Russia instead seem comfortable with a fluid continuum between poems as written and poems as performed."[40] If, as the editors of *Russian Performances: Word, Object, Action* argue, the dominant "emphasis on textuality in Russian studies . . . has been guided by formal, structural, and semiotic frameworks and methodologies," the actual experience of performance "moves far beyond" the foundational models that govern essentially all available histories of Russian culture.[41] And of course, the story of Russian performance overlaps tightly with that of the avant-garde:

> Landmarks in Russian studies' genealogy of performance are linked to the artistic avant-garde of the early twentieth century. . . . Prerevolutionary spectacles such as the poet Vladimir Mayakovsky's eponymous *Vladimir Mayakovsky: A Tragedy* (1913) and the futurist opera *Victory over the Sun,* also 1913 by Aleksei Kruchenykh, represented the innovation and daring of such life creation in what the critics and artists both called "the new theater," exhibiting a performative sensibility that the young Bolshevik state sought to adapt to its revolutionary purposes. . . . The performativity of the early Soviet era found in the work of such figures as Vsevelod Meyerhold, Sergei Eisenstein, and Kazimir Malevich is matched by newer discoveries made by the postwar Leningrad Underground, the Moscow Conceptualists in the 1970s and 1980s, and Actionism, which flourished in the 1990s.[42]

A poetic practice such as Osminkin's is therefore more readily described by terms such as event, embodiment, and relational art than unpacked through textual close reading. Indeed, there is a wealth of references to political theory throughout Osminkin's essays (Foucault, Rancière, Butler, and others on sub-jectivization in particular); so too his deceptively simple poems demand theo-retical accompaniment. In *Interactive Art and Embodiment: The Implicit Body as Performance*, Nathaniel Stern describes the performing body as "a dynamic form, full of potential. It is not 'a body,' as thing, but *embodiment* as incipient activity."[43] I similarly try to use the term relational, rather than interactive, when discussing political or protest performance to conceptualize the disso-lution of the performer-audience dichotomy: a distinction between the two terms highlights "what digital and interactive artworks *cannot* do, as well as what they have the potential to do, outside of purely technical terms."[44] The trouble with "interactive" lies in what the term prettifies and obfuscates in commercial use: the "idea that interactivity's supposed provision of choice means it is intrinsically more democratic (or freeing) than other media," given that "such language . . . has been coopted by commercial companies trying to sell us products."[45] Osminkin's performances and demands of his audiences establish modes of relation, not choose-your-own-adventure, consumer-oriented interactivity.

Nicolas Bourriaud builds on the notion of the primacy of relation as-serted by Jean-Luc Nancy to define relational artworks broadly as "invita-tions, casting sessions, meetings, convivial and user-friendly areas, ap-pointments, etc. . . . vehicles through which particular lines of thought and personal relationships with the world are developed."[46] Conceived as "public encounters, events, and collaborations," relational art strives to move beyond aesthetic consumption.[47] Poetic practices that aspire to sim-ilar modes of embodiment and relational affect therefore necessarily rely on performance, audience presence and participation, and site-specific experience—rather than on the poetry book as object and commodity (poor commodity that it is). We can imagine the chasm of difference be-tween reading Osminkin's "Poetic manifesto of the movement 'Occupy Abai'" on the page (reprinted in *Comrade Word*) and participating in the performance of the same piece at the Occupy Abai encampment during the protests of 2012.[48] It is no surprise, then, that those who have experi-enced the latter count Osminkin as one of the most important figures and aesthetic influences of the vibrant new Russian Left, whereas those who have only experienced a few examples of his work in written form remain slightly stumped by the fervor of his fan base.

FIGURE 5.6 Roman Osminkin performs "it happens you meet an underage girl . . ." at the Free Internet protests in 2013. SERGEI YUGOV.

I give below an image of Osminkin reading "it happens you meet an underage girl . . ." inside a circle of activists gathered to protest the changing internet laws in the pivotal and grim summer of 2013.

Бывает повстречаешь малолетку
и сразу принимаешь строгий вид
быстрее проходите мимо детка
от вас половозрелостью фонит

а я законы новые читаю
и мне педофилию не пришьешь
будь вы похои трижды на данаю
но возраст ваш не совершенен все ж

it happens you meet an underage girl
and right away you make a stern face
walk faster past me child
I smell sexual maturity's reek

but I read all the new laws
for pedophilia you won't get me
you could have thrice the charms of danae
but your age is insufficient still

This performance, which I had the opportunity to witness firsthand, transformed the energy of the otherwise listless crowd within minutes and made
of the minor protest an event with legs and aftershocks—especially through
the ongoing digital dissemination of photos and videos of varying quality
taken by the spectators (myself included, I later realized when asked for a copy of
my smartphone video). Osminkin prefaced his reading with the apology that
his poems were about the wrong laws, noting that even he could not write fast
enough to keep pace with changes in the Russian legislation. His piece spoke
instead to the still recent (and then shocking) laws targeting "sexual devi-
ancy," purportedly intended to protect the nation's youth from corrupting influences. The list of encounters Osminkin's lyric persona "sternly avoids"
includes an underage girl, a skulking foreign agent, and lesbians; in the last
section, Osminkin again uses the term *maidens* before switching in the final
stanza to the untranslatable *baba* (very roughly something like *broad*) a Russian woman is doomed to remain:

бывает повстречаешь лесбиянок
и сразу принимаешь строгий вид
будь трижды вы девицы без изъянов
от вас гоморрой за версту фонит

а я законы новые читаю
гейпропагандаю меня не прошибешь
в россии пол себе не выбирают
родилась бабой—бабой и помрешь

it happens you meet some lesbians
and right away you make a stern face
if you were maidens blameless three times over
I'd still smell gomorrah's reek

but I read all the new laws
for gay propaganda you won't get me
in russia you don't pick your gender
if you're born a broad, as a broad you croak

The crowd howled, filmed, posted—and protested.

Clearly, poetic performances and performative behavior on the part of experimental poets predate by far the early teens of the twenty-first century—we need think not only of the futurists' shock tactics but Symbolist *zhiznetvorchestvo*, or life-creation. However, such practices today occur and read differently after the widespread reception and recognition of five decades of international performance art, body art, and feminist art—which Osminkin and fellow poets draw on avidly, queering the Russian poet in ways other artists have been quick to seize on as possible and productive directions for Russian poetry. For example, Galina Rymbu, as I discuss in the coda to this book, shares the intense interest in gender and sexuality present in Osminkin's performative poetics but makes it overt and central to her own stunning, powerfully political, but far more neo-Romantic work. Indeed, gender- and sexuality-based critiques are proving to be some of the most aesthetically and politically interesting movements in Russia, and all over the former Second World. Rymbu and the next generation of Russophone left feminist poets leap off even the springboard *[Translit]* has offered to forge their own vision of the future. But in my view Osminkin and Chukhrov are right there with them, well ahead of the times.

Richard Schechner writes that performance art asks the question, "'Who is this person doing these actions?'—unlike theater, which asks about the character doing the actions. Insisting that spectators regard not a character but an actual person (even if the artist embellishes that persona, as Spalding Gray did) actualizes the slogan, 'the personal is political.'"[49] That old activist slogan is in turn borrowed from the title of Carol Hanisch's 1969 essay, explaining her bra-burning protest of the Atlantic City Miss America pageant, and reminding us of performance art's roots in feminist art and theory.[50] This is how I ultimately understand Osminkin: identifying without pause with women, sexual minorities, and "decadent" local and foreign thinkers. The latest return of the Russian avant-garde bursts bodily out of local counter-traditions, reinvigorated by the output of years of international theory and art practice.[51]

On Cuteness and Gender

Sianne Ngai has inspired many with her by now often quoted insight that po-etry's powerlessness in commodity society reflects "its distinctive ability to theorize powerlessness in general."[52] Even as I write these words, Russia, the complicated exception that proves the rule, offers what could be thought of as either example or counterexample: in June 2021, international media spread the word that liberal opposition mainstream poet and television personality Dmitry Bykov (born 1967) was the most recent target of a seeming govern-ment assassination attempt through poisoning. Bykov, presumably, had ac-cumulated enough influence to catch the Kremlin's eye. It remains the first suspected attempted government assassination of a poet since the darker days of the Soviet Union.

Fortunately, Roman Osminkin has attracted less attention. And here I want to turn to the other key concept articulated in Ngai's essay, cuteness, as a very close if unexpected match to Osminkin's subversive avant-garde poetic prac-tice. Ngai writes,

> The avant-garde's lack of political consequentiality is typically attributed to the short or limited range of its actual address, often taken as sign of its elitism as a mode of "restricted production" (the critical position of Pierre Bourdieu); its susceptibility to becoming routinized, in spite of its dynamism and commitment to change, and thus to being absorbed and recuperated by the cultural institutions it initially opposes (the crit-icisms of Raymond Williams, Peter Bürger, and Paul Mann); and a so-cial overambitiousness signaled by the incomplete or unfinished nature of all its projects. . . . [Yet] cuteness allows us to conceive the powerless-ness of both poetic forms and the social formations built around their production in the arena of political action as the source of an unsus-pected power in the domain of political imagination: a fantasy about the very capacity to fantasize or imagine an *otherwise*.[53]

Ngai foregrounds cuteness ("simple or formally non-complex and deeply associated with the infantile, the feminine, and the unthreatening")[54] as one strangely subversive way forward. The strategy of cuteness, while present to some extent in the work of several other poets discussed in this book (notably in Arseniev's collaborations with Osminkin or other experiments during the Laboratory of Poetic Actionism era), proves uniquely central to Osminkin's work. (It is markedly absent in the work of either Chukhrov or Rymbu.)

As I hope to have convinced readers by this point, nearly all the poets associated with *[Translit]*—certainly all the poets chosen as case studies for this book—identify the rich and diverse traditions of the avant-garde as among Russia's greatest contributions to world culture and politics. Nearly all also take seriously critiques of the avant-garde that document its dangerous and frequent slides into the opposite of its emancipatory ideals. The line in the sand shifts from case to case and time to time, as the examples of "grandfather of Russian protest culture" Eduard Limonov and other uneasy red-brown ideologues show.[55] Around the world the extreme right today co-opts for its own purposes what were once progressive, leftist forms of critique. Such appropriations seem part of a general cultural phenomenon that echoes the previous century's rise of fascism in tandem with the Futurist moment.[56] It is not enough for the *[Translit]* poets to use the legacies of the avant-garde against the global present: they must also respond to the lessons of the present to improve upon the tools of the past.

Nationalism and masculinism form two axes of the familiar slide from left to right that the most perceptive members of the new Russian avant-garde are so determined to avoid. Osminkin, who, as he puts it in biographical statements, hails from the "rich agricultural regions along the Volga River in Russia and in the Zhitomir region of Ukraine,"[57] was immediate in his responses to the annexation of Crimea—thereby joining the exceedingly small minority of artists and intellectuals who have stood in consistent and firm opposition to what has been referred to as the "Crimean consensus." He has since left the country in response to the 2022 invasion of Ukraine. Yet it is his more subtle undermining of the masculinity of the Russophone avant-garde poet that may prove more lastingly subversive and emancipatory. From his collaborations with his partner, the feminist artist Anastasia Veprova, to the scores of deliberately effeminizing gestures that consistently punctuate performances of political militancy, Osminkin undermines the performative maleness of much of "serious" Russian poetry in general. His singing, dancing, and love of costume tiptoe in the direction of drag, if ambiguously so; his bodily performance, often described as athletic or acrobatic, also emphasizes youth and smallness. If the red-brown punks who follow Limonov and National Bolshevism seek to inspire fear through costume and visual iconography, Osminkin succeeds in being extremely likable—more than that, *cute*. Gender expectations of the Russian avant-garde be damned.

6

Art Must Be Communist

THE VOICES OF KETI CHUKHROV

*I*N FEBRUARY OF 2015 the exhibition *Specters of Communism: Contemporary Russian Art* opened simultaneously in two New York locations: the James Gallery at the CUNY Graduate Center and *e-flux*. Curated by Boris Groys, the show presented work by a number of prominent Russian cultural figures: Keti Chukhrov, the Chto Delat collective, Anton Vidokle of *e-flux*, and Pussy Riot, among others. Groys's introductory essay made clear the premise of his curatorial selection: taking inspiration from Jacques Derrida's *Specters of Marx* (1993), Groys chose works that suggest "communism continues to haunt Russia as well as the West." The conceptual work suggested by "haunting," however, goes only so far: Groys's conceit, with its characteristic emphasis on the transformation of life into art, suits some contemporary Russian art very well. But the most compelling work in the show looks forward as well as backward and imagines a far more dynamic relationship between aesthetics and politics: Chukhrov's video-verse-drama "Love Machines" (2013) in particular is less driven by trauma or nostalgia than a desire to explore the potential reemergence of radical art and politics after the Soviet Union.[1]

Chukhrov (born in Soviet Georgia, in 1970) has become increasingly visible internationally in recent years, through art world events, translated poetic texts in English-language literary journals (*n + 1; Common Knowledge*), and through numerous conferences and academic publications.[2] A closer look reveals that over the past two decades, Chukhrov has been developing a distinctive practice that makes her at once paradigmatic and exceptional, a challenging representative of the Russian poetic avant-garde. She shares political stances and theoretical underpinnings with her *[Translit]* collaborators, but her work is entirely distinct from that of other members of the circle, spilling well past the bounds of the journal and its platforms, and her stance vis-à-vis historical avant-gardes is, on the whole, more openly critical.

The curator of an influential portion of the contemporary Russian poetry scene once allegedly declared, "There is no such poet as Keti Chukhrov." Indeed, Chukhrov is neither quite Russian nor quite a (lyric) poet, but she plays with the honorific and its implications as she does with her other roles of academic, public intellectual, performer, and collaborative artist. Her work slides fluidly between poetry, drama, contemporary art, political philosophy, and cultural criticism; her very name is a well-crafted line (as was said of Anna Akhmatova) that speaks to equally fluid national identifications. Born Ketevan Chukhrukidze in Tbilisi, Chukhrov moved from Soviet Georgia to the capital of the crumbling anti-imperial empire to study literature and philosophy at Moscow State University. After decades in Moscow, she teaches today in the cultural studies department of the prestigious Higher School of Economics; other recent appointments include a curatorial stint at the Moscow Museum of Contemporary Art and the Marie Skłodowska-Curie fellowship at the University of Wolverhampton in the United Kingdom. Given her equal ease with global art and theater worlds and Russian-language poetry, and eloquence across many (imperial) languages—were I to predict today a steady rise to international fame for any poet whom I follow, it would be for Keti Chukhrov.

Chukhrov's political values, intellectual interests, and extraordinary erudition are all in evidence in her (usually staged and remediated) poetic works, which tend toward long dramatic verse forms and collect the voices of Moscow's subalterns: migrant workers, sex workers, and precarious surplus populations who can find no work at all. In a 2015 interview, Chukhrov explained that her choice of form and attraction to theater were driven by dissatisfaction with other genres and their institutions, for "contemporary art is too constrained by the gallery and by fixation on the art object, lyric poetry is too focused on the experience of the individual, and neither is an effective means for moving people to political insight or action."[3] Borrowing from an assemblage of aesthetic and critical practices from the past, com-

FIGURE 6.1 Keti Chukhrov's video art piece *Love Machines* screens at the *Specters of Communism* exhibit curated by Boris Groys at *e-flux* and the James Gallery in New York City.   JULIA SHERMAN.

bined with their carefully historicized study, Chukhrov forges a distinctive hybrid practice as a bulwark against the creeping fascisms of the present and the lost hope for a different future. Her work probes in a very different way the central questions of any post-Soviet avant-garde: Who dares to dream again of a global egalitarian society? And what have we learned?

In form as in content, Chukhrov's contribution to the *Specters of Communism* exhibit reads as a wildly imaginative exercise in collectivity formation. The 2013 video "Love Machines" is based on Chukhrov's text, a verse drama structurally familiar to readers of her other poetic work.[4] Chukhrov's classically trained and strikingly beautiful voice is also heard throughout the piece. But the video was shot and edited by others (Sergei Shilov and Viktor Alimpiev, respectively); the actors include other poets and artists well known in Russian leftist circles (Dina Gatina and Arseny Zhilyaev, the latter also featured in Groys's show), as well as the group Truppa Rupor and the artistic director Semen Filipov. "Love Machines" is thus hardly video art by Chukhrov so much as it is a collaborative coproduction based on her written work and

made with her full participation. Relinquishing solo authorship alongside
lyric subjectivity, Chukhrov foregrounds each interpretation, performance,
and translation as the cocreation of a new collective. The resulting ephemeral pieces take on new life and draw in new audiences and participants with
each performance—a form most adequate to the kind of Deleuzian logic that
informs Chukhrov's academic and artistic work alike.

The experimental verse drama at the heart of the video, meanwhile, reads
as an allegory that refuses to fully signify its secondary meaning. The love
machines in question are presumably the futuristic androids that have been
sent to intervene in (accelerate? seduce and destroy?) the meaningless lives
of contemporary Muscovites. A cow is also involved. As Anastasiya Osipova
puts it in a perceptive review: "*Love Machines* casts all of its characters—
robots and cow included—as political subjects in a collective vision of responsibility."[5] We appear to see three coexisting stages of development: the
animal, the human, and the Futurist-machine. The human remainder, as delineated and differentiated from the (abused, loving) animal and (brutal,
seductive) machine, is mostly unappealing. Yet the elite formation of futurist-
androids, who would eliminate all who fall short of standards, hardly maintains the moral higher ground. Before we even hear the androids' wind-down
exercises of "dyr bul schyl" (*zaum*, or beyond-sense syllables that are Aleksei
Kruchenykh's most-quoted line of avant-garde assault on Russian poetry
from 1912), the piece has registered as a mocking rebuke of one kind of avant-
garde teleology.

There is a tautological whiff here of Groys's *Total Art of Stalinism: Avant-
Garde, Aesthetic Dictatorship, and Beyond* (1988), which asserted a direct line
of descent from the revolutionary Russian avant-garde to the terrors of high
Stalinism—and which may explain Groys's attraction to Chukhrov's piece.[6]
However, the two visions rapidly diverge, in my view: studied as a coherent
body of work, Chukhrov's ongoing explorations read neither as totalitarian
fearmongering (they are fundamentally Marxist) nor as Soviet nostalgia
(they are deeply critical of false utopias). Chukhrov directly confronts the
seeming impossibility of her position, probing the fears of her generation of
left-wing post-Soviet (and, arguably, peculiarly postcolonial) intellectuals
to imagine—and at least momentarily to conjure on a microlevel, through
art—a future that ends neither in the total dominion of converging global
elites nor in the not-so-proverbial gulag. Even as she explores the fears left

behind by the traumas of the past, her work prompts unalike individuals to come together in the present to engage in something aesthetic, social, meaningful—and oriented toward the future.

Throughout this book, I conceptualize the *[Translit]* circle as a contemporary avant-garde, arguing that radical post-Soviet Russian poets revive historical avant-gardes in search of a paradoxically timely path forward. The most compelling and recent revivals, I try moreover to stress, include correctives along lines of nation and gender. Chukhrov—perhaps unsurprisingly, as Georgian and a woman—presents a particularly compelling case study within the *[Translit]* constellation: her doubly marginalized yet instantly globally legible work, in nearly all instances, contains unflinching and merciless critiques of utopian clichés and overreaches. And yet, as she has declared in lectures, Chukhrov still believes that "art must be communist."[7] Indeed, it is as if the verse dramas probe the limits and possible failings of her political stances in content, while simultaneously working to affirm them through form. In other words, while the fabulae of her poetic experiments genuinely question how artistic and literary practices can hope to escape their political, financial, and cultural entrapments (doing the work of relentless self-questioning critique, as Chukhrov sees it), their forms and many afterlives in genuinely collectivity-forming performances tell a story of boundless optimism and local transformation. The underlying motto of such work might be best summarized through the Beckettian invective to "Fail better," here explicitly politicized. In my view, few fail so well.

Read alongside her critical essays, Chukhrov's poetic experiments reveal an extended multigenre and multimedia investigation into post-Soviet subjectivization. She remains a scholar and follower of Deleuze, in her estimation still one of the most radical thinkers of the past half century. That stance itself is striking in our reactionary postmodernist present, where the weapons of left and right appear to have traded sides, and poststructuralist epistemological critiques are readily appropriated into ominous "post-truth" stances. But Chukhrov bases in Deleuze her suspicion of singularity and universality in favor of the "centrifugal politics of multiplicities, repetitions, seriation, and temporal procedures," which she reads as both fundamentally communist and continually relevant to the global present.[8] Chukhrov moreover uses Deleuze to conceptualize the event as a political, aesthetic, ethical moment of conversion radically open to all, including to those for whom no active struggle is currently possible: "[Deleuze] sees [a revolutionary mode] as an act of conversion on all levels—the empirical, mental, conscious, unconscious, and spiritual. And what is most important is that his focus on the event pre-supposes the potentiality of emancipatory change, the procedure of gener-ating strength, not only in case of a possible and given situation of struggle and its institutional or administrative framework, but even where there can be no such possibility of struggle—i.e. in the conditions of utmost social weakness."[9] It is through this enormously optimistic reading of Deleuze—for a kind of inclusive, flexible, left-leaning populism—that Chukhrov views the future of struggle in post-Soviet Russia, and not only Russia.

Chukhrov's oeuvre inevitably faces all the by now familiar critiques: that it is not poetry; that it is not Russian; and that it is not politically effective. Again, Sianne Ngai has responded to that last and lingering critique by showing us how to reframe the powerlessness of poetry in commodity society as instead a unique opportunity to theorize powerlessness itself.[10] Chukhrov tries to theorize powerlessness in her work in ways that are both deeply local and globally familiar, while simultaneously providing a model of subjectivization and collectivity formation in action. Some of this is by now familiar: Medvedev tries to build new collectives through his activism and organizing; Arseniev through the social network provided by [Translit]; Skidan through Chto Delat and other literary and artistic collaborations; Golynko through more academic forms such as teaching and translation; Osminkin through rapport with audiences at his performances. By writing pieces that essentially demand actors and staging, Chukhrov consistently builds that work into her very forms. Yet, despite the many voices speaking her work, Chukhrov's theses remain consistent: all desire, even faked, is political eros; art must be communist; and the post-Soviet subject is not even dead. Chukhrov is and is not avant-garde, I suspect, even in her own estimation: she embeds her politics in institutional critique, lends her labor to collectives and collaborations, and refracts her poetic voice into multi-tudes. But she also rejects dated teleologies, militarized metaphors, and models of modernity projected by powerful metropoli onto spaces with their own nonmodern stories to tell.[11] She takes responsibility for her words by voicing them, lending her actants (never entirely genre-appropriate characters, always creatures made up tangibly of words) her own haunting vocals in the most thrilling performances of her work. What if Dostoyevsky was right—and radical—all along, Chukhrov seems to ask, and beauty will save the world?

Political Eros

Chukhrov's best-known dramatic poem to date, "Afghan-Kuzminki" (2008), gives voice to its own post-Soviet Hamlet—quite literally. Written as a kind of dramatic duet in mostly free verse and named after a notorious unregulated Moscow street market (many of which are Central Asian, Caucasian, or otherwise "Soviet Oriental"), the approximately three-thousand-word text includes no authorial interventions or anything resembling a lyric persona. First published in 2008 in *[Translit],* the piece was reprinted alongside six similar experiments by Chukhrov in a 2010 chapbook, *Just People: Dramatic Poems.* Like her other dramatic poems, it has taken on many more lives in performance and video formats.[12]

Chukhrov's choice to debut her first book of dramatic poems with the lo-fi Kraft series, the poetry chapbook arm of *[Translit],* was itself a statement, particularly given her many options and prestigious literary and academic connections. As the reviewer Danila Davidov notes, such a choice is clearly motivated by politics: "The series, organized by several leftist-by-conviction authors, is an example of a new *samizdat.* The publishing notes declare: 'The paper on which this booklet is printed is called "craft" by the printing industry. It is the same paper as used by postal workers and many other technical industries. . . . Perhaps it is because poets, as a rule, have not engaged in material labor that what you hold in your hands does not seem like a "normal" book of poetry.'"[13] Davidov finds continuity in the text inside with the Soviet avant-garde OBERIU poet Alexander Vvedensky as well as with Samuel Beckett, suggesting that similarly "irreconcilable participants in the shredded social field" appear to be the only important actants in Chukhrov's works.[14] Davidov emphasizes the evident socioeconomic critique in a piece about a migrant worker and a woman offering sex in exchange for better conditions in an uncontrollable street market.

And yet, from the perspective of the present, "Afghan-Kuzminki" indeed already reads as a text written in better times, reflecting the surge of political energy in Moscow and St. Petersburg that ultimately bubbled over in the "new Decembrist" rallies and the years of political protest in 2011–2012.[15] Chukhrov was part of that energy since the formation of the Chto Delat collective in 2003—at a time when, as her frequent collaborator Aleksandr Skidan has put it, you had to be crazy to be a Marxist in post-Soviet Russia.[16] Against the fallout of the financial crisis and Putin's rise to power on the creeping cult of the new stability, however, the ranks of left-leaning intellectuals grew. A mere year or so later, they took to the streets. Chukhrov's best-known text to date brims with the hope and the desire to come together, so characteristic of those game-changing years.

The subtitle of the dramatic poem is "An Attempt to Engage in Sex." The two voices belong to Hamlet and Galina, the former a Dagestani migrant worker with some capital in the market (*rynok*) where both sell goods. Hamlet trades in fur and vaguely criminal entrepreneurship; Galina, a Russian hawking underwear at the bottom of the market's social ladder, sells herself. Or so she tries: for the duration of the piece, the two attempt to trade sex for a better gig, but the primal scene of exchange is continually deferred. Instead, within and through Chukhrov's rhythmic and occasionally rhymed lines, some form of unexpected subjectivization seems to occur. The borders around "Hamlet" and "Galina" prove permeable. "Afghan-Kuzminki" ends at dawn, outside the market, with a call to wipe the woman's face clean of cheap makeup and thus to see her for the first time.

The text opens with irreconcilable differences and rough linguistic registers. Hamlet regrets picking Galina for his advances but reasons that "the broads here are just all sweaty pieces of crap anyway" (Bab'e zdes' vse ravno odno potnoe govno). Galina grumbles that she has to sleep with "another wog, but who else here is going to bite? / I'll suffer through it somehow" (Chernyi opiat', nu kto eshche kliunet zdes' / Kak nibud' poterpliu). We end with inexplicable power reversals and radical empathy: the coming together of undesirables, the immigrant and (failed) sex worker. Faked desire becomes real political eros: Hamlet's opportunism and Galina's materialism alike reveal an impossible-to-eradicate longing for human connection and a better life. The titular "attempt to engage in sex," which initially reads as black comedy and inevitably provokes audience titters, by the end seems serious and moving. Intercourse is hard; under the conditions of metastasizing twenty-first-century capitalism, it feels impossible.[17]

Hamlet cedes most of the philosophizing to Galina, who retells soliloquies in her own tragicomic words: "To be is necessary. / Being ill is forbidden"

(Byt'—nado. Bolet' nel'zia). She interrupts their first attempt unexpectedly with a description of a television series currently showing on the archconservative national Channel One. The show's protagonist is a modern-day superfluous man:

Работа вроде хорошая у него,
На жизнь хватает.
Непонятно одно—зачем сама жизнь,
чтобы что?

He's got a good job sort of:
It's enough to live on.
Only one thing ain't clear: what's the point of life itself,
What are you supposed to do with it?

Popular mutations of literary clichés seep into the text from the media that thoroughly saturate the characters' lives: "Television my bodyguard, / Watch over me always" (Televidenie moi telokhranitel', smotri na menia vsegda). In place of sex, the two begin to connect through watching music videos of garish Russian pop and anticipate the Georgian-born journalist Tina Kandelaki's (surely no accidental Caucasus reference) next outfit. Chukhrov's verse drama actively includes example after example of culture as spectacle, underlining what it refuses to sell us: namely, seduction.

The high-art market likewise makes a cameo: Hamlet catches on quickly about contemporary art: "In Moscow people know what this art is, / That it's something profitable and cool" (A v Moskve etot *art* chto takoe / chto eto denezhnoe i krutoe, / znaiut). In identical terms, he evaluates women based on the estimated market cost of their bodies (the pop star Friske, a hundred thousand, whereas Galina's cellulite should be nearly free). Galina picks up the theme, but slides from one archetype of the oldest profession to another:

А я бы если пошла на панель,
Только бесплатно.
Интересно, если бы девчонка полюбила всех
Так же сильно как Христос,
Она бы бесплатной проституткой что ли стала,

Она бы совсем что ли не разбирала,
Кто ее в разнос, а кто взасос.
Сильно бы плакала, страдала,
Но всем разрешала.
А если б я рисовать как художница стала
Детям бы с картинами своими
Играть разрешала

If I worked the streets,
I'd do it only for free.
I wonder, if a girl loved everyone
As deeply as Christ,
Would she become a free whore?
Would she care less
Who abused her and who wooed her?
She would suffer and cry,
But let everyone do her.
And if I started drawing like an artist,
I'd let children play
With my pictures.

The artist-Galina would give away her work for free, like a girl Christ giving away her love. Here Galina joins a procession of holy harlots and martyrs: Galina the Corinthian mixed with Marina Tsvetaeva's Mary Magdalene by way of Lars von Trier.[18] Such communist-adjacent holy harlotry contrasts with the self-serving politics of Hamlet's mother, whom he calls the worst of whores:

партию любишь,
А теперь любишь то, чего теперь дают,
ларек, например, свою поставку, лоток,
сожителя Леху.
Была бы вся страна—монастырь, бля.

you loved the Party,
And now you love what's given you—

A kiosk, say, your own supplier, a stall,
Your live-in lover Lyokha.
Fuck, if only the whole country were a monastery.

Hamlet's mother now believes only in the *rynok,* visually represented by the hawker's stand with which the poem opens. This market is literally broken: Hamlet the guest worker tries to keep it together with nails he holds in his mouth. At the start of Chukhrov's text, he removes those nails when he begins to speak.

Further spectacle, in a dramatic turn, enters through the text's only included external voice, a televised speech by Vladimir Putin, all cadences and invocations of foreign enemies:

Дорогие сограждане, мешают нам враги
понять великую сердечную простоту,
Мешают нам
Любить и верить.

My fellow citizens, our enemies prevent us
From understanding the heart's great simplicity.
They prevent us
From loving and believing.

Repeating the acronyms and abbreviations "WTO, WTO, / IMF, ABM, / UN, OSCE, O," Galina begins to weep: "How can I love this country? That's why I'm crying. / How can I call it my own?" Hamlet, tellingly, has nothing to say on the subject.

As the registers blur and polyglossia builds—after many lines of substandard, colloquial, obscene, but evocatively chosen and loosely rhymed language—Marina Tsvetaeva's poetry suddenly enters the mix. In the startling climax, Galina recites verses from Tsvetaeva's 1936 cycle "Verses to an Orphan" over Hamlet's sleeping body, as if casting a love spell.

Что для ока—радуга,
Злаку—чернозем—
Человеку—надоба,
Человека—в нем.

What rainbow is to the eye,
Black soil to grain,
A man's need
For man is to man.

Some event occurs: upon waking, Hamlet tells her that he dreamed of a world without walls and, in an ambiguously violent vision, simultaneously emancipatory and flaying, that he could see through her very skin. Political subjectivization, as Jacques Rancière writes, is always "the denial of an identity given by an other, given by the ruling order of policy."[19] Galina and Hamlet must cease to cohere and conform to become political subjects, much less to commune.

Whence Galina's radical ethics, whence Hamlet's dream in "Afghan-Kuzminki"? It is hard to avoid the reading that Tsvetaeva's verses serve as a catalyst, and one that genuinely exists in a different economy than the book market or art gallery sales. Chukhrov renders startlingly literal and immediate the conversion made possible by an artistic event: were it not for the piece's explicit rejection of realist poetics and psychological verisimilitude, the effect would be jarring or comical. Retold in plot summary, the slim narrative of "Afghan-Kuzminki" might read as relatively transparent propaganda for solidarity and inclusivity. (Indeed, one marker of Russia's new left is the rediscovery of socialist tropes from the other side of the Soviet century and of the impossibility of recovering their shocking innocence.)[20] But the oddly virtuoso poetry of her hybrid forms informs the content and makes the larger meaning of the piece harder to retell than the fabula would suggest. Indeed, despite Chukhrov's layered theoretical underpinnings, her works are surprisingly accessible compared with some other contemporary Russian avant-garde poetry: they simply mean what they say on multiple levels. Some event has occurred, both aesthetically and politically, to allow Hamlet and Galina to break out of their individual prisons and see each other and an open, shimmering future: Chukhrov tries to show the simultaneous universality of the longing and alterity of transformation.

In a 2009 manifesto published in *[Translit]*, Chukhrov lays out her aesthetic and political agenda, which has remained consistent in the decade since: "Recently, I came to the clear understanding that art cannot but be communist. This is not at all a manifestation of ideology, as it may seem to some. It is also not a dogma. It just suddenly became obvious to me that the whole of art—from ancient Greece to the present day—the art that overcame selfishness and conceit—contains in itself communist potentiality."[21] Her definition of art is inherently political, regardless of overt content or even the professed politics of the artist, and pluralistic in essence: the artist must become many. Her list of writers and artists that achieve this highest level of communist potentiality begins with Dostoyevsky—echoing Bakhtin, ever present in Chukhrov's commitment to polyphony and dialogue—but also includes such odd fellow travelers as Beckett, Beethoven, Brecht, Khlebnikov, Mayakovsky, Mozart, Platonov, Shakespeare, and of course Vvedensky, the historical avant-garde poet most proximate to the twenty-first century in her view. Like Skidan, with whom she is close, she writes against what she sees as a tradition of a hermetic, individual-oriented (indeed individual-fetishizing) line of Russian lyric poetry.

Form follows content in many provocative ways in "Afghan-Kuzminki": the text reads as poetry after language and drama after character. The incongruent voices each fail to hold together just as Chukhrov herself disavows lyric forms. She anticipates the critique that her events and conversions are not "real" or "convincing" by rejecting psychological naturalism as ideologically as well as aesthetically conservative. The center does not hold; identity is not stable; language moves through men like air. In his review of Chukhrov's dramatic poems, Davydov draws attention to their "stylistic aggression and deliberate linguistic shapelessness," which he suggests "demonstrate the total impossibility that different 'others' can meet each other."[22] I agree but find Chukhrov ultimately less interested in deconstructing literary practices than in forcibly critiquing a political order in which hard shells of identity are forged and sold—and with which the institutions, practices, and common forms of aesthetic production are fundamentally complicit.

The trouble is of course that the two economies, of ideas and institutions, are both distinct and entangled. Hence Chukhrov's interventions nearly always veer into critiques of cultural elites: her actants often exist on the edges of the art world, exposing failures even as they inspire participants and onlookers to long for something better. As her essay "The Mobile Communist Theater" makes clear, Chukhrov turns to performance and to theater to challenge the conventions of both poetry and contemporary art: "The inevitable transition to theater came to me on the one hand from the direction of poetry, and on the other, from contemporary art. In poetry, the encumbering factor was the monologue, some sort of doomed attachment to acmeism, lyricism—that is, in the end, the tendency to talk only about oneself, even when talking about the world, and even often castrating the legacy of the avant-garde and modernism."[23] Russian poetry's attachment to the lyrical subject (what Chukhrov calls the victory of the acmeist line over the "castrated" avant-garde) privileges one individuated voice, one unrepeatable consciousness, one liberal subject. In response, Chukhrov's attempt to reenchant poetry is viscerally political and interpersonal, tellingly invoking Tsvetaeva as another nomad, another woman, and moreover one with politics resistant to appropriation by either Soviet or anti-Soviet literary historians.

Chukhrov's critique of Russia's contemporary art scene is even fiercer than her dismissal of mainstream lyric poetry. Both are in bed with nationalism, but the former also with power and real money. Echoing Peter Bürger's account of commercialized neo-avant-gardes, Chukhrov suggests that contemporary art has so thoroughly incorporated critique into the institution as to remain mired in the repetition of its own commentaries.[24] Moreover, in a 2011 art review titled "Art after Primitive Accumulation: Or, on the Putin-Medvedev Cultural Politics," she writes that while contemporary Russian literature and theater retained some ties to late Soviet dissident culture, contemporary artists have chosen more powerful patrons: "Despite the initial expectation . . . that contemporary art's modernist and avant-garde background would draw the cultural milieu away from supporting the government, Russian cultural politics—as well as contemporary art and its practices—became, voluntarily or not, oriented towards power. . . . [With certain exceptions] Russian contemporary art today keeps away from the vulnerable and problematic zones of post-Soviet reality."[25]

Chukhrov's manifesto for *[Translit]* calls instead for a poetic practice grounded in Vsevolod Meyerhold's theater of cabotinage, a moving assemblage loosened from chains to time and place. Chukhrov insists that theater works differently than other media, contemporary art, literature, or lyric poetry: it includes the possibility for an encounter, for dialogue, for performances by "the injured or the oppressed themselves. . . . Such is the political, aesthetic, and communist potential of theater."[26] Without hearing, magnifying, and allowing ourselves to be transformed by the voices that surround us, we have

FIGURE 6.2 Keti Chukhrov prepares to sing the entirety of her dramatic poem "Afghan-Kuzminki" as a liturgy.   CHTO DELAT.

no chance of understanding "what has happened or is happening among us, in our country, in our state, in the world. . . . (Doesn't Hamlet launch his 'theater' with just such a purpose?)"[27] It is with the revolutionary potential of the stage in mind that Chukhrov tries to reclaim a radical potential for contemporary Russian-language poetry.

In one reading of "Afghan-Kuzminki" recorded as a duet with Skidan, Chukhrov chants Tsvetaeva's verses in dramatic declension, differentiating this moment from the rest of the dramatic poem.[28] In other live and recorded performances, she has chanted the entire text as a liturgy; as if song, once allowed in, takes over the entire work.[29] In yet another recorded and digitally disseminated adaptation for the gallery, "Viktoriia," many participants (including the curator Andrei Parshchikov, the director Ksenia Peretrukhina, and about twenty other artists) combined the dramatic poem with video interviews of workers from a Caucasian market, expanding the dramatic poem from within to include a multiplicity of participants and works of art.[30] As Chukhrov says of this performance: "All of us were the writers."[31]

Art Must Be Communist

The astonishing optimism of Chukhrov's "Afghan-Kuzminki" teeters, for some, on the brink of false consciousness. It is hard to shake the suspicion that emancipatory encounters with poetry are possible only for a small network of people writing for each other as we await the end of the world. Indeed, and increasingly, the fear of false consciousness takes center stage in Chukhrov's poetic works. Unlike for example, Kirill Medvedev, with whom she also often collaborates and performs, Chukhrov appears less concerned about sliding from left- to right-wing populism than with the pursuit of the ever-receding post-Soviet subaltern. Both poets, however, interrogate the tightening choke hold of globalized twenty-first-century nationalism and the complicit role of seemingly all media, literature, or visual culture alike.[32]

The post-Soviet subaltern dominates "Communion" (2009), another dramatic poem from Chukhrov's *Just People* collection and of similar length and structure. The title, a neologism in the original (*Kom'ionion,* something like Commie-Union) plays on religious communion but seems composed equally of the words *communism* and *union*. It thereby resembles the name of its heroine, Diamara, a Soviet-era charmer of a given name deriving from "dialectical materialism." "Communion" is a darker, more self-ironizing piece than the defiantly Romantic "Afghan-Kuzminki": this time the dialogue takes place among three women, but again most often tends toward duet form. No male voices interrupt the flow of feminine chatter—about fashion, lovers, remodeling, class difference, and the divine reasons for all the above—and their chiasmatic reversals of spiritual seduction. Sons, fathers, husbands, and lovers are referred to and occasionally spoken to on the phone, but as Diamara puts it, this time it's "just girls, / more like 'we're sisters, angels, poems, dreams.'"[33]

The entire dramatic poem is contained within the nesting layers of the Russian art world. It begins in the glamorous Moscow apartment of Nita, the gilded-youth progeny of a New Russian businessman. Nita is a photographer; her sidekick Ira is an art critic and poet; and Nita has hired Diamara, a migrant worker ("guest" worker) from Nazran, a city in Ingushetia in the Caucasus, to repaint her apartment. As "Afghan-Kuzminki" was and was not about sex, "Communion" is and is not about art and spiritual union across class—and race.

Faith is as central to Nita's identity as her astonishing material wealth, to which her vulgar take on Russian Orthodox Christianity is very much linked. Ira admires Nita's independence as a list of assets:

Зачем тебе мужчина, если есть машина у тебя
И деньги есть, и в Бога веришь и понимаешь Его
Так точно порой интерпретируешь писание,

И ноги есть и грудь на месте,
И гучи носишь и прекрасный художник ты
И вид с окна великолепен,
А пахнешь как райская трава,
И причищаешься и благодать имеешь вроде
И любишь родину и роду аристократическому принадлежишь

What do you need a man for, if you have a car
and money too, if you believe in God and understand Him
and you interpret scripture so precisely,

your legs and breasts are all in place,
you wear Gucci, you're an artist,
the view from your apartment is glorious,
you smell like flowers from the heavens,
you take communion and have grace it seems
and love the motherland and are aristocratic.

Nita has it all and it is all the same: car, money, God, body, fashion, real estate, and grace intercut with nationalism. Somehow this post-Soviet heiress has blacked out an entire century to claim aristocracy and a living bond between church and state, reimagined for the twenty-first century and buttressed with "ultramodern technologies": Nita is a false princess Anastasia, with a smartphone. She seduces the awestruck Diamara with a reactionary postmodernist version of Christian Orthodoxy: the love that she offers is supposed to be that of a godmother, a mother in Christ.

Говорит молча
Сопровождает в темноте

Ему не надо платить
Только упоминать
И просить можно у него почти все

Ира:
А ноги как у Наоми Кэмпбелл тоже?

He speaks without words,
He's by your side in the dark,
you never have to pay Him,
just say His name,
and you can ask for almost anything.

Ira:
Even legs like Naomi Campbell's?

Chukhrov lays the ridicule on thick, sliding mercilessly from religious rhetoric to a vulgar patois of women's fashion magazines and aspiring oligarch intrigues. Diamara, the only foil we are given to Nita's world, just has more dated competing clichés to offer: while her employers humiliate her and deny her humanity, Diamara sings the secular hymns of her childhood, celebrating a past that increasingly seems unbelievable. Did people in this same Moscow not so long ago really sing such words?

Мы коммунисты тем,
что ногами в сегодня стоящие,
тянемся к завтру в темя
и тянем его в настоящее.

Мы коммунисты тем,
что слышим класс безгласый
всех, кто разрознен и нем,
собираем в поющую массу.

We're truly communists because
It's here and now we plant our feet,

Yet reach out for the future's peak,
And make today tomorrow meet!

We're truly communists because
It's we who hear the voiceless classes
All those who, cast away and sundered,
We unify in singing masses.

The only break in the unintentional, painful hilarity that follows many of
Diamara's utterances comes in the form of an unexpected prose interruption
in the verse text. Diamara searches for her own words to describe her family's
arrival in Moscow as guest workers—and the lyrical form of "Communion"
makes way to accommodate her truth:

We were supposed to move into the dorm straight from Kazansky Station, everything was fine, we had handed over our passports when suddenly the assistant director says, we're under construction, he says, you
can't move in until November, not for six months, and we only had
enough money for food until we found work, so we left. . . . I waited on a
bench with Genka and the suitcases on Gogolevsky Boulevard, where
can you go with a kid, I thought. . . . We spent seven hours on that bench.
Genka would run around, then nap on a suitcase, or on my lap. And I
felt so calm, calm for myself, for everyone, everything's fine, I thought,
there's no pain, misery is impossible if you bear it all with grace.

The mood of the piece changes, as we glimpse a fissure not of psychological
but socioeconomic verisimilitude. Russia's metropoli are fueled by migrant
labor, quietly freezing to death on benches and in entryways, beaten to death
by fascist youth and complicit police. All of it is true, despite the arch styl-
ization. We suddenly grasp the tone and indeed, the genre of the text quite
differently: this isn't satirical drama, but something else, both lyric and antilyric. To keep us in that space of suspended interpretation, Chukhrov plays
with registers of ridicule and piety without fully committing to either,
showing the coexistence of both.

In another of the text's many strange asides, one that again breaks the flow
established elsewhere and foreshadows the even more bewildering finale,

Diamara speaks to her husband (offstage, as it were) on the phone and tries to impart what she's learning of God from her new friends. Telling him to stare at the void between things, she explains: "People, Sanya, don't see shit in it, / it's boring, dreary, there is nothing in it." To have faith means to look into the void and see life and spring. And yet, shit is precisely what her mistress, Nita, is all too good at seeing. When Diamara accidentally uses the bathroom reserved for Nita and her guests, rather than the one relegated to Diamara and other workers, all illusions of fairy godmothering vanish. Nita's disgust shocks Diamara, whose attempts at plebian theology only further enrage her mistress. Diamara has clearly failed to grasp the essence of materialist Christianity.

Without warning, Diamara hysterically declares it all to have been a farce, that she has stayed on out of love for Nita. But this is the wrong confession: there is no Diamara at all. The next-to-final twist reveals the entire post-Soviet guest worker persona as a fraud: a mask lifts to show another equally implausible mask. After she leaves Nita's apartment, Diamara places one more phone call and slips back into being "an ostentatious Moscow metrosexual" (or hipster), as she is described in the opening cast of characters. Diamara is not a migrant worker at all but an urban artist, who has been filming the new Russian elites for her own purposes, planning to screen their vulgarities and hypocrisies for her own profit.

Кем была в этот раз?
Маляршей из Назрани.
Сработало еще как. Иду к тебе в Ваниль, позвони Диме,
пусть подгонит мою машину туда же,
Нет, маленькую. Ощущение кульное, придешь все расскажу.
Я даже камеры ставила.
Смонтирую сначала, потом покажу.

Who was I this time?
A house-painter from Nazran.
It worked like you wouldn't believe. Let's meet in "Vanilla," call Dima,
tell him to bring my car around,
no, the smaller one. It was really cool, I'll tell you when we meet.
I even had cameras hidden.
I'll edit first, and then show you.

Diamara inhabits the same grotesque world as Nita, or at least an intersecting one: her medium (video art), method (deceit and intrusion), and politics (an exposure of the new moneyed elite) mark her as a somewhat edgier member of the contemporary art scene. But her words are intended to strip away all audience sympathy, transforming this post-Soviet Cinderella into another unpleasant Moscow archetype. We miss the house painter from Nazran who provided the only voice of innocence—and are thereby forced to catch ourselves fetishizing the "noble savage" by way of Soviet nostalgia.

It is difficult not to read "Communion" as self-critique, probing an art world with which Chukhrov is intimately if critically familiar, and which is also the venue for her work. We begin to read the piece as an exposé of the absurd reactionary postmodernist world we now share; and the post-Soviet migrant worker seems the hero-victim, an authentic remainder and an exception to this theater of cruelty. And then this idealized subaltern is revealed as just another mirage and appropriation by an artist looking to increase her cultural (and actual) capital. How can anyone escape the apparatus?

Chukhrov's dramatic poem, alongside its many incarnations and remediations, feels particularly timely. The changing mood from 2010 to 2020 reflects a new pessimism in Russia and around the globe, with the collapse of the years of international protest into rightist victories such as Brexit, the 2016 American presidential election, the 2018 Russian presidential election, the ensuing waves of global techno-pessimism and hacker-phobia, the resurgence of demonizing rhetoric with painful echoes of the past on both sides of the old Cold War—and all of it leading up to a global pandemic with a latest death count of 5 million worldwide. Chukhrov's work also reflects familiar fears of avant-gardes ending badly—that these flickers of political and aesthetic passion end in one of three ways: sliding from the left into right populism and nationalism (Eduard Limonov; arguably the group Voina); riding a wave of popularity all the way to *Vogue* and Bloomingdale's department store (Pussy Riot; Russian avant-garde art refashioned into handbag advertisements); or sitting tight in academic or art-world insularity (arguably Chto Delat, and Chukhrov's own highbrow art). The drawbacks associated with the avant-garde are as persistent as its potential advantages and emancipatory energies. There is a reason, as Paul Mann theorized, that avant-gardes die as frequently as they are reborn.

However, Chukhrov chooses not to end "Communion" with open mockery or nihilistic complacence in the face of plural failures. The text ends with one more phone call: Nita has rung, breaking character, to ask Diamara for forgiveness. Diamara, back in the role we preferred, responds with something like a recipe for, as in the title, "Commie-Union":

Ты, Нита?
Да. Да. Да. Каждый через себя—два.
Я—ты. Ты—я.
Так пусть поступит вся страна.
[. . .]
Теперъ ветку любую с земли подними,
Не просто так, а служебно учась, и беги
Ветку, смотри, не урони.
Так до меня дойди.

Hello, Nita. Is it you?
Each in herself is two.
I am you. You are me.
Let the whole country be as we.
[. . .]
Now take any branch up from the earth,
not in just any way, but be shy,
as if you were learning how, now run,
don't drop the branch, hold it in front,
and like that, come and find me.

The moment is unmotivated and fails to fit the frame of the urban artist's deception. The text does not end when it should—the form evades genre, coherent interpretation, and closure again; and through that excess textual matter, communion remains an unexpectedly real possibility, available for the audience and characters alike.

Where does all this leave us, or Russian avant-garde poetry? Artists are, more often than not, villains in Chukhrov's work. Gender themes are central to all her art and interventions, but never in entirely comfortable forms. The single-gender construction of "Communion" on the surface purifies the focus of oppression onto class and more subtly race (too often ignored in the Russian context), though the language of all three women in the dramatic poem remains that of patriarchy in various refractions. Chukhrov scoffs at liberal myths of female solidarity, going a step further here than in her other works to clarify the extent to which Putin's Russia (and so many other nation-states) consists of perpetrator-victims. The women are no better than the men, as far as policing oppressive hierarchies goes. Likewise, Chukhrov's Russian texts are peppered with Caucasian actants and intrusions, but she shies away from anything resembling self-satisfied Western poetics of inclusion. What relationship, if any, exists between the urban artist playing Diamara and a real post-Soviet subaltern? The question remains unanswered, nor is the ethnicity of the artist specified: she has cast a Russian actress uncomfortably in the role of Diamara, but she has also performed all the roles in the piece herself—which would seem to dramatically influence the reading, perhaps usefully ambiguating it from one staging to the next.[34] Performance for Chukhrov thus maintains a double edge, at once emancipatory and dangerous, an easily perverted gesture of reaching out that can never guarantee a desirable response but that must be made, and questioned, again and again.

I would like to end with a brief and perhaps jarring comparison between Chukhrov's work and that of the Canadian poet Anne Carson. I see unexpected but enticing parallels in a poetics based on drama and song, as contemporary as it is archaic, and on a politics of erotics that has been described as a feminine sublime—a sublime that erases itself, that does not domesticate violence, that arises from the kenosis of the vanished lyric subject. For Carson, creation, or rather decreation, which is the same thing as love, is both rapture and personal negation: love / decreation "dares the self to leave itself behind, to enter into poverty."[35] Dan Disney, in "Sublime Disembodiment? Self-as-Other in Anne Carson's *Decreation*," writes: "Carson has no use for a centre, and herein harnesses the sublime as a powerful creative energy. . . . There is something of the ascetic to her poetic modes of glimpsing realities, and her immersion never entails overcoming the wonder of apprehension. Instead, Carson overcomes historicized, masculine, canonical impulses to make a certain kind of sense."[36] Chris Jennings, in turn, in "The Erotic Poetics of Anne Carson" relates Carson's kenosis to Patricia Yaeger's definition of the feminine sublime as directed toward others, "spread[ing] itself out into multiplicity."[37]

Chukhrov shares Carson's poetics of kenosis and fascination with the radical potential of a feminine sublime: however, she pushes similar formal strategies toward an explicit politics, a post-Soviet Marxism convergent with radical feminism. Art is always communist: and I would remind us again of Chukhrov's rejection of the dominant lyric tradition of Russian poetry in favor of Vvedensky's and Tsvetaeva's avant-gardes. In an essay titled "Nonsense as an Instrument of the Sublime," Chukhrov reads avant-garde nonsense as a "radical defamiliarization of the world of objects and meanings," rife with metaphysical and political concerns.[38] But if previous avant-garde incarnations reveal a recurrent tendency to slide from left to right along the twin channels of nationalism and masculinism, Chukhrov's work probes socialist feminist strategies: multiplicity, decreation, empathy, and doubt serve as the points of departure for a new avant-garde poetics.

Moreover, she uses the archaic, the pre- and nonmodern to challenge a dominant narrative of European modernity that so often limns and limits the energies of the avant-garde: the Caucasus and Caucasians in her work function as an outside to the European modernity project throughout, challenging through their very recurrent and haunting presence Russia's pretensions to inclusion within that project. As Chukhrov writes in an essay for the *Chto delat'?* newspaper: "It isn't necessary to throw anyone or anything from the steamship of modernity. We just have to understand that everything has been given to and for everyone. Otherwise, life on this earth has no meaning."[39]

Not Even Dead

In 2014, amid the global tremors of Russia's unexpected annexation of Crimea and internal war against "sexual deviants" and other so-declared undesirables with the legislative acts of 2013, Chukhrov debuted a new piece.[40] Unlike for some artists and writers in Russian left circles, the pace of Chukhrov's production has stepped up considerably rather than slowed after 2012; likewise, more and more collaborators eagerly stage and adapt the works in real time. "Not Even Dead," a half-Russian and half-English verse drama, is set in a post-Soviet, post–civil war present that could be nearly anywhere (Donbass, Armenia, Azerbaijan, Ossetia, Abkhazia; with a quick language change, Bosnia; the list goes on) and offers an equally open ending. It is the rare piece by Chukhrov to date to be set outside Moscow: a closer reading reveals the frequent references to Georgian and Megrelian to suggest that this particular post-collapse hell is an aftermath of the Georgian-Russian war. Chukhrov locates us among those who supported "the side of those that besieged the place," who have refused to relocate after losing, and who can expect only sporadic supplies of humanitarian aid from Russia. These lingering post- (post-Soviet, perhaps postimperial, certainly postapocalyptic) losers are the not-even-dead.

The title refers therefore to the sorriest imagined incarnations of the post-Soviet subject, in this dramatic poem also the subject of an exploitative documentary art piece by a Dutch crew led by Ilona, another once local girl turned cosmopolitan artist. In the middle of the piece, however, a character suddenly shares an alternative potential origin for the title: "If we now take the Georgian-Megrelian kvart-kvintaccord—this will be the key to cure and convalescence, it was even used to revive the dead, if the dead were children. Like in the song 'Sisa.' A mother steals the body of the baby, who is already in the coffin, and rushes into the forest to hide there and to sing this song to her son Bondo until he resurrects. Whether or not she succeeded nobody knows."[41] The Georgian musical insertion into the endless grappling between two languages of empire appears linked to the theme of possible resurrection: the not-even-dead may well rise again, especially if they are children. As Golynko has speculated and as their frequent Chto Delat collaborator, the philosopher Oxana Timofeeva, theorized in her provocative essays on the post-Soviet precariat as zombies: the undead are a real political force to be reckoned with, for they have nothing left to lose.[42] Perhaps the same could be said for the post-Soviet youth.

Chukhrov's Caucasus, so often haunting the margins of her other work, or present through displaced persons turned denizens of Russia's crumbling imperial capital, here takes center stage. The piece, about unending post–Cold War war, is arguably her darkest yet, but all the more powerful in confronting audiences with non-Russia as a necessary component of any contemporary Russian-language aesthetic project. Chukhrov's piece reads as a kind of Brechtian theater (see especially one of the choose-your-own-ending choices: Ilona "enters the sea with the rest of the characters, we think that this is a collective suicide, but suddenly they all begin to perform a synchronized swimming number"). It shares in this turn much with the filmed dramatic performances by Chukhrov's frequent collaborators in the Chto Delat collective. However, the very textuality of her work appears to offer Chukhrov an out whenever she wants it: unlike her protagonist, Ilona, Chukhrov does not in the end entirely rely on any one of the many structures and institutions that occasionally support her work. She always has the choice to publish in the Kraft series, on plain Kraft paper, instead. In the end, her hybrid practice of transmedial boundary-crossing illustrates the very practical and lasting potential of poetry as a relatively autonomous art and serves as a model of intellectual survival strategies amid the stranglehold of interlocking complicities.

Once again, we are reminded that we cannot write post-Soviet literary history without interrogating large-scale transnational phenomena and the specificities of local struggle alike.[43] So too Chukhrov remains cautiously poised in her precarious position, walking a tightrope between Russian poetry and performance and the cosmopolitan, global English institutions of academe and contemporary art. (It might be noted that Chukhrov is about as Russian as I am American; when we speak, we choose one of two imperial languages in which to communicate.) One way or another, she still depends on state or private funds—in a familiar late-Soviet fashion, using the very stipend allotted to the arts and humanities to engage in a sophisticated critique legible initially to a smaller group, but steadily growing and filled with unexpected connections and strange solidarities, inside and outside the former Second World. Rather than an unquestionably heroic advance guard, Chukhrov attempts to conjure a new model for aesthetic and political resistance that is as pre- as postmodern, at once hopeful and perpetually questioning and critical. Chukhrov's verse dramas, perhaps more than any other poetic practice I explore in this book, ironize and question the alternative international networks I may be in danger of romanticizing here: however, with every invitation to collaborate, Chukhrov conjures more unexpected collectivities into existence.

Coda

THE PASSION OF GALINA RYMBU

*I*N THE WINTER OF 2020, I joined socialist feminist poet / academics Anjuli Fatima Raza Kolb and Lindsay Turner to write collaboratively about Galina Rymbu's recently released English-language anthology *Life in Space* (translated by Joan Brooks and published by Ugly Duckling Presse just after the start of the coronavirus pandemic).[1] In language later cut from the published review, we struggled to articulate the feeling of being able to breathe again, deeply and ecstatically, reading Rymbu's poetry from cover to cover in quarantine and isolation. After a season of overheated interiority, someone quipped, Rymbu's words were welcome thundersnow. Reencountering Rymbu's work for the second time in English translation and observing it land so intimately with audiences very different from her initial readers felt transformative yet again, confirming gender- and sexuality-informed approaches as the frontier of emancipatory Russophone poetics. It seems to me without doubt that the fiercest and most innovative political poetry currently being written in Russian sits at the intersection of socioeconomic, decolonial, and gender-based critique. Moreover, it is already distinct, if also stemming from what I have here termed the post-Soviet avant-garde: for, as Kirill Korchagin noted, Rymbu (born in Omsk, 1990) and her generation grew up reading Kirill Medvedev and comrades as contemporary classics.[2]

I have sought to show how contemporary Russian poets rediscovered through the study of historical avant-garde blueprints for resistance against global capitalism and twenty-first-century fascisms. Shocking precisely for their refusal of cynicism and vulnerable position of hope, contemporary Russian

avant-gardists mine rich local countertraditions with tools from international Marxist theory and art practice—the unexpectedly left canon portion
of the world culture so longed for during the decades of Soviet isola-
tionism. Each of the poets whose work has been explored in this book has
developed a distinct and unique practice, a different set of formal solutions
to the burning questions raised by the future commons and its emergent
aesthetics. Each explores facets of a shared set of fears: of appropriation; of
lack of differentiation from a far more rapidly growing radical right; of
failing particular constituencies (the uneducated poor, women, migrants,
younger radicals); of intellectual, political, and aesthetic complacency; of
elitism and irrelevance. Each tries and fails, time and again; each explores
and learns from past failures. Most find a way to keep going.

   While nearly all the protagonists of this book recognize feminist art and
theory as critical to an emancipatory canon of potential precursors, the last
three in particular—Osminkin, Chukhrov, and Rymbu—locate gender-
based critique near or at the center of their Marxism. Socialist feminism, in
many ways, has the most direct and ready response for how it differs ideologically from the state socialist past: a revolution that leaves patriarchy in-
tact is no revolution. Rymbu, moreover, already reads as a post-*[Translit]*
poet, in both her work and biography. Rymbu moved from Omsk to Moscow
and then to St. Petersburg for study; for a moment she seemed not only central to the group's activities but indeed poised to take over the journal as its
next showrunner. Then paths diverged; she moved once more; and along
the way she launched her own journal instead: *F-pis'mo,* or *F-Writing.* After
a year or so of collective meeting and planning, *F-pis'mo* exploded into
public view in 2018 as Russia's first-ever platform dedicated to feminist and
queer writing. As a concluding case study, I choose Rymbu as a purposefully paradoxical one: emerging from the *[Translit]* circle (in one possible
narrative about her life and work), she simultaneously proves its productive
influence and presents a limit case to my argument about the resurgence of
the Russian avant-garde. For Rymbu is as Romantic as avant-garde; and
while her work certainly fits many definitions of the latter term, it has little
tolerance for masculinist military fantasies or metaphors of elite scouting.
Likewise, the Siberian-born Rymbu, of highly mixed ethnic (Russian, Ukrainian, Roma) descent, and now an émigré sheltering in place in Ukraine, pushes
us to switch out terms like Russian poetry for Russophone. *F-pis'mo,* and

FIGURE C.1 Galina Rymbu speaks at a meeting of the Russian Socialist Movement (RSD). YOUTUBE.

the (from the start) international collectivities it calls into view, deserves its own book-length study and belongs to the future.

*   *   *

RYMBU FIRST CAPTURED THE IMAGINATION of Russian literary society in 2014–2015 with poems such as the untitled "the dream is over, Lesbia, now it's time for sorrow." Moving from youthful publications in local Omsk journals to leading Russian literary platforms in the space of a few years, Rymbu was recognized by one cultural arbiter after another as the leading voice in Russian poetry of her generation. She has held that position since and added an international readership stretching from Siberia to San Francisco. Her poems in English have appeared widely online over the past five years. In December of 2020 she was profiled in *Time* magazine, along with other founding members of the *F-pis'mo* feminist writing collective; *The Los Angeles Review of Books* in the same month called Rymbu the voice of feminism.[3] Through classical references, sliding pronouns, formal play, and oblique treatment of grammatical gender in Russian, Rymbu's work highlights gender and sexuality as central to understanding her region's histories and on contemporary possibilities for cultural and political change. Rymbu's gender politics inspire her doubled critique: of the neoliberal global present from its left margin; and of much of the left from feminist sidelines. As the world polarizes, Rymbu proves that the poetic voice—a cold Romantic lyricism forged in a dis-individuated but intimate poetic subjectivity—can be fresh, queer, and dangerous.

Russian American poet, translator, and scholar Eugene Ostashevsky describes eloquently the shock of the new that he (a seasoned reader of contemporary Russian poetry, and familiar with the work of all the other poets in this book) nevertheless experienced when encountering Rymbu's poetry for the first time:

> I first came across a poem of [Rymbu's] shortly after she posted it on LiveJournal, a social network popular in Russia, on February 27, 2014. It was the day that Russian troops started operating in Crimea, and several days after the victory of the Maidan Revolution in Kyiv and the tawdry close of the Sochi Olympics. . . . It felt strange that a work of this artistic sophistication and power could be composed and posted on the Web simultaneously with the events it responded to. Its viewpoint was that of the minuscule and very young Russian Left—roughly the same political alignment as those of the poet-activist Kirill Medvedev and of Pussy Riot, to cite figures known to some Western readers. But the poetry was different. It was Big Poetry, very much grounded in tradition but also propelling it forward, into the terra incognita of the now.[4]

Where did Russophone poetry's newest radical prodigy come from? Hardly one of Russia's much-maligned cosmopolitan gilded youth, Rymbu studied philology and theology in Siberia before relocating to Moscow and the Gorky Literary Institute; she went on to focus on political philosophy at the graduate level at the European University in St. Petersburg. In 2018 she left Russia, perhaps permanently, to resettle in Lviv, Ukraine, for reasons she cites as personal and political. Over the last eight years, her poetry catapulted to publication in leading Russian journals and venues such as *[Translit], New Literary Review, Snob,* and Colta.ru; her work has since found its way in English translation into the likes of *n+1, Arc Poetry, The White Review, Berlin Quarterly, Music & Literature, Asymptote, Powder Keg,* and several others.

The recipient of many awards herself, Rymbu is the cofounder of the Drag-omoshchenko Poetry Prize. As long as I have known of Galina Rymbu, she has identified publicly as both a socialist and a feminist.

In an interview with Joan Brooks, Rymbu highlights both the similarities and differences her upbringing had with that of the generation immediately prior, before ultimately describing her childhood in the 1990s as post-Soviet apocalyptic: "When I was a child I didn't feel like I was living in a world that was principally different from the late Soviet period, which my parents were always talking about, which survived in books, in a lot of institutions, and in general in all the material artifacts of daily life. . . . The everyday life of simple post-Soviet people was criminalized, the social situation didn't change, it even got worse. . . . Poor people today live in a condition of permanent so-cial catastrophe. They've lost their place in time and history."[5] Rymbu shares this generational trauma with the younger *[Translit]* poets, including Med-vedev, Arseniev, and perhaps especially Osminkin. But these others remain profoundly Moscow and St. Petersburg poets, deriving a not insignificant portion of their authority and style from the great underground traditions of the cities they love (and critique). Rymbu resembles Chukhrov more in placelessness: she has lived in both Moscow and St. Petersburg, but remains unhooked from these locales, independent from their siren call, fundamen-tally translocal and ultimately, like Chukhrov, transnational. As I have written elsewhere about a rising generation of Russian women filmmakers, gender politics plays no small role in this nonidentification: as Henry James's best villainess Madame Merle put it, women belong to place differently.[6]

While her astonishingly rapid rise to visibility (in the limited fields repre-sented by literary and leftist circles, to be sure) coincides with the period when she joined the *[Translit]* collective, Rymbu has since distanced herself some-what from the journal and its projects—as well as from Russia—in search of her own independent path. As Elizabeth Frost has written in *The Feminist Avant-Garde in American Poetry,* doubly marginalized feminist avant-garde poets tend to share the "fundamental" belief that "language shapes conscious-ness and that, in its accepted, 'correct' forms, language restricts. Yet . . . they also believe that language can *change* consciousness; each weds radical poli-tics to formal experiments—the most fundamental gesture of any avant-garde practice."[7] If feminist avant-garde poets share this fundamentally avant-garde understanding of language with their male counterparts, what distinguishes their efforts is the added "desire to extend conceptions of what feminism might consist of."[8] Thus it is with Rymbu, who asks, What can feminism teach Russian avant-garde poetry? and, What can Russian avant-garde poetry teach feminism?

Gender and sexuality must be at the forefront of contemporary discussions of cultural and economic injustice: in Russia today,

> Women make up 70 percent of the unemployed. And of these unemployed women, 85 percent have higher or specialized educations. Now the placement officers say they should be cleaners or nurses, the lowest-paid, least prestigious jobs. They say women under 18 or over 45 should not be trained or retrained, because there are no jobs for them. The paradigms of women's lives are changing. Why should they get a higher education? . . . Through the media of the new Russian market, sexual freedom is being purveyed as a heterosexist male prerogative, with women enjoined to consume their own commodification as a means of earning value in men's eyes.[9]

This time around, the gendering of revolution and of the new left alike must be seriously rethought. And it is from this direction that Rymbu's poetry bursts violently into view. She gives vibrant, unforgettable voice to anonymous lines that have appeared in Cyrillic and Latin graffiti alike across the former Second World: *If the revolution is not feminist, it will not be.*

The poem that many of Rymbu's admirers first encounter, in Russian or in translation, is the untitled "the dream is over, Lesbia, now it's time for sorrow." Brooks's English translation grows and bleeds in response to the original, giving the impression that we are witnessing not only a transubstantiation but a conversion, an answering echo to what we termed Rymbu's clarion call:

сон прошёл, Лесбия, настало время печали,
время сбросить кольца и платья на пире кровавом
во славу доброй памяти сестёр наших
будем бить бокалы!

о, Лесбия, время войны настало,
покупать травматику у мужичков коренастых,

в чехол от макбука прятать лезвие, шило
и двигаться, стиснув зубы, через ряды фашни тёмной.

the dream is over, Lesbia, now it's time for sorrow,
time to throw off our rings and dresses at the bloody feast
in honor of the memory of our sisters
let's smash our glasses!

o, Lesbia, the time of war has come,
time to buy guns from thick-set men
and hide a blade or a shiv in your macbook case
and move with clenched teeth through the dark fascist ranks.[10]

Ostashevsky makes several observations in an introduction accompanying the English-language translation, points he fears American readers might miss: most crucially that in Russia, the "Western classics" to which Rymbu alludes remain "associated with Enlightenment values, and are consequently politically anti-government."[11] As the opening lines make clear, Rymbu makes evident and surprising allusions to Catullus, to Sappho, and Ostashevsky points out an echo of classical meters in her free verse. However, the language she uses for her allusions is something else entirely, contemporary and elementally wild. Like Golynko and Osminkin, she seizes on slang and political clichés such as the "Putinist slogan 'Russia rises from her knees,'" but renders them literal, obscene, and shockingly living speech.[12]

If Osminkin offers one example of how younger Russian radical poets study and move past Conceptualist experimentation with language and bared device, Rymbu offers another with overtly high stakes. Moreover, unlike Osminkin, Rymbu does not appear to find her subject matter particularly funny or ironic at all:

такое время, что любовь и политика—одно и то же,
а полиция и ненависть—это что-то другое.
где открытые лекции сменяются уроками уличной борьбы,
где дыхание на морозе превращается в воображаемые
    свободные университеты
и на коленях стоит олимпийский мишка,

а рядом с ним на коленях стоит ребёнок,
вижу, Лесбия, в руке твоей бритву, волосы спутались, взгляд
    безумен.

it's a time when love and politics are one and the same,
while police and hate are something different.
where open lectures give way to lessons in street fighting,
where frosty breath turns into imaginary free universities
and the olympic bear is on his knees,
and next to him a child is on his knees,
I can see a razor in your hand, Lesbia, your hair is tangled, your
    gaze is mad.

Rymbu merits comparison with other radical feminist artists from Russia,
such as the graphic-reportage visual artist Victoria Lomasko, who seemingly
effortlessly revitalizes select Soviet mores (including the profoundly anticapitalist and viscerally held stance that art "belongs to everybody") with the
most vivid description of contemporary horrors.

Despite the ferocious forward drive of her hymnic repeated imperatives,
Rymbu's defiantly lyric persona leaves room for self-interrogation over the
problem of language:

я не знаю, какие нужно прочесть книги,
какой политической борьбой здесь нужно заняться,
когда вокруг все ни мёртвые ни живые,
по сговору, в небытие устанавливают один порядок
[. . .]
когда не знаешь языка другого,
вставай, Лесбия! хватит, вставай с колен!
вставай, любимая, даже если на смерть идёт дело

I don't know what books I should read,
what kind of political struggle I should practice,
when everyone around is neither living or dead,
colluding, establishing the kind of order in non-being
[. . .]

when you know nobody's language,
rise, Lesbia! enough, get off your knees!
rise, beloved of mine, even if it means death

Rymbu explains in interviews that she refuses to condescend to an imagined, naive working-class populace. She believes it a dangerous illusion that "the oppressed have a simple language, that we should employ a series of reductions . . . to be comprehensible as poets and artists"; instead, she weaves together a "rat's nest of complexity" from the languages of students and streets.[13] The result she presents, like a bloody offering, as the language of a people dreaming of freedom.

"the dream is over, Lesbia" captures the common characteristics of nearly all of Rymbu's poetic works, which otherwise range over a variety of styles and formal experiments, trying on something new in nearly every poem. Yet her signature is unmistakable: a Rymbu poem tends to be marked by blood and fearless in the connections drawn between the personal and political. Rymbu understands the body itself as a constituted and emergent thing that is "historical—and consequently fluid—in essence": "For there is no border between my body and the multiple processes of historical change, which are enacted through me, who am at once the mouth and the word of their polyglot glossolalia. If 'revolution' is history projecting itself into the future, 'my' revolution is history immanent in me as desire and anticipation. It is why the blood that comes out of the body is red."[14] Hence too the importance of the doubly valenced classical allusion in her most famous poem: an invocation of the origins of lyric poetry but also of queer subjectivity in Russia at a time when that has been rendered nearly illegal. She mentions American novelist Kathy Acker as a kindred spirit who unflinchingly conjures this "feminine (and sometimes queer) subject, who enters into sexual relations that are suffused with violence. . . . Only by giving herself up to them completely can she critique them. We can't live in a world without violence, we are born as subjects into a world of violence, we are formed by violence, and so is our desire. . . . This is what I want to write about."[15] The historical body and the queer body alike are bloody battlegrounds for Rymbu, scarred by violence and liberated through violent resistance.

Rymbu describes poetry in the same terms, showing the fundamental centrality of the lyric (not song, not theater, not performance) for her understanding of subjectivity formation. Poetry, she insists, must struggle against systemic, all-pervasive, internalized violence "with the help of a certain violence of its own, fiercely struggling with those languages for a future of peace."[16]

> The task of political poetry is to subvert . . . narratives and values that block any sense of class belonging, that power continues to impose on people in its effort to suppress class consciousness and block the possibility of a second great socialist revolution. . . . Leftist, engaged political poetry must practice its own reevaluation of the revolutionary past and the socialist experiment in order to find a way to produce a genuinely alternative revolutionary culture, one that corresponds to the class identity of the future revolutionary subject, liberating the majority's political vision, its sensuous perception of things.[17]

Across her manifestos (and nearly every poem, essay, or speech by Rymbu reads as the continuation of one larger manifesto) she states directly and unflinchingly what all the poets of the [Translit] circle seem to be after: a reevaluation of the revolutionary past that not only allows for but necessitates the formation of a new revolutionary culture.

Fragments from the Future

In the winter of 2018, Galina Rymbu made a tour of American universities and institutions hosted by scholars, translators, and fellow poets intrigued by her unique blend of poetry and politics. She was a guest of honor at a conference I organized at Yale University on the topic of "Pointed Words: Political Poetry in the Global Present." Rymbu participated doubly, reading and discussing her own poetry (with the help of her partner and translator, the Ukrainian poet Yanis Sinayko) and engaging more broadly with the central questions of the conference. How should politically leftist poetry today engage with the desire for a new world? Her final speech on the topic, delivered to an audience of international academics and poets as well as friends and collaborators (including Kirill Medvedev, Pavel Arseniev, Dmitry Golynko, and Keti Chukhrov), brought the room to silence.

Rymbu's first answer addresses time. Thinking through the conceptual promise of utopia, she suggests that today, "we are deprived of the past, because it became a manipulative space for reactionary forces ('winners write the history'). Those forces urge us to return to the past reinvented by them (as in Russia) when we have no future."[18] Art more generally and poetry in particular, as the densest form of artistic experimentation with language, offer the promise of plural and alternative ways of experiencing time. Poetry moreover offers a way to survive in the wasteland of catastrophe capitalism:

The space of a catastrophe (planetary, ecological, political) is a given. And it is material. Poetry works with the materiality of the catastrophe, the fear of death, loneliness and defeat, creating special places— communities, environments, shelters where our strength can be restored and destroyed languages (including mental) can be revitalized. This is where the new ways of "being together" or "being near" can be found and proposed. . . . Poems make up a mental map of movement in the wasteland. And it seems to me that this is more productive than simply to acknowledge the failure and defeat of poetic language and art in the era of postcapitalism.[19]

Ultimately, she explains why poetry must play this special role of mapping movement in the wasteland: as a "special form of linguistic action and thinking, [poetry] puts forward the logic of transformation against the logic of deadly antagonism."[20] The very (counter)logic of poetry is the logic of "transfiguration, transformation, which concern not only a person, a subject, but also all ecosystems, worlds, political spaces. This is how the cosmists saw the transformation of the revolutionary subject and the world. That is how I see the proximity of revolution and poetry. They both transform the world."[21]

Rymbu's speech at Yale was movingly framed by musing on its own limitations, as an illustration of the stolen space of emancipatory thought under nearly impossible circumstances. Having no permanent position, no steady source of income (unlike nearly all the US- or European-based academics and even students in the room), Rymbu was only able to travel and subsist during that travel on funds made immediately available by foreign institutions. Needing to work constantly to eke out a living for herself and her son, she had no time before her flights to write, with the exception of stolen hours in the hotel room as the conference was already underway, and even then making sure there was ample time left for translation into the common but unmastered language, English. This speech on utopia, she said, was the best she could manage to think under the (unchanging, usually worsening) circumstances of oppressed and persecuted precarity.

In March 2019, I next had the opportunity to translate collectively "Fragments from the Book of Decline"—in my view Rymbu's masterwork to date—alongside Rymbu herself, Ostashevsky, Anastasiya Osipova, Stephanie Sandler, and several other poets, translators, and scholars.[22] I was struck again by the difference between Rymbu's work and that of the other avant-garde poets explored in this book. For by the time we arrive at Rymbu's poetry, born entirely of the new millennium, the distinction between the lyric and its avant-garde opposition has entirely vanished. Lyric poetry *is* avant-garde in a world defined by this late stage of capitalism. Subjectivity is no longer the victimizing illusion of the bourgeois but a near impossibility. The formation of both new subjectivities and collectivities—in a more immediate, somehow visceral understanding of Rancière's logic of subjectivization—seem one and the same. To find the time and focus to think *is* revolution.

Wandering in the wilds of Rymbu's postapocalyptic "Fragments from the Book of Decline," we come to understand that the impossible landscapes of her nightmares darkly mirror our current world. Yet it is only by looking closely at the terrible that we might glimpse a trace of the revolutionary moment creeping closer. Rymbu writes:

несу на приём свой сон. пусть. пусть посмотрят, что не так,
что стало, эти,
    животные с красными глазами, преображенные
        лекарственным ветром,
    сопротивлением, именно эти, которые одним мутным
        взглядом
    поднимают танкеры над водой, а ту черную жидкость
        заставляют
    обратно втекать, внутрь земли. они лечат? знают
    Гею так, как ты? как в том сне, где хотим, когда она
        коротким дном-лезвием

провела по твоей голове, и все свернулось в отснятое. мы
     держим,
лежим, изменяясь, ночь, обнимая книгу упадка.

I take my dream in for examination. let them see. let them check what's
    wrong, what came of it, these
animals with red eyes, transformed
        by medicinal winds,
by resistance, namely these ones, who with a single blurred
        gaze
lift tankers above the water and force that black liquid to flow
backward, into the earth. are they healers? do they know
Gaia like you do? like in that dream of desire, when she drew
        a hull, short, razor-sharp,
across your head, and everything wound back into the reel. we
        hold on,
lying there, transforming, the night, clutching the book of decline.

What is perhaps most shocking in this moment is the unapologetic Romanticism of Rymbu, retaining all the bold wildness of earlier centuries, as well as a Blakean reach and synthesizing bird's-eye vision. If the speaker and subjects suffer differently, they also fight and commune under shared conditions of extractive labor and landscapes emptied of recognizable forms of life.

In an interview with Osipova and myself recorded at the same time as our work on the collective translation of the cycle, Rymbu described her new work as reflecting a world in which catastrophe on a planetary scale has already struck. The transformations that have already ensued have altered politics, tectonics, and the very fiber of being—including relationships between the beings she calls "the survivors" and language itself. Yet even in this world, poetry maintains for Rymbu an ecstatic function, "an escape from the language of the possible, that can answer questions about our political future and about those languages that we will use in that future."[23] Or as she puts in the beyond-sense language of poetry:

мой мобильник почти разряжен, я пишу чтобы зафиксировать:
край ночи

другой, с другими, и снова
книга упадка взорвана,
вблизи от огня.

my phone is almost out of charge, I write to
record all this: the brink of night
is the other, with others, and again
the book of decline blasted open,
next to fire.

We end with fire, and with a socialist feminist poetics that reads as shockingly close here to Blake, there to Hölderlin: to a renewed understanding of poetry as that human technology that proves lastingly capable of imagining a global egalitarian future. Now come, fire.

Coda to a Coda: It's No Good But It's Not Over

On March 1, 2022, just over a week after the Russian Federation invaded Ukraine and seemingly changed the geopolitical world order overnight, Skidan posted a poem on Facebook that was translated within hours by Kevin Platt and made the rounds of the politically like-minded within days. Skidan left Russia not long after, but chose to return after the death of Golynko to help settle his friend's affairs. I will include the poem and translation here in entirety:

поздно листать новости и фейсбук поздно писать о личной и
    коллективной вине
поздно читать ханну арендт и карла шмитта влюбленных в
    шварцвальд поздно становиться ректором чрезвычайного
    положения
поздно стоять на троицком мосту и смотреть на самый
    прекрасный город в мире поздно смотреть на лед самой
    прекрасной реки в мире
поздно выходить на лед самой прекрасной реки в мире и писать
    на нем хуй войне поздно поднимать и разводить мосты

поздно оплакивать мосты поздно строить мосты поздно
    говорить поздно любимым поздно их обнимать
поздно переименовывать троицкий мост в мост имени
    троцкого поздно говорить ни мира ни войны
поздно говорить моя бабушка родилась в полтаве в 1909 году
    поздно говорить ее фамилия была трепке фон трепке
поздно говорить что мы ссым
поздно вспоминать 2001 год валерия подорогу после вручения
    премии белого в кафе на литейном и его слова кого мы
    выбрали и не просто выбрали а вот этими вот руками и
    помогли глебу павловскому и его медиа
поздно говорить блокада отечественная война лидия
    гинзбург
поздно говорить я предупреждал в 2003 году осторожно
    религия осторожно
поздно говорить геноцид первая мировая обратим штыки
    против империализма как учили бакунин кропоткин и
    опарыши в снах бруно шульца когда он шел по улицам
    винницы чтобы выпить с аркадием
поздно говорить расчеловечивание
мобильные крематории
спецоперация
остается говорить
перечитай антигону верни нам наших мертвых
я хочу их оплакать
это раньше полиса раньше его насилия и закона закона-как-
    насилия это сестра это брат ставшие бездонной могилой и
    обещаньем любви
вот это еще не поздно может быть остановить мобильные
    крематории
похоронить наших детей

*   *   *

too late to scroll through news on facebook too late to write about
    personal and collective guilt

too late to read hannah arendt and carl schmitt in love with the
    schwarzwald too late to be provost of the state of emergency
too late to stand on the troitsky bridge and gaze at the loveliest city
    in the world too late to gaze at the ice of the loveliest river in the
    world
too late to go out on the ice of the most beautiful river in the
    world and write fuck war on it too late to raise and lower the
    bridges
too late to cry over bridges too late to build bridges too late to say
    too late to loved ones too late to hug them
too late to rename the troitsky bridge as the trotsky bridge too late
    to say neither peace nor war
too late to say my grandma was born in Poltava in 1909 too late to
    say her name was trepke von trepke
too late to say we are pissing our pants
too late to remember valery podoroga in 2001 after getting the Bely
    Prize in that café on leteiny and him saying who have we elected
    not only elected but with these very hands helped gleb pavlovsky
    and his media outlet
too late to say blockade patriotic war lydia ginzburg
too late to say i warned you in 2003 watch out religion watch out
too late to say genocide wwi turn the bayonets against imperialism
    as bakunin kropotkin taught and bruno schulz dreaming of
    maggots when he walked vinnytsia's streets to drink with arkady
too late to say dehumanization
mobile crematoria
special operation
it remains to be said
reread antigone return our dead
i want to lament them
this precedes the polis precedes its violence and the law the law as
    violence this is sister this is brother becoming a bottomless grave
    and a promise of love
and maybe it's still not too late to stop the mobile crematoria
to bury our children

To end without acknowledging that one story ends with air strikes, bodies in Bucha, police terror recalling grandparents' whispered stories of 1937, the growing, uncountable numbers of refugees fleeing Ukraine, Belarus, Russia in despair, the First Wave of the twenty-first century—would dishonor the unflinching clarity with which the protagonists of this book spent the past two decades predicting rivers of blood ("too late to say I warned you in 2003"). Yet despite the devastatingly changed circumstances, despite the untimely loss of Golynko—like Skidan's metaphor of radical poets appearing briefly, like worms in the rain—I believe that the republic of letters called into being in the years 1999–2022 was not a failure but a cultural formation whose truly transnational, political, and aesthetic influences are far from over. Maybe it is still not too late.

Medvedev, who has no intentions of leaving Moscow, wrote the following Facebook post to his friends leaving the country in February 2022:

Хочется сказать тем, кто сейчас уезжает, особенно тем, кто сохраняет свою любовь к рождению при этом. Не могу никому ничего посоветовать, у всех своя жизнь и она одна, но все же. Все же напомню, что вынужденным посещением вне родины можно заниматься не только для публичной и иной помощи и солидарности сегодня, но и для подготовки к тому, чем мы, надеемся, будем заниматься потом.

На практике, как работает в других странах местное самоуправление, независимые профсоюзы, политическое просвещение среди бедных и малообразованных, как выявлены на уровне бюджетов, как всякие малые дела покрывают с борьбой за большое общественное благо. И речь далеко не только о Западе, есть множество стран, от Индии до Чили, где на пересечении каких-то событий и крупных универсалистских проектов связано много лет дел, что-то такое, что нам стоит поучиться из первых рук.

Последние годы очевидны, что у нас появилось новое поколение тех, кого назвали демократической интеллигенцией, люди, готовые уже перейти от этакой вечной оторопи перед своей страной или от этического протеста к тому, чтобы взять на себя ответственность, идти в политику, в депутаты, в лидеры экодвижений и профсоюзов.

Мы думали (я, по мере необходимости, думали), что этот эво-
люционный процесс неизбежно какое-то время и что в основном
мы на верном пути. Сейчас он кажется изуверски прерванным, но
есть и шанс, что в конечном итоге вся наблюдаемая дикость ускорит
его во много раз. И что будет отброшено к чертовой матери из
того, что бросило идти вперед и вот сейчас добровольно показало
свою мёртвость и разрушительность.

Уверен . . . что если мы все не сгинем, то у нас будет шанс на
новую страну и новое общество. И вот тогда нам нужно будет
много новых людей—новых политиков и чиновников, судей и
депутатов, даже новых священников и милиционеров. Так что
будьте готовы возвращаться и детей тоже настраивайте

I would like to say something to those who are leaving now, especially
those who still claim to love their country while doing so. I can't tell
anyone what to do, everyone has their own life to live and just the one,
but still. So let me remind you that forced excursions from the home-
land aren't only useful for public opinion and raising solidarity, but also
to prepare for what we hope will happen after. So go and study how local
self-government works in other countries; study independent trade unions,
political education among the poor and poorly educated, how budgets are
allocated, how all sorts of small things contribute to the struggle for a
greater public good. And not only in the West, but in many countries,
from India to Chile, where years of work have gone into the intersection
of events and large universalist projects, something that we should learn
first-hand. .

In recent years, it became obvious that we do have a new generation
of what we've called the *democratic intelligentsia,* people who are already
ready to move on from eternal stupor in response to their country and
also from individual acts of ethical protest to taking responsibility, going
into politics, becoming deputies, leaders of eco-movements, and trade
unions.

We thought (I thought) that this evolutionary process was inevitable
and that we were basically on the right track. Now it seems savagely interrupted, but there is also some chance that in the end this unchecked
savagery will speed it up many times over. And we'll send back to hell

all that has prevented us going forward, and that has now openly shown its dead and destructive nature. And I am sure . . . that if we all do not perish, we will have a chance to build a new country and a new society. And at that point we are going to need a lot of new people to help us—new politicians and officials, judges and deputies, even new priests and policemen. So be ready to come back, and get your children ready, too.

NOTES

Preface

1. Alain Badiou, *The Communist Hypothesis* (London: Verso, 2010), 6.

Introduction

1. For an expanded reading of lyric forms in the age of other media, see Marjorie Perloff, *Radical Artifice: Writing Poetry in the Age of Media* (Chicago: University of Chicago Press, 1991).

2. I join several recent scholars in attempting to trace the interpenetrations of poetry with politics, economics, and remediation. I take inspiration from Fred Moten's body of work, but see also Jasper Bernes, *The Work of Art in the Age of Deindustrialization* (Stanford, CA: Stanford University Press, 2017); Walt Hunter, *Forms of a World: Contemporary Poetry and the Making of Globalization* (New York: Fordham University Press, 2019); and increasingly many others.

3. Marija Hlavajova and Simon Sheikh, eds., *Former West: Art and the Contemporary after 1989* (Cambridge, MA: MIT University Press, 2017); Francis Fukuyama, "The End of History?," *The National Interest* 16 (1989): 3–18; Stephen Crowley, "Russia: The Reemergence of Class in the Wake of the First 'Classless' Society," *East European Politics & Societies* 29, no. 3 (2015): 699.

4. Marijeta Bozovic and Rossen Djagalov, "Post-Soviet Aesthetics," in *After Marx: Literary Criticism and the Critique of Value,* ed. Colleen Lye and Christopher Nealon (Cambridge: Cambridge University Press, 2021), 143–160.

5. Quoted in Joan Brooks, "A Conversation with Galina Rymbu," *Music & Literature,* February 4, 2016, https://www.musicandliterature.org/features/2016/1

/31/a-conversation-with-galina-rymbu. I am indebted to Joan for years of collaboration, debate, and dialogically sharpened insight on poetry and the new Russian left.

6. Crowley, "Reemergence of Class," 699.

7. Crowley, "Reemergence of Class," 703.

8. For English language examples, see Andrew Scott Barnes, *Owning Russia: The Struggle over Factories, Farms, and Power* (Ithaca, NY: Cornell University Press, 2006); David Hoffman, *The Oligarchs: Wealth and Power in the New Russia* (New York: Public Affairs, 2002); and Branko Milanović, *Income, Inequality, and Poverty during the Transition from Planned to Market Economy* (Washington, DC: World Bank Regional and Sectoral Studies, 1998).

9. Crowley, "Reemergence of Class," 707.

10. Names to watch for and that share or intersect with the *[Translit]* orbit include Elena Kostyleva, Nikita Safonov, Nikita Sungatov, Evgeniya Suslova, and at one time Dina Gatina; the prolific contemporary Russian poetic scene more broadly also includes such stars as Maria Stepanova, Elena Fanailova, and many talented others whose names are sprinkled throughout this text.

11. The Russian Socialist Movement (Rossiskoe sotsialisticheskoe dvizheniie, or RSD) is a left-wing political organization in Russia, emerging out of several earlier organizations (including Vpered, or Forward) in 2011. Unrecognized as an official political party, the organization nevertheless has ten regional branches and has been involved in causes ranging from independent trade unions to the campaign to save Khimki forest.

12. Nearly all the artists and theorists in this study view "the West" as an ideological construction that depended on the continued existence of the Soviet Union, its spectral afterlives, or an imperfect substitute. I introduce and use quotation marks to emphasize distance from the construction. See, e.g., the collaborative Berlin-based project Former West, in which several Russian and eastern European artists, poets, and theorists included in this book participated directly (https://formerwest.org/Front).

13. Mike Sell, *The Avant-Garde: Race, Religion, War* (London: Seagull Books, 2011), 41.

14. Hal Foster, *The Return of the Real: The Avant-Garde at the End of the Century* (Cambridge, MA: MIT Press, 1996).

15. Fukuyama, "The End of History?," 3–18; Pascale Casanova, *The World Republic of Letters* (Cambridge, MA: Harvard University Press, 1999).

16. Keith Gessen, "Kirill Medvedev: An Introduction," in *It's No Good: Poems / Essays / Actions,* by Kirill Medvedev, trans. Keith Gessen, with Mark Krotov, Cory Merrill, and Bela Shayevich (New York: Ugly Duckling Presse, 2012), 18.

17. Kirill Medvedev, "'They Treat Us Like Shit': The Cult of Navalny," trans. Keith Gessen, *London Review of Books* 34, no. 4 (February 2012): 238. A central goal of the Free Marxist Press, in keeping, has been "self-enlightenment": "One of the reasons I started the publishing house was that I realized that there was a lot about leftist thought and leftist history that I simply didn't know; it was not available in Russian. I wanted to translate it and publish it and learn it myself." See Emma Goldhammer and Kirill Medvedev, "Direction Expression" interview, *Boston Review,* July 29, 2013, www.bostonreview.net/world-poetry/direct-expression.

18. Medvedev, "'They Treat Us Like Shit,'" 129: "The goal of today's left artist must be to use one or another link to the outbursts of the oppressed and their underground movements—to discover his link to history, to those artists, philosophers, and fighters who have been cast aside or castrated in the contemporary 'post-political' world" (244).

19. Evgeny Dobrenko and Mark Lipovetsky, eds., *Russian Literature after 1991* (Cambridge: Cambridge University Press, 2017), 3.

20. See Maksim Hanukai and Susanna Weygandt, eds., *New Russian Drama* (New York: Columbia University Press, 2019). My simplification by media of course glosses over important counterexamples and hybrids: arguably, Russian television series also appear to be experiencing a golden age. Many current *serialy* tackle pressing social issues (e.g., class stratification), albeit in a relatively mainstream way compared with the avant-garde poets.

21. Dobrenko and Lipovetsky, *Russian Literature,* 9. See also Bradley Gorski, "Authors of Success: Cultural Capitalism and Literary Evolution in Contemporary Russia" (PhD diss., Columbia University, 2018).

22. See Elizabeth Frost, *The Feminist Avant-Garde in American Poetry* (Iowa City: University of Iowa Press, 2005), xi; the doubly marginalized feminist avant-gardists not infrequently "position themselves in ambivalent relation to the predominantly male avant-garde movements with which they are often associated; further, they distinguish their work from that of feminist poets writing in more traditional forms."

23. Fredric Jameson, *Postmodernism, or The Cultural Logic of Late Capitalism* (Durham, NC: Duke University Press, 1989).

24. Theodor W. Adorno, "Lyric Poetry and Society," in *Critical Theory and Society: A Reader,* ed. Stephen Eric Bronner and Douglas Kellner (New York: Routledge, 1989), 155.

25. The highly American-dominated if international discipline of Slavic studies seemed poised on the verge of distancing itself from older models of "enemy studies" while already beginning to flirt with new incarnations of Cold War rhetoric. It is imperative if devilishly difficult to chart an alternative course that looks instead to patterns of interconnections, mutual influence, and cross-pollination.

26. Ernst Bloch, *The Principle of Hope* (Cambridge, MA: MIT Press, 1995); Heather Love, "Close but Not Deep: Literary Ethics and the Descriptive Turn," *New Literary History* 41, no. 2 (2010): 371–391.

27. I have in mind Rancière's *The Ignorant Schoolmaster: Five Lessons in Intellectual Emancipation* (1987) as well as his famous break with Althusser over whether protesting workers need to be "given" theory.

28. Alain Badiou, *The Communist Hypothesis* (London: Verso, 2010), 6.

29. Jodi Dean, *The Communist Horizon* (New York: Verso, 2012).

30. Ernesto Laclau, *On Populist Reason* (New York: Verso, 2005). See Benjamin McKean, "Toward an Inclusive Populism? On the Role of Race and Difference in Laclau's Politics" *Political Theory* 44, no. 6 (2016): 797–820.

31. Etienne Balibar, *Citizen Subject: Foundations for Philosophical Anthropology* (New York: Fordham University Press, 2017).

32. Warren Montag, "On Etienne Balibar's Foundations for Philosophical Anthropology," *Radical Philosophy,* June 2018, https://www.radicalphilosophy.com/article/between-subject-and-citizen.

33. Jacques Rancière, *The Politics of Aesthetics,* ed. and trans. by Gabriel Rockhill (London: Bloomsbury, 2013), 8.

34. Rancière, *The Politics of Aesthetics,* 13.

35. Sianne Ngai, "The Cuteness of the Avant-Garde," *Critical Inquiry* 31, no. 4 (2005): 838.

36. Ngai, "The Cuteness of the Avant-Garde," 59. See also, "There are historical reasons, in other words, for why an aesthetic organized around a small, helpless, or deformed object *that foregrounds the violence in its production as such* might seem more ideologically meaningful, and therefore more widely prevalent, in the culture of one nation than in that of another" (78). Ngai seems to have Japan and South Korea in mind primarily, but her observation proves insightful for Russian cultural productions as well.

37. Jacques Rancière, "Politics, Identification, and Subjectivization," *October* 61 (1992): 62.

38. Rancière, "Politics, Identification, and Subjectivization," 62.

39. See for example, Clement Greenberg, "Avant-Garde and Kitsch," *Partisan Review* 6, no. 5 (1939): 34–49. Greenberg suggests that it was "no accident" that "the birth of the avant-garde coincided chronologically—and geographically, too—with the first bold development of scientific revolutionary thought in Europe."

40. Foster, *Return of the Real,* 15. In Hal Foster's formulation, critical oppositions of art and life tend to "position life at a point beyond reach. . . . the avant-garde project is predisposed to failure, with the sole exception of movements set in the midst of revolutions (this is another reason why Russian constructivism is so often privileged by artists and critics on the left)."

41. Peter Bürger, *Theory of the Avant-Garde*, trans. Michael Shaw, foreword by Jochen Schulte-Sasse (Minneapolis: University of Minnesotta Press, 1984), xv.

42. Bürger, *Theory of the Avant-Garde*, 72.

43. Bürger, *Theory of the Avant-Garde*, 73.

44. Paul Mann, *The Theory-Death of the Avant-Garde* (Bloomington: Indiana University Press, 1991), 3. See also the similar vision expressed in Julia Kristeva, *Revolution in Poetic Language* (New York: Columbia University Press, 1985).

45. Sell, *Avant-Garde*, 14. See also: Foster, *Return of the Real*, 16; and Jochen Schulte-Sasse's foreword, "Theory of Modernism versus Theory of the Avant-Garde," in Bürger, *Theory of the Avant-Garde*: "Only when confronted with the potential of post-avant-garde art does Bürger apparently fail to pursue the logical conclusions of his own analysis and relate it to a body of texts that has begun exploring this potential (e.g., leftist radical literature of the twenties; Brecht; broad sectors of contemporary Latin American literature; the films and stories of Alexander Kluge; or literature emerging from feminist movements in the United States)" (xlv).

46. Sell, *Avant-Garde*, 14. See also Foster on Jürgen Habermas's sharp critique of the avant-garde project: "Not only did the avant-garde fail, Habermas argues, it was always already false, 'a nonsense experiment'" (Foster, *Return of the Real*, 16).

47. Sell, *Avant-Garde*, 14–15. John Roberts summarizes the continuing debate as bifurcating around two opposing positions: "those who think that the avant-garde (constructivism, productivism, Dada, surrealism) is a purely historic category that has now been superseded, and those who think that the avant-garde is still very much an unfinished project. . . . In the first category there are those who mourn the passing of the avant-garde, as well as those who have no wish to see it return in any form whatsoever and are therefore certainly dismissive of any claims that its ideals might still be with us"; John Roberts, "Revolutionary Pathos, Negation, and the Suspensive Avant-Garde," *New Literary History* 41, no. 4 (2010): 717–730.

48. Boris Groys, *The Total Art of Stalinism: Avant-Garde, Aesthetic Dictatorship, and Beyond*, trans. Charles Rougle (London: Verso, 2011).

49. Sell, *Avant-Garde*, 13. Burden had himself shot in the arm by a .22 rifle.

50. Sell, *Avant-Garde*, 31.

51. Foster, *Return of the Real*, 25.

52. Sell, *Avant-Garde*, 4.

53. Sell, *Avant-Garde*, 48.

54. Foster, *Return of the Real*, 11.

55. Foster, *Return of the Real*, x.

56. Foster, *Return of the Real*, 20.

57. Foster, *Return of the Real*, 29.

58. See also the conferences on which the volumes *The Idea of Communism* were later based: Costas Douzinas and Slavoj Žižek, eds., *The Idea of Communism,* vols. 1 and 2 (London: Verso, 2011–2013).

59. Fukuyama, "The End of History?," 3–18.

60. Marc James Léger, *Brave New Avant-Garde: Essays on Contemporary Art and Politics* (Winchester, UK: Zero Books, 2012), 1.

61. Marc James Léger, ed. *The Theory of the Avant-Garde and What It Means Today* (Manchester: Manchester University Press, 2014). I joined the chorus for the second volume with an essay on Kirill Medvedev, an earlier version of the first chapter.

62. Léger, *Brave New Avant-Garde,* 1.

63. Andrew Kahn, Mark Lipovetsky, Irina Reyfman, and Stephanie Sandler, eds., *A History of Russian Literature* (Oxford: Oxford University Press, 2018), 611.

64. Kahn et al., *History of Russian Literature,* 611. See also Katerina Clark, *Petersburg: Crucible of Cultural Revolution* (Cambridge, MA: Harvard University Press, 1995).

65. Kahn et al., *History of Russian Literature,* 612.

66. Gerald Janecek, *The Look of Russian Literature: Avant-Garde Visual Experiments, 1900–1930* (Princeton, NJ: Princeton University Press, 2014), 41. See also Harsha Ram, "Futurist Geographies: Uneven Modernities and the Struggle for Aesthetic Autonomy; Paris, Italy, Russia, 1909–1914," in *The Oxford Handbook of Global Modernism,* ed. Mark Wollaeger and Matt Eatough (Oxford: Oxford University Press, 2012).

67. John E. Bowlt and Olga Matich, eds., *Laboratory of Dreams: The Russian Avant-Garde and Cultural Experiment* (Stanford, CA: Stanford University Press, 1996), 4.

68. Bowlt and Matich, *Laboratory of Dreams,* 4.

69. See Graham Roberts, *The Last Soviet Avant-Garde: OBERIU—Fact, Fiction, Metafiction* (Cambridge: Cambridge University Press, 1997), 179. See also Charles Russell, *Poets, Prophets, and Revolutionaries: The Literary Avant-Garde from Rimbaud through Postmodernism* (Oxford: Oxford University Press, 1985).

70. Julia Vaingurt, *Wonderlands of the Avant-Garde: Technology and the Arts in Russia of the 1920s* (Evanston, IL: Northwestern University Press, 2013), 6. See also Marjorie Perloff, *The Futurist Moment: Avant-Garde, Avant Guerre, and the Language of Rupture* (Walden, MA: Wiley-Blackwell, 2003), 74.

71. The era saw the rise of cinema and development in the fields of knowledge production, anthropology, and ethnography. See Brian Hochman, *Savage Preservation* (Minneapolis: University of Minnesota Press, 2014).

72. Deborah Wye, "Art Issues / Book Issues: An Overview," in *The Russian Avant-Garde Book, 1910–1934,* ed. Margit Rowell and Deborah Wye (New York:

MoMA, 2002), 15. See also Kristin Romberg, *Gan's Constructivism: Aesthetic Theory for an Embedded Modernism* (Oakland: University of California Press, 2019).

73. Nina Gurianova, "A Game in Hell, Hard Work in Heaven: Deconstructing the Canon in Russian Futurist Books," in *The Russian Avant-Garde Book,* 26. See also Nina Gurianova, *The Aesthetics of Anarchy: Art and Ideology in the Early Russian Avant-Garde* (Berkeley: University of California Press, 2012).

74. Kahn et al., *History of Russian Literature,* 620.

75. Aleksandr Skidan, "The Resistance of / to Poetry," *boundary 2* 26, no. 1 (1999): 247.

76. Kahn et al., *History of Russian Literature,* 624.

77. Kahn et al., *History of Russian Literature,* 631.

78. Dobrenko and Lipovetsky, *Russian Literature,* 4.

79. Kahn et al., *History of Russian Literature,* 639. The authors note the continuation of Dragomoshchenko's work as "particularly well carried on in the poetry, theory, and translation work of Aleksandr Skidan and Anna Glazova." See also Stephanie Sandler, "Dragomoshchenko, Hejinian, and the Persistence of Romanticism," *Contemporary Literature* 46, no. 1 (2005): 18–45; and Aleksandr Skidan, "Poznanie pyli: A. Dragomoshchenko," in *Summa poetiki* (Moscow: Novoe literaturnoe obozrenie, 2013), 119–126.

80. Kahn et al., *History of Russian Literature,* 632.

81. Kahn et al., *History of Russian Literature,* 633.

82. See Ilya Budraitskis (a former mentee of Osmolovsky, member of Chto Delat, and activist for RSD circles), *Art and Theory of Post-1989 Central and Eastern Europe* (New York: MoMA, 2018), 245. See also Joan Brooks, "Hysteria or Enjoyment? Recent Russian Actionism," in *Cultural Forms of Protest in Russia,* ed. Birgit Beumers, Alexander Etkind, Olga Gurova, and Sanna Turoma (London: Routledge, 2017), 141.

83. From Dmitry Prigov's *Manifesty,* translated and summarized by Dobrenko and cited here from "Prigov and the Aesthetic Limits of Sots-Art"; Evgeny Dobrenko, "Socialist Realism, a Postscriptum: Dmitrii Prigov and the Aesthetic Limits of Sots-Art," in *Endquote: Sots-Art Literature and Soviet Grand Style,* ed. Marina Balina, Nancy Condee, and Evgeny Dobrenko (Evanston, IL: Northwestern University Press, 1999), 96.

84. See Skidan, "Golem Sovieticus: D.A. Prigov" in *Summa poetiki,* 264–258. See also Medvedev: "Post-Conceptualism comes after the radical word-play and author-assassination of writers like Dmitri Prigov and Vladimir Sorokin (in his early work)—that is, after the Russian representatives of early postmodernism had become canonical." Post-Conceptualism (called sometimes the "New Sincerity") "senses acutely the postmodern death of the author and the necessity for his resurrection and rehabilitation" (Medvedev, "'They Treat Us Like Shit,'" 206).

85. Igor Chubarov, *Kollektivnaia chuvstvennost': Teorii i praktiki levogo avangarda* (Moscow: Vysshaia Shkola Ekonomiki, 2014), 13–14. See also Roberts, "Revolutionary Pathos, Negation, and the Suspensive Avant-Garde," 730.

86. Arseniev, "nam pridetsia zakryt' universitety," *Nozh*, March 14, 2020, https://knife.media/coronavirus-poetry/. My translation.

1. The Poetics of Refusal

1. Portions of this chapter were first published in an early article I wrote on Kiril Medvedev's poetry: Marijeta Bozovic, "Poetry on the Front Line: Kirill Medvedev and a New Russian Poetic Avant-Garde," *Zeitschrift für Slavische Philologie 70.1* (2014): 89–118. Reprinted in Marc Léger, ed., *The Idea of the Avant-Garde and What It Means Today*, 2nd ed. (Bristol, UK: Intellect Ltd., 2019). His name has since spread well beyond literary and academic journals to appear with some frequency in *The New York Times* and *Guardian*, as well as to return about 4 million Google search results in Russian and English languages combined.

2. Ilya Kukulin, "Documentalist Strategies in Contemporary Russian Poetry," *Russian Review* 69, no. 4 (2010): 601–602.

3. Aleksandr Skidan, *Summa poetiki* (Moscow: Novoe Literaturnoe Obozrenie, 2013), 104.

4. For recorded clips of these appearances, see https://www.youtube.com/watch?v=VF3zDG-2c10; and http://tvkultura.ru/video/show/brand_id/20929/episode_id/428523/video_id/428523/.

5. Kirill Medvedev, "Diary: State of the Russian Left," *London Review of Books* 35 no. 12 (June 2013); Kirill Medvedev, "'They Treat Us Like Shit': The Cult of Navalny," *London Review of Books* 34, no 4 (February 2012); Kirill Medvedev, "Beyond the Poetics of Privatization," *New Left Review* 82 (2013): 64–83. See the recent clip of the song performed by Sergei Tikhanovskii and Kosmos in Belarus: https://www.youtube.com/watch?v=8X89s6ni7GU.

6. See Roman Jakobson's famous essay, "On a Generation That Squandered Its Poets" (1931), in Roman Jakobson, *Language in Literature,* ed. Krystyna Pomorska and Stephen Rudy (Cambridge, MA: Harvard University Press, 1987), 273–300.

7. English translations are drawn, when available, from Kirill Medvedev, *It's No Good: Poems / Essays / Actions,* trans. Keith Gessen, with Mark Krotov, Cory Merrill, and Bela Shayevich (New York: Ugly Duckling Presse, 2012). Translations of unpublished material are mine.

8. Chris Cumming, "Revolting Russians," *BOMB Magazine,* March 28, 2013, https://bombmagazine.org/articles/revolting-russians/.

9. Keith Gessen, "Kirill Medvedev: An Introduction," in *It's No Good,* 15.

10. Gessen, "Kirill Medvedev," 20.

11. Gessen, "Kirill Medvedev," 20.

12. Ilya Matveev, "The Two Russias Culture War: Constructions of the 'People' during the 2011–2013 Protests," *South Atlantic Quarterly* 113, no. 1 (2014): 188.

13. By no means does such a position exempt us from an obligation to trace and study the effects of various interpenetrating hierarchies of power, or of the rise, fall, interactions, and unforeseen effects of specific collectivities and institutions.

14. Aleksandr Skidan, "The End of the Cease-Fire: Notes on the Poetry of Kirill Medvedev." Originally published in 2006 on the site Polit.ru and reprinted in a 2013 volume of collected essays, *Summa Poeticae* (Skidan, *Summa poetiki,* 104).

15. For an overview of Medvedev's break with Dmitry Kuzmin, his former mentor and publisher in English, see Jeff Parker, "Delirious Light: Kirill Medvedev's *It's No Good,*" *The Los Angeles Review of Books,* February 6, 2013, https://lareviewofbooks.org/article/delirious-light-kirill-medvedevs-its-no-good/. Parker writes: "Kuzmin's important literary clearinghouse *Vavilon* gave many young poets, including Medvedev, their early break. . . . Medvedev formed a close association with Kuzmin and shared his ideas about contemporary poetry, admiring his open, inclusive approach. As time passed, however, he began to see certain authoritarian tendencies in Kuzmin's operation that troubled him."

16. Kirill Medvedev, "Pokhod na meriiu" i drugie stikhotvoreniia," *Novoe literaturnoe obozrenie* 111 (2011); Medvedev, *Pokhod na meriiu* (Moscow: Svobmarksizd-Translit, 2014).

17. I served on the jury from 2013 to 2016 and witnessed firsthand the discussions of the perceived "turn to the left" of the Andrei Bely prize. Aleksei Tsvetkov discusses the phenomenon in an interview about political change in Russia: see Ian Shenkman, "Aleksei Tsvetkov: Dostatochno neskol'kih protsentov chtoby obshchestvo vozvralos,'" November 7, 2015, https://www .novayagazeta.ru/articles/2015/11/07/66279-aleksey-tsvetkov-171-dostatochno -neskolkih-protsentov-chtoby-obshcestvo-vzorvalos-187.

18. For an overview of the aesthetics of the New Russian Left, its significance and turbulent rise from the ashes of the Soviet experiment, see the earlier coauthored essay, Marijeta Bozovic and Rossen Djagalov, "Post-Soviet Aesthetics," in *After Marx: Literary Criticism and the Critique of Value,* ed. Colleen Lye and Christopher Nealon (Cambridge: Cambridge University Press, 2019).

19. Kirill Medvedev, "Communiqué," September 22, 2003; Medvedev, *It's No Good,* 101.

20. Medvedev, *It's No Good,* 101.

21. Greg Afinogenov, "Review," *BookForum,* April 9, 2013, https://www
.bookforum.com/review/11396.

22. Medvedev, "'They Treat Us Like Shit,'" 136.

23. Medvedev, "Communiqué"; Medvedev, *It's No Good,* 102.

24. Kirill Medvedev, "Manifesto on Author's Rights," November 30, 2004;
Medvedev, *It's No Good,* 147.

25. See also Lucy McKeon, "New Emotion: On Kirill Medvedev," *Paris Review,*
April 8, 2013.

26. Medvedev, *It's No Good,* 162. Verso expressed interest in releasing the volume
in Europe, but Medvedev felt that he could not sell or sign away rights he had
disavowed. As Keith Gessen explains, Verso relies financially on the sales of foreign
rights; it was willing to take on a British edition of Medvedev's book, provided it
could sell the rights in Europe. In contrast, *n+1* and Ugly Duckling Presse followed
Medvedev's stipulation and indicated no copyright (hence taking on personal risk)
on the copyright page (personal communication, November 12, 2013).

27. Ian Dreiblatt, "In Russia a Poet Declares His Candidacy," *Melville House,*
May 24, 2017, https://www.mhpbooks.com/in-russia-a-poet-declares-his
-candidacy/.

28. Walt Hunter, "Planetary Dejection: An Ode to the Commons," *symploke*
24, nos. 1–2 (2016); Anne Boyer, *Garments Against Women* (Boise, ID: Ahsahta
Press, 2015).

29. Kirill Medvedev, "What's Behind Russia's Left-Wing Turn?," March 12,
2020, https://www.opendemocracy.net/en/odr/social-democracy-russia-kirill
-medvedev/.

30. Progressive Marxist in this context identifies newer (and on the whole
younger) Marxist groups from the hardly forward-looking or internationally
minded remains of the Communist Party of the Russian Federation. Some of
the most vivid examples of Medvedev's community-building efforts include
his work with *[Translit]* and the Russian Socialist Movement.

31. Kirill Medvedev, *Vse plokho* (Moscow: Klub Proekt OGI, 2000).

32. See also Brian James Baer, *Translation and the Making of Modern
Russian Literature* (New York: Bloomsbury Academic Press, 2015).

33. See Jon C. Hopwood's review of the exhibit *Charles Bukowski: Poet on the
Edge* at the Huntington Library in *Yahoo Voices,* June 3, 2010.

34. See also Eleonory Gilburd, *To See Paris and Die: The Soviet Lives of Western
Culture* (Cambridge, MA: Harvard University Press, 2018).

35. Medvedev, *It's No Good,* 118.

36. Medvedev, "'They Treat Us Like Shit,'" 123.

37. Interview with Emma Goldhammer, "Direct Expression: An Interview with
the Dissident Russian Poet and Activist Kirill Medvedev," *Boston Review,* July 29,
2013, http://bostonreview.net/world-poetry/direct-expression.

38. See Parker, "Delirious Light."

39. See https://fmbooks.wordpress.com/category/%d0%ba%d0%bd%d0%b8%
d0%b3%d0%b8/.

40. Viktor Serzh, *Soprotivlenie,* trans. Kirill Medvedev (Moscow: Free
Marxist Press, 2015).

41. Gleb Morev, "Serzh, eto vypavshee zveno evoliutsii russkoi
intelligentsia," interview with Kirill Medvedev, Colta.ru, August 12, 2015,
https://www.colta.ru/articles/literature/8204-serzh-eto-vypavshee-zveno
-evolyutsii-russkoy-intelligentsii.

42. Kirill Medvedev, *Vtorzhenie* (Moscow: ARGO-RISK, 2002). For some
overview of the diverse poetry scene of the post-Soviet period, from which the
leftist avant-garde group both emerges and stands out, see Andrew Kahn, Mark
Lipovetsky, Irina Reyfman, and Stephanie Sandler, *A History of Russian Literature* (Oxford University Press, 2018), 766.

43. Kukulin, "Documentalist Strategies," 596.

44. Mikhail Gronas, "Why Did Free Verse Catch On in the West, but Not in
Russia? On the Social Uses of Memorized Poetry," in *Cognitive Poetics and
Cultural Memory: Russian Literary Mnemonics* (London: Routledge, 2011), 143.
He adds, "As one might expect, [rhyme and meter are used] more so on the
traditionalist than on the avant-garde flank."

45. Skidan, *Summa poetiki,* 106.

46. Brian McHale, "Weak Narrativity: The Case of Avant-Garde Narrative
Poetry," *Narrative* 9, no. 2 (2001): 162.

47. McHale, "Weak Narrativity," 162.

48. As retold in Gessen, "Kirill Medvedev," 17.

49. Medvedev, *It's No Good,* 117–118.

50. Medvedev, *It's No Good,* 117.

51. Medvedev, *It's No Good,* 136.

52. Kirill Medvedev and Nikolay Oleynikov, "On Propaganda in Art," in
"Special Issue: The Urgent Need to Struggle," *Chto delat'?,* 2010, https://chtodelat
.org/category/b8-newspapers/12-70-1/. I tell more of the aims and origins of Chto
Delat in Chapter 3.

53. See Ilya Budraitskis, *Dissidenty sredi dissidentov* (Moscow: Free Marxist
Press, 2017).

54. Cumming, "Revolting Russians."

55. See Mark Lipovetsky, "Russian Literary Postmodernism in the 1990s,"
The Slavonic and East European Review 79, no. 1 (January 2001): 31–50, for an
overview of Russian postmodernism from the 1960s to the 1990s and the
gradual merging of internally contradictory trends toward conceptualism and
the neobaroque.

56. Medvedev, *It's No Good,* 254.

57. See Ellen Rutten, *Sincerity after Communism: A Cultural History* (New Haven, CT: Yale University Press, 2017). While Medvedev has been associated with "new sincerity," he was early to critique new sincerity as complicit with right-wing populism.

58. Medvedev, *It's No Good,* 237.

59. Kirill Medvedev, "Ob 'upriamstve liriki' Vsevoloda Nekrasova," *Novoe literaturnoe obozrenie* 5 (2009): https://magazines.gorky.media/nlo/2009/5/ob -upryamstve-liriki-vsevoloda-nekrasova.html.

60. Medvedev, "Ob 'upriamstve liriki' Vsevoloda Nekrasova."

61. Medvedev, *It's No Good,* 137–138.

62. "По дороге на защиту леса," originally published on Facebook; republished in the journal *Novoe literaturnoe obozrenie;* Medvedev, *It's No Good,* 267–268.

63. I have in mind the historically revisionist *Inglourious Basterds* (2009) and *Django Unchained* (2012). The enthusiastic reception of Tarantino by politically right-leaning audiences complicates the comparison but highlights yet again a recurrent problematic in avant-garde aesthetics.

64. Patrick Rumble and Bart Testa, *Pier Paolo Pasolini: Contemporary Perspectives* (Toronto: University of Toronto Press, 1994), 152.

65. See also Artemy Magun, *Negative Revolution: Modern Political Subject and Its Fate after the Cold War* (New York: Bloomsbury Academic Press, 2013).

66. Bozovic and Djagalov, "Post-Soviet Aesthetics"; see also a forthcoming essay on Bykov and media rivalries.

67. After 2014, the majority of the country rallied around Putin's regime in both enthusiastic response to the annexation of Crimea and indignation over the international condemnation of Russia. Konstantin Gaaze, "Why the Crimean Consensus Is Over (And What Comes Next)," (Carnegie Moscow Center blog), September 29, 2018, https://carnegie.ru/commentary/77310.

68. From a personal exchange in November 2018. Medvedev, in my view, has been consistent in trying to reach out, engage in discussion, reorient—and convert—those who he sees as interested in populism but lacking the guardrails of Marxist theory. For example, Medvedev participated in the protests on Alexei Navalny's arrest on January 23, 2021. While distancing himself from Navalny's pro-business, "Russia for Russians" rhetoric, Medvedev explains his participa-tion in such protests: "All of this opens up great opportunities for leftist politics, which . . . could produce a far more powerful wave of discontent and a far more coherent program of change than Navalny's eclectic populism." See the discus-sion "Navalny's Return and Left Strategy" on the LeftEast platform, January 22, 2021, https://www.criticatac.ro/lefteast/navalnys-return-and-left-strategy.

69. Ernesto Laclau, *On Populist Reason* (New York: Verso, 2005). See Ben-jamin McKean, "Toward an Inclusive Populism? On the Role of Race and Difference in Laclau's Politics," *Political Theory* 44, no. 6 (2016): 797–820.

70. Goldhammer, "Direct Expression."

71. Skidan, *Summa poetiki*, 109.

72. Aleksandr Skidan, "Derzhat' distantsiu, dezhat' udar," in Medvedev, *Pokhod na meriiu*, 50.

73. More recently, debates and critiques at international conferences have challenged Russian leftists to expand their canon of Western Marxism in ways that lend greater prominence to Black feminism and postcolonial studies—increasingly important to a new Russophone Left reeling after Crimea, Belarus, and the war in Ukraine to better address the post-Soviet subaltern. Chukhrov and Rymbu in particular appear oriented in this direction.

74. Jay D. Bolter and Richard Grusin, *Remediation: Understanding New Media* (Cambridge, MA: MIT Press, 2000), 49.

75. First disseminated on Medvedev's Facebook page; planned for reprinting in *Novoe literaturnoe obozrenie;* also reposted on the Russian social media site VKontakte. While the realities of the technocratic market problematize, and in some ways rehearse, the problems of print media, they at least offer a transnational alternative to locally dominated and inflexible platforms. Many activists globally use Facebook and Twitter in increasingly inventive and subversive ways while remaining well aware of the platforms' complicities and surveillance dangers.

76. Medvedev's November 2015 arrest took place at a protest organized by striking long-distance truck drivers. For his work on LeftEast, a politically leftist platform dedicated to news and analysis of Russia and eastern Europe, see http://www.criticatac.ro/lefteast/author/kirill-medvedev/.

77. Danny Witkin and Kirill Medvedev, "From the Underground, with Love," *PYXIS: Wesleyan Journal of the Humanities* (May 23, 2013).

78. Kirill Korchagin, "Poeticheskoe *my* ot avangarda 1920-kh godov do noveishei politicheskoi poezii," *Kritika i semiotika* 2 (2019).

2. The Avant-Garde Journal 2.0

1. David Lau, "Avant-Garde Cooptation," Harriet (blog), Poetry Foundation, April 7, 2014, http://www.poetryfoundation.org/harriet/2014/04/avant-garde -cooptation/.

2. Lau, "Avant-Garde Cooptation."

3. The comparison with MFA poetry illuminates the differences: academia-adjacent creative writing in the United States is supported by major institutions, funding, and has unexpected roots in the politics of the Cold War. See Eric Bennett, *Workshops of Empire: Stegner, Engle, and American Creative Writing During the Cold War* (Iowa City: University of Iowa Press, 2015). I hardly mean to suggest that MFA writing cannot be political; moreover, several poets from

[Translit] have held or currently hold academic positions, and several have visited, among others, the Iowa Writers' Workshop. The difference in degree of precarity, and in marginalization from academic institutions as loci of cultural capital, however, is hard to dispute.

4. Kevin Platt, introduction to *Reported Speech,* by Pavel Arseniev (New York: Cicada Press, 2018), 7.

5. See "Otkrylas' Moskovskaia shkola novoi literatury," Colta.ru, April 13, 2020, https://www.colta.ru/news/24092-otkrylas-moskovskaya-shkola-novoy -literatury.

6. Molly Thomasy Blasing, "Polyphonic Transpositions: Pavel Arseniev's *Reported Speech," Reading in Translation,* June 21, 2019, https:// readingintranslation.com/2019/06/21. Besides the bilingual anthology, Arseniev also recently published a chapbook of English translation. Pavel Arseniev, *Spasm of Accommodation* (Oakland, CA: Commune Editions, 2017), https:// communeeditions.com/spasm-of-accomodation/.

7. The project is a collaboration between Arseniev and *[Translit]* theorist Mikhail Kurtov. See Pavel Arseniev, "Dora Vei," *Premiia Arkadiia Dragomosh-chenko,* https://atd-premia.ru/2017/09/21/dora-vey/. See also Jana Kostincova, "Dora Vey Lives and Works in St. Petersburg: Russian Poetry Written by People and Algorithms," *Novaia Rusistika* 1 (2020): 37–43.

8. Sergei Zavialov, afterword to Arseniev, *Reported Speech.*

9. Denis Larionov, "Soobshchestvo zavedomo nesoglasnykh drug s drugom liudei," Colta.ru, November 13, 2014, http://www.colta.ru/articles/literature /5351.

10. Giorgio Agamben, Aleksandr Skidan, Aleksei Penzin, and Dmitry Novikov, "Poeticheskii sub'ekt dolzhen kazhdyi raz byt' proizveden zanovo— tol'ko dlia togo, chtoby zatem ischeznut'," *[Translit]* 8 (2010): 4–11.

11. Larionov, "Soobshchetsvo zavedomo nesoglasnykh drug s drugom liudei."

12. Arseniev has presented on *[Translit]* at numerous international institutions and festivals. In the United States, *[Translit]*'s champions have included translators, scholars, and poets, with *n+1* and Cicada Press again in leading roles.

13. For an introduction to the culture of (often Russia-based) "shadow" libraries, see Dennis Tenen and Maxwell Foxman, "Book Piracy as Peer Preservation," *Computational Culture* 4 (November 9, 2014): http://computationalculture .net/book-piracy-as-peer-preservation/.

14. Larionov, "Soobshchetsvo zavedomo nesoglasnykh drug s drugom liudei."

15. See Stephanie Sandler, "Dragomoshchenko, Hejinian, and the Persistence of Romanticism," *Contemporary Literature* 46, no. 1 (2005): 18–45; and Aleksandr Skidan, "Poznanie pyli," in *Summa poetiki* (Moscow: Novoe Literaturnoe Obozrenie, 2013), 119–126.

16. Larionov, "Soobshchetsvo zavedomo nesoglasnykh drug s drugom liudei."

17. For a history of St. Petersburg's literary significance, see Julie Buckler, *Mapping St. Petersburg: Imperial Text and Cityshape* (Princeton, NJ: Princeton University Press, 2005). For the city as palimpsest, see the classic essay by Michel de Certeau, "The Practice of Everyday Life," in *The Blackwell City Reader,* ed. Gary Bridge and Sophie Watson, 2nd ed (Malden, MA: Blackwell Publishing, 2002), 111–118.

18. As suggested by Joan Brooks in the roundtable discussion, "Post-Soviet Political Performance: Counterculture, State Power, and Mainstream," *ASEEES* national convention, November 21, 2015.

19. Platt, introduction to *Reported Speech.*

20. Kevin Platt, "Pavel Arseniev, the Laboratory of Poetic Actionism, and Remediation," MLA convention paper, 2016; Boris Groys, *The Total Art of Stalinism: Avant-Garde, Aesthetic Dictatorship, and Beyond,* trans. Charles Rougle (London: Verso, 2011).

21. Mike Sell, *The Avant-Garde: Race, Religion, War* (London: Seagull Books, 2011), 41.

22. Arseniev, *Reported Speech,* 157–158.

23. Robert Frost, "A Servant to Servants," in *North of Boston* (New York: Henry Holt and Company, 1915). *[Translit]* omits the word "out" from the original quotation. The full line reads: "He says the best way out is always through."

24. See the following definition of 1990s translit, accessed via the Wayback Machine: "TRANSLIT is the 'grandaddy' of all Cyrillic text conversion programs. It was developed by Jan Labanowski in the early 1990s. TRANSLIT is a shell program from an era that required the user to type rather long and tedious command lines, but the tedium is more than made up by the configurability and flexibility of the program. TRANSLIT is / was . . . a self-extracting archive"; https://web.archive.org/web/20050526034052/http://www.qsl.net/kd4whz /russian/translit.html.

25. Giuliano Vivaldi, "You Cannot Even Imagine Us," *Tribune Magazine,* May 21, 2019, https://tribunemag.co.uk/2019/05/you-cannot-even-imagine-us.

26. Blasing, "Polyphonic Transpositions." She continues: "Those familiar with the work of American poet Kenneth Goldsmith may recognize this compositional process of repurposing existing text ('creative unwriting') as a growing transnational model, one adapted from earlier surrealist and avant-garde writers and reasserted in the post-postmodern digital age."

27. My thanks to Ania Aizman for pointing out the Los Indignados precedent.

28. Vivaldi, "You Cannot Even Imagine Us."

29. Platt, introduction to *Reported Speech,* 10.

30. Platt, introduction to *Reported Speech,* 10. In a version presented at the MLA convention in 2016, Platt added that Russian art "has been depoliticized and reinstitutionalized by markets, galleries and universities . . . the political legacy of Soviet-era aesthetic dissent is subject to cooptation by an establishment that is only too happy to celebrate 'present liberal freedoms' by exhibiting the non-conformist art of the past (consider, for instance, oligarch and Kremlin-insider Roman Abramovich's acquisition of Ilya Kabakov's archive for some 60 million dollars in recent years)."

31. Eric Bulson, *Little Magazine, World Form* (New York: Columbia University Press, 2019), 2.

32. Bulson, *Little Magazine,* 4, 7.

33. Suzanne Churchill and Adam McKible, *Little Magazines and Modernism: New Approaches* (Aldershot, UK: Ashgate, 2007), 5.

34. Sell, *The Avant-Garde,* 26.

35. I have written elsewhere about the interwar Yugoslav avant-garde journal *Zenit:* see Marijeta Bozovic, "Zenit Rising: Return to a Balkan Avant-Garde," in *After Yugoslavia,* ed. Radmila Gorup (Stanford, CA: Stanford University Press, 2013).

36. Brent Hayes Edwards, *The Practice of Diaspora: Literature, Translation, and the Rise of Black Internationalism* (Cambridge, MA: Harvard University Press, 2003), 9.

37. Bulson, *Little Magazine,* 7.

38. Bulson, *Little Magazine,* 14.

39. Bulson, *Little Magazine,* 15.

40. See also Hans Günther, "Lef i stanovlenie sovetskoi kul'tury," *Russian, Croatian and Serbian, Czech and Slovak, Polish Literature* 40, no. 1 (1996): 19; Maria Gough, "Paris, Capital of the Soviet Avant-Garde," *October* 101 (2002): 53–83; Jeremy Hicks, "Worker Correspondents: Between Journalism and Literature," *Russian Review* 66, no. 4 (2007): 568–585; and Ann Komaromi, *Uncensored: Samizdat Novels and the Quest for Autonomy in Soviet Dissidence* (Evanston, IL: Northwestern University Press, 2015).

41. *Krytyka polityczna* planned Russian issues (there have been a number of print and online Ukrainian issues since Maidan), and the Polish editors initially turned to *[Translit]*—as Arseniev recounted to me in an interview in 2015. The collaboration fell through after an issue in the end along practical, though some might also say ideological, lines: ultimately, the mainstream left-liberal success of *Krytyka polityczna* inspires suspicion in Russian leftist circles.

42. Larionov, "Soobshchetsvo zavedomo nesoglasnykh drug s drugom liudei."

43. Larionov, "Soobshchetsvo zavedomo nesoglasnykh drug s drugom liudei."

44. Evgeny Dobrenko and Mark Lipovetsky, eds., *Russian Literature after 1991* (Cambridge: Cambridge University Press, 2017), 11.

45. Medvedev comments that, "in this, as in so much else, [Kuzmin] was so far ahead of the rest of the literary field as to be playing in some different game entirely" ("'They Treat Us Like Shit': The Cult of Navalny," *London Review of Books* 34, no 4 [February 2012], 184).

46. Medvedev, "'They Treat Us Like Shit,'" 198, 199.

47. I am indebted here to the research of Jacob Lassin on religious and nationalist presentations of Russian poetry online. See Jacob Lassin, "Sacred Sites: The Russian Orthodox Church and the Literary Canon Online" (PhD diss., Yale University, 2019).

48. See also Jonathan Crary, *24 / 7: Late Capitalism and the Ends of Sleep* (London: Verso, 2013).

49. Bulson, *Little Magazine,* 29.

50. Bulson, *Little Magazine,* 31.

51. Paul Mason, *Why It's Kicking Off Everywhere: The New Global Revolutions* (London: Verso, 2012), 75. See also Paolo Gerbaudo, *Tweets and the Streets: Social Media and Contemporary Activism* (London: Pluto, 2012), 3. In the Russian context, Facebook and its Russian-language rival VKontakte tend to cater to "Western-leaning" and "nationally oriented" users (echoing the nineteenth-century Westernizers and Slavophiles, respectively), albeit with overlap.

52. See also Matthew Fuller and Andrew Goffey, *Evil Media* (Cambridge, MA: MIT Press, 2012).

53. Pavel Arseniev, "The Pragmatic Paradox as a Means of Innovation in Contemporary Poetic Speech," trans. Cement Collective, in "Poetry after Language" on Stanford University's ARCADE digital salon, http://arcade .stanford.edu/content/pavel-arseniev-poetry-and-prose.

54. See John MacKay, *Dziga Vertov: Life and Work (Volume 1: 1896–1921)* (Boston, MA: Academic Studies Press, 2018).

55. Arseniev, "The Pragmatic Paradox."

56. We might compare this with Skidan's physics-inflected title, *Red Shifting.*

57. Thomas Campbell's translation, in Arseniev, *Reported Speech,* 29–33. In more recent crises, the European University's administration was accused of a series of minor infractions, such as neglecting to supply staff with sufficient athletic facilities: "EUSP is an independent and globally engaged institution that has attracted much negative attention from Russian state agencies—most recently when it was evicted from its campus and deprived of its license to operate for over a year in 2017–2018" (Platt, introduction to *Reported Speech,* 8).

58. Pavel Arseniev, "Poema solidarnosti," from *Poeziia priamogo deistviia* in *Bestsvetnye zelenye idei iarostno spiat* (Moscow: Svobodnoe marksistskoe izdatel'stvo and *[Translit],* 2011), 7.

59. Vivaldi, "You Cannot Even Imagine Us."

60. See for example the poem, "Stay with Us, Little Boy, You'll Be Our Ph.D." (Ostavaisia mal'chik s nami, budesh' nashim Ph.D.) in Arseniev, *Reported Speech*, 112–113.

61. Pavel Arseniev, "Sergey Tretyakov between Literary Positivism and the Pragmatic Turn," trans. Ingrid Nordgaard, in *Russian Literature* (forthcoming).

62. Arseniev, "Sergey Tretyakov."

63. Arseniev, "Sergey Tretyakov."

64. Arseniev, "Sergey Tretyakov." See also Katerina Clark's "Boris Pilniak and Sergei Tretiakov as Soviet Envoys to China and Japan and Forgers of New, Post-Imperial Narratives (1924–1926)," *Cross-Currents: East Asian History and Culture Review* 28 (2018): 27–47, https://cross-currents.berkeley.edu/e-journal /issue-28/clark; as well as the discussions on Tretyakov in Katerina Clark, *The Fourth Rome: Stalinism, Cosmopolitanism, and the Evolution of Soviet Culture, 1931–1941* (Cambridge, MA: Harvard University Press, 2011).

65. Pavel Arseniev, "Performative Knowledge," in "Knowledge in Action," *Chto delat'?*, September 2008, http://chtodelat.org/b8-newspapers/12-53 /performative-knowledge/.

66. Arseniev, "Performative Knowledge."

67. Arseniev, "Performative Knowledge."

68. Novaia literaturnaia karta Rossii, "Pavel Arseniev" entry, http://www .litkarta.ru/russia/spb/persons/arseniev-p/.

69. Published in issue 4 of *[Translit]* in 2008; here in Ainsley Morse's translation, in *Reported Speech*, 25.

70. Platt, introduction to *Reported Speech*, 10.

71. Roman Jakobson, "Linguistics and Poetics," in *Style in Language*, ed. T. Sebeok (Cambridge, MA: MIT Press, 1960), 350–377.

72. Jasper Bernes, *The Work of Art in the Age of Deindustrialization* (Stanford, CA: Stanford University Press, 2017), 15.

73. Arseniev, "Sergey Tretyakov."

74. Arseniev, "Sergey Tretyakov."

75. "Matthew Kirschenbaum has used the phrase 'formal materiality' in reference to digital media, and like N. Katherine Hayles before him, he's interested in the way that the physical properties of any medium play an integral role in how it can be adapted for artistic ends. This continued emphasis on new and old media's materiality, whether it involves typewriters, computers, hard drives, record players, screens, and books, has made it impossible for us to ignore how mediation itself is so intimately tied up with the experience of touch, smell, taste, and sound" (Bulson, *Little Magazine*, 21–22).

76. Platt writes of the latter that it "transform[s] poetry that was essentially a form of private existential or artistic investigation into one of the oldest known forms of street art, the graffito," Platt, "Pavel Arseniev." See also: "By comparing this process to 'hacktivism,' they underline the subversive nature of their poetic actions, which should lead to critical reflections on language when citizens pass the art works in the street." Dorine Schellens, "Time to Speak: Pavel Arseniev and the Laboratory for Poetic Action," *Leiden Rusland Blog,* December 4, 2015, http://leidenruslandblog.nl /articles/time-to-speak-pavel-arsenev-and-the-laboratory-for-poetic-action.

77. Anna Landikhova, "Poetic Performance: Literature or Politics," ArtUkraine .com, November 16, 2011, https://artukraine.com.ua/eng/a/poeticheskiy -performans-literatura-ili-politika/#.ZBnSEXbMI2x.

78. See also Schellens, "Time to Speak."

79. Marjorie Perloff has argued that citational and constraint-based poetry is more accessible and even personal than the hermetic poetry of the 1980s and 1990s: see *Unoriginal Genius: Poetry by Other Means in the New Century* (Chicago: University of Chicago Press, 2012).

80. One of the Manifesta curators, Joanna Warsza, describes the dilemma as follows: "We are confronted with the old political dilemma: engagement or disengagement? As much as we, of course, clearly and without doubt oppose the Russian military intervention in Crimea and the position of the Russian government, we also oppose the tone of west-centric superiority. . . . The projects will obviously not represent the position of the Russian government. I believe that as long as we can work in the complex manner and in the context-responsive way, as long as we—curator, artists, team—are not exposed to self-censorship, not intimidated or restricted, we will do so." Juste Kostikovaite, "Ghosts and Manifesta 10: A Conversation with Joanna Warsza," *Echo Gone Wrong,* October 15, 2014, http://www.echogonewrong.com/interview-from-lithuania /ghosts-and-manifesta-10-a-conversation-with-joanna-warsza/.

81. Sally McGrane, "Allowed a Space in Russia for Criticism, Artists Have Fun with It," *New York Times,* October 10, 2014, http://www.nytimes.com/2014/10/10 /world/europe/allowed-a-space-for-criticism-artists-in-russia-have-fun-with-it .html; see also "Manifesta 10: Curatorial Approach and Artists Announced," March 25, 2014, http://manifesta.org/2014/03/manifesta-10-curatorial-approach -and-artists-announced/.

82. Kostikovaite, "Ghosts and Manifesta 10."

83. Pavel Arseniev, "Den' Rossii," in *Reported Speech,* 80–92.

84. "In his rejection of the stances of subjective lyricist or postmodern ironist, Arseniev also sidesteps the role of the martyr poet who speaks truth to corrupt power. Instead, he adopts the anti-pathetic role of the discursive technician, placing all the tools of the poetic at the service of socially meaningful

utterance, applying ironic critique not to deflate, but to inoculate political commitment" (Platt, introduction to *Reported Speech,* 11).

85. Zavialov, afterword to *Reported Speech.*

86. Arseniev, "nam pridetsia zakryt' universitety," *Nozh,* March 14, 2020, https://knife.media/coronavirus-poetry/. My translation.

3. Language Poetry Is Leftist

1. See "Aleksandr Skidan's *Red Shifting* Reviewed by Will," *Poetry New York* (blog), 2007–2008, http://archives.evergreen.edu/webpages/curricular/2007 -2008/poetryny/aleksandr-skidans-red-shifting-reviewed-by-will.html.

2. Aleksandr Zhitenev, "Megafon kak orudiie proizvodstva," Colta.ru, July 12, 2013, http://archives.colta.ru/docs/27338. Zhitenev's piece offers little in the way of novel argumentation, relying instead on perceptions of authenticity and sincerity. What Kevin Platt has summarized as "the tediously repeated question of whether 'true' art can concern itself with the mundane matter of politics" seems dated to the point of implausibility a decade of global crisis and polarizing artistic production later. Kevin Platt, "Foreword: Pavel Arseniev's Intervention in Lyric," in *Reported Speech* by Pavel Arseniev (New York: Cicada Press, 2018), 9.

3. For example, when Skidan presented on the poetry of a younger generation for the Yale conference "Political Violence: Militant Aesthetics after Socialism" in 2015, he used the opportunity to introduce his international audience to the work of then relatively unknown Galina Rymbu.

4. See a summary of the Adorno / Lukács debate in Peter Uwe Hohendahl, "Art Work and Modernity: The Legacy of Georg Lukacs," in *Reappraisals: Shifting Alignments in Postwar Critical Theory* (Ithaca, NY: Cornell University Press, 1991), 53–74.

5. Skidan was instrumental in establishing a prize and publishing series in Dragomoshchenko's name. He explains that Dragomoshchenko "turns out to be very important for young authors as a poet—as researcher of the boundaries of language and the world. . . . [Moreover, Dragomoshchenko] paid a lot of attention to young authors, conducted a seminar with young writers and critics, met them with enthusiasm and tried to promote them; the idea of generational connection was always present" (quoted in Tatiiana Vol'tskaia, "Drugaia poetika," *Radio Svoboda,* November 13, 2014, http://www.svoboda.org/content /article/26630913.html).

6. Jacob Edmond, *Common Strangeness: Contemporary Poetry, Cross-Cultural Encounter, Comparative Literature* (New York: Fordham University Press, 2012), 7–8.

7. Philip Metres, "The Healing Art: An Interview with Elena Fanailova," *The Normal School,* November 12, 2015, https://www.thenormalschool.com/blog /2015/9/12/the-healing-art-an-interview-with-elena-fanailova. That "the world" meant mostly Western Europe is a critique that needs be made again and again while acknowledging what was progressive, emancipatory, and thrilling in that imperative to become "world citizens."

8. Stephanie Sandler, "Arkadii Dragomoshchenko, Lyn Hejinian, and the Persistence of Romanticism," *Contemporary Literature* 46 (2005): 18–45.

9. Gennadii Katsov, "Aleksandr Skidan: 'Kazhdyi avtor svoi pravila, svoi zakon,'" *Runy Web,* June 20, 2014, http://www.runyweb.com/articles/culture /literature/alexander-skidan-interview.html.

10. The establishment of the Dragomoshchenko prize for Russian-language poets under twenty-seven, established in 2014, symbolically recognized and confirmed Dragomoshchenko's seminal role for contemporary Russian poetry.

11. Philip Metres, "Interview: Aleksandr Skidan," *Cosmonauts Avenue,* accessed March 1, 2017, http://www.cosmonautsavenue.com/the-poetics-of -being-torn-asunder-an-interview-with-aleksandr-skidan/.

12. Metres, "Interview: Aleksandr Skidan."

13. Metres, "Interview: Aleksandr Skidan."

14. Chto Delat website: https://chtodelat.org/.

15. Pauline Tillman, "Art: This Is War," *Fair Observer,* March 2, 2012, http://www.fairobserver.com/region/europe/art-war/.

16. Alexander Skidan, "Trans-formation: The Poetic Machines of Alexander Vvedensky," trans. Lyn Hejinian and Lucas Stratton, *Floor,* August 6, 2015, http://floorjournal.com/2015/08/06/trans-formation-the-poetic-machines-of -alexander-vvedensky/.

17. Skidan, "Trans-formation."

18. Skidan, "Trans-formation."

19. Skidan writes,

As we know, Bakhtin examined multi-voicedness and polyphony only in the novel and in prose, virtually denying poetry this "privilege" and disqualifying poetry as "naïve monologism" (and this in spite of a close relationship with Vaginov and, perhaps, a familiarity with the work of other OBERIU writers). However, this does not prevent us from extending the principle of hetero-glossia into poetry, especially since Bakhtin himself, writing under the name of his friend V. N. Voloshinov, encourages us to do so. In the essay originally titled "The Word in Life and the Word in Poetry" and first published in the journal *Zvezda* (1926), the theorist writes: "A form especially sensitive to the position of the listener is the lyric." (Skidan, "Trans-formation")

20. Skidan, "Trans-formation."

21. I use the term futurist rather than accelerationist throughout despite the evident desire here "to accelerate" knowledge and social relationships to emphasize the correct lineage. See Benjamin Noys, *Malign Velocities: Accelerationism and Capitalism* (Winchester, UK: Zero Books, 2014).

22. Skidan, "Trans-formation."

23. Skidan, "Trans-formation."

24. Alain Badiou, *The Communist Hypothesis* (New York: Verso, 2010).

25. Skidan, "Trans-formation."

26. He names as paradigmatic new poets of desubjectification a younger generation of *[Translit]* authors: Nikita Safonov, Denis Larionov, and Evgeniya Suslova. Skidan, "Trans-formation."

27. Metres, "Interview: Aleksandr Skidan."

28. Metres, "Interview: Aleksandr Skidan."

29. Metres, "Interview: Aleksandr Skidan."

30. Skidan's dream of world culture—like that of so many of his generation—is undoubtedly confined to a Western European canon.

31. Unless otherwise stated, translations in this chapter are from Aleksandr Skidan, *Red Shifting,* trans. Genya Turovskaya with Eugene Ostashevsky, Evgeny Pavlov, Jacob Edmond, and Natasha Randall (New York: Ugly Duckling Presse, 2008).

32. "Aleksandr Skidan's *Red Shifting* Reviewed by Will."

33. Metres, "Interview: Aleksandr Skidan."

34. Sandler, "Arkadii Dragomoshchenko."

35. Sandler, "Arkadii Dragomoshchenko."

36. I have had the opportunity to witness this in real time at the series of workshops and events at the University of Pennsylvania: see "Your Language—My Ear: Russian and American Poets at Close Quarters," organized by Kevin Platt, February 26–18, 2015, http://ccat.sas.upenn.edu/slavic/events/slavic _symposium/poster_2015.pdf.

37. Katsov, "Aleksandr Skidan."

38. "Interview with Dmitry Golynko," *Calque,* June 2008, http://calquezine .blogspot.com/2008/06/interview-with-dmitry-golynko.html.

39. "Interview with Dmitry Golynko."

40. "Interview with Dmitry Golynko."

41. "Interview with Dmitry Golynko." Golynko's understanding of the motivating power of "belatedness" and the possibilities for Russian literary acceleration echoes no one so much as the late Vladimir Nabokov. I write about Nabokov and Russian literary belatedness in *Nabokov's Canon: From Onegin to Ada* (Evanston, IL: Northwestern University Press, 2016). By curious convergence, Golynko wrote his dissertation on Nabokov as well.

42. "Interview with Dmitry Golynko."

43. Dmitry Kuzmin, "Fragging: Dispersing and Reassembling the Lyrical Subject in Aleksandr Skidan's Poetry," *Russian Literature* 109–110 (2019): 203–220. Kuzmin identifies the influences of Deleuze, Agamben, and Jean-Luc Nancy as especially central to Skidan in this period.

44. As in the title of Fredric Jameson's study *The Prison-House of Language: A Critical Account of Structuralism and Russian Formalism* (Princeton, NJ: Princeton University Press, 1972).

45. See for example, David Lehman, "Apollinaire's 'Zone,'" *Virginia Quarterly Review* 89, no. 2 (2013): 58.

46. See http://www.vavilon.ru/textonly/issue4/moreino.htm for Sergei Moreino's Russian translation. "With your hand full of hours, you came to me. / I said, 'Your hair is not brown'" in Paul Weinfeld's translation, https://paulweinfieldtranslations.wordpress.com/2014/12/06/paul-celan-with-your-hand-full-of-hours/. See also Amir Engel, "Renewal in the Shadow of the Catastrophe: Martin Buber, Hannah Arendt, and Paul Celan in Germany," *German Studies Review* 39, no. 2 (2016): 297; and Antti Salminen, "On Breathroutes: Paul Celan's Poetics of Breathing," *Partial Answers* 12, no. 1 (2014): 107–126.

47. Leonid Livak, "Peter and the Walrus, or *Petersburg* at the Limits of Intertextuality," *The Russian Review* 79 (January 2020): 46.

48. Dante Alighieri, *Purgatorio,* trans. John Sinclair (Oxford: Oxford University Press, 1939), 197.

49. Marijeta Bozovic, "'I'll Permit Myself to Continue for Pasternak': Reflections on Olga Sedakova's Long Modernist Century," in *Festschrift for Alexander Zholkovsky,* ed. Denis Ioffe, Marcus Levitt, Joe Peschio, and Igor Pilshchikov (Boston, MA: Academic Studies Press, 2017).

50. See Stephanie Sandler, "Mirrors and Metarealists: The Poetry of Ol'ga Sedakova and Ivan Zhdanov," *Slavonica* 12, no. 1 (2006): 4.

51. Joshua Cohen, "Aleksandr Skidan Sees 'Red,'" *Forward,* February 6, 2008, http://forward.com/culture/12618/aleksander-skidan-sees-red-01240/.

52. "Aleksandr Skidan's *Red Shifting* Reviewed by Will."

53. Benjamin Paloff, "A Sliver of a Sliver: Aleksandr Skidan in America," *Harp and Altar,* http://www.harpandaltar.com/interior.php?t=r&i=4&p=26&e=43.

54. Paloff, "A Sliver of a Sliver."

55. Jacques Rancière, "You Can't Anticipate Explosions: Jacques Rancière in Conversation with Chto Delat," *Rethinking Marxism* 20, no. 3 (2008): 402–412. Vilensky's response: "Art and emancipatory politics always have a surplus that cannot be appropriated by the institutions of power. Another thing is that we should think not only of the market's totality, but also of the emancipatory practices that constantly break this totality. I think that the avant-garde is indelibly connected to political events or movements that prepare its way. But if we look at these movements, we can see that their form is historical and that it changes."

56. Aleksandr Skidan, "The Resistance of / to Poetry," *boundary 2* 26, no. 1 (1999): 244–247.

57. Skidan, "The Resistance of / to Poetry."

58. Cohen, "Aleksandr Skidan Sees 'Red.'"

59. Margarita Shalina, "Three Percent Review: Aleksandr Skidan, *Red Shifting*," *Three Percent,* accessed March 1, 2017, http://www.rochester.edu /College/translation/threepercent/index.php?id=983.

60. Walter Benjamin, "A Short History of Photography" (1930), "Author as Producer" (1934), "The Work of the Art in the Age of Mechanical Reproduction" (1936); *Moscow Diary* (1926–1927).

61. Jodi Dean, "Politics without Politics," *parallax* 15, no. 3 (2009): 20–36.

62. Cohen, "Aleksandr Skidan Sees 'Red.'" See also Kuzmin, "Fragging."

63. Aleksandr Chantsev, "Punkt naznacheniia," *Kul'turnaia initsiativa,* November 12, 2014, http://kultinfo.ru/novosti/1745/.

64. Rudolf Arnheim, *Visual Thinking* (Berkeley: University of California Press, 1969), 246.

65. Marie-Laure Ryan, ed., introduction to *Narrative across Media: The Languages of Storytelling* (Lincoln: University of Nebraska Press, 2004), 27. See also Marshall McLuhan and Bruce R. Powers, *The Global Village: Transformations in World Life and Media in the Twenty-First Century* (Oxford: Oxford University Press, 1989), 56.

66. Guy Debord, *The Society of Spectacle,* trans. Donald Nicholson-Smith (New York: Zone Books, 1994).

67. Aleksandr Skidan, "Poetry in the Age of Total Communication," trans. Thomas Campbell, *nypoesi,* November 30, 2007, https://www.nypoesi.net/?id =tekst&no=43.

68. "Aleksandr Skidan's *Red Shifting* Reviewed by Will."

69. See Kevin Platt, organizer of the Your Language My Ear Project, "Preface. Aleksandr Skidan: Two films, Two Poems, and an Interview," *Jacket2,* March 2, 2018, https://jacket2.org/feature/aleksandr-skidan-two-films-two-poems-and -interview. My translation of Kino Eye is included and published here: https:// jacket2.org/poems/kino-eye.

70. Aleksandr Skidan, "Kevin M. F Platt and Aleksandr Skidan in Conversation," *Jacket2,* March 2, 2018, https://jacket2.org/interviews/kevin-m-f-platt -and-aleksandr-skidan-conversation..

71. Skidan, "Kevin M. F. Platt and Aleksandr Skidan in Conversation." See also John Mackay, *Dziga Vertov: Life and Work (Volume 1: 1896–1921)* (Boston, MA: Academic Studies Press, 2018).

72. Julian Murphet and Lydia Rainford, eds., introduction to *Literature and Visual Technologies: Writing after Cinema* (New York: Palgrave Macmillan, 2003), 23.

73. Julian Murphet, *Multimedia Modernism: Literature and the Anglo-American Avant-garde* (Cambridge: Cambridge University Press, 2009), 13.

74. Murphet, *Multimedia Modernism,* 30.

75. Katsov, "Aleksandr Skidan."

76. Skidan, "Poetry in the Age of Total Communication."

77. Skidan, "Poetry in the Age of Total Communication." See also Jacob Edmond, *A Common Strangeness: Contemporary Poetry, Cross-Cultural Encounter, Comparative Literature* (New York: Fordham University Press, 2012), 229n84.

78. Matvei Yankelevich, "The Works and Days of Aleksandr Skidan," *Common Knowledge* 26, no. 2 (April 2020): 333–335. Yankelevich introduces the translated cycle, "The Works and Days of Daniil Ivanovich," trans. Aleksandr Skidan and James McGavran, *Common Knowledge* 26, no. 2 (April 2020): 336–352.

79. Yankelevich, "The Works and Days of Aleksandr Skidan," 334.

80. Nelli Muminova, "Aleksandr Skidan: 'Poeziia bessil'naia, no v etom i sostoit ee neveroiatnaia moshch,'" *O-kulture,* November 9, 2014, http://o-culture.com/literatura/item/482-aleksandr-skidan-poeziya-bessilna-no-v-etom-i-sostoit-ee-neveroyatnaya-moshch.

4. Dmitry Golynko

1. He lost his university position and survived for a while, like most of the rest, on wits and freelancing.

2. Artemy Magun has even referred to Golynko's influence on a younger generation as "Golynkoism." ASEEES convention, 2019.

3. As Hal Foster writes: "After the climax of the 1968 revolts," critical theory came to occupy "the position of cultural politics, at least to the extent that radical rhetoric compensated a little for lost activism (in this respect critical theory is a neo-avant-garde in its own right)." Hal Foster, *The Return of the Real: The Avant-garde at the End of the Century* (MIT Press, 1996), xiv.

4. Eireene Nealand, "Dmitry Golynko's *As It Turned Out,*" *Tarpaulin Sky,* December 2008, https://tarpaulinsky.com/2008/12/dmitry-golynkos-as-it-turns-out-reviewed-by-eireene-nealand/.

5. Jacob Edmond and Cilla McQueen, "Spanners in the Wrong Works," *ka mate ka ora: a new zealand journal of poetry and poetics,* March 2012, http://www.nzepc.auckland.ac.nz/kmko/11/ka_mate11_jedmond.asp.

6. Il'ia Kukulin, "Ischeznoveniie spektaklia," Vavilon.ru, 2006, http://www.vavilon.ru/texts/kukulin2.html.

7. Quoted in Stanislav Lvovsky, "Ne nazyvat' poetami," *Poetry News Weekly,* October 14, 2011, http://os.colta.ru/literature/projects/10038/details/31065/.

8. Kevin Platt, "Now Poet: Dmitry Golynko and the New Social Epic," *Jacket2,* August 8, 2014, http://jacket2.org/article/now-poet-dmitry-golynko-and-new -social-epic. See also Nealand, "Dmitry Golynko's *As It Turned Out.*"

9. Dmitrii Bak, "Sto poetov nachala stoletiia: O poezii Dmitrii Golynko-Vol'fson i Timura Kibirova," *Oktiabr'* 9 (2011), http://magazines.russ.ru/october /2011/9/ba11.html.

10. See Erin McKnight, "Review: *As It Turned Out* by Dmitry Golynko, Translated by Eugene Ostashevsky and Rebecca Bella, with Simona Schneider," *Bookslut,* December 2008, http://www.bookslut.com/poetry/2008_12_013793 .php; and Bak, "Sto poetov nachala stoletiia."

11. Translations in this chapter, unless marked otherwise, are from Dmitry Golynko, *As It Turned Out,* trans. Eugene Ostashevsky and Rebecca Bell, with Simona Schneider (New York: Ugly Duckling Presse, 2008).

12. Dmitry Golynko, "Socially Applied Poetry," written in Berlin on May 1, 2011, translated by Marijeta Bozovic, in collaboration with Golynko, in "Poetry after Language" on Stanford University's ARCADE digital salon, http://arcade .stanford.edu/content/dmitri-golynko-poetry-and-prose.

13. Golynko, "Socially Applied Poetry."

14. Dmitry Golynko, "Interview with Dmitry Golynko," *Calque,* 2008, http://calquezine.blogspot.com/2008/06/interview-with-dmitry-golynko.html. Dmitrii Golynko-Vol'fson, *Homo scribens* (St. Petersburg: Borey-Art, 1994).

15. "Interview with Dmitry Golynko."

16. "Interview with Dmitry Golynko." Dmitrii Golynko-Vol'fson, *Betonnye Golubki* (Moscow: Novoe literaturnoe obozrenie, 2003).

17. "Interview with Dmitry Golynko."

18. "Interview with Dmitry Golynko." The Iowa Writers' Workshop, let it be noted, has been the recipient of CIA funding in recent cultural Cold War history. See Eric Bennett, *Workshops of Empire: Stegner, Engle, and American Creative Writing during the Cold War* (Iowa City: University of Iowa Press, 2015).

19. Dariia Pasichnik, "Dmitrii Golynko-Vol'fson: Nesovremennye zametki o statuse literaturnogo truda," *[Translit]* 8 (2010): http://syg.ma/@daria -pasichnik/dmitrii-golynko-volfson-niesvoievriemiennyie-zamietki-o-statusie -litieraturnogho-truda.

20. Dmitriy Golynko-Vol'fson, "New Russian Millennium Experience of Post-eschatological Consciousness," Guelman.ru, 1998, reprinted in *Moscow Art Magazine* 22, http://www.guelman.ru/xz/english/XX22/X2206.HTM; see also Rosalind J. Marsh, *Literature, History, and Identity in Post-Soviet Russia, 1991–2006* (Oxford: Peter Lang, 2007).

21. Golynko-Vol'fson, "New Russian Millennium Experience."

22. Marshall Berman, *All That Is Solid Melts into Air: The Experience of Modernity* (1982; repr., London: Verso, 2010).

23. Golynko-Vol'fson, "New Russian Millennium Experience."

24. Golynko, "Applied Social Poetry." Originally in Russian in *[Translit]* 10 / 11 (2012). Translated by Bozovic with Hanukai (Arcade, Stanford University). The Polish was translated by Golynko into Russian first.

25. Golynko, "Applied Social Poetry."

26. Golynko, "Applied Social Poetry."

27. Golynko, "Applied Social Poetry."

28. Golynko, "Applied Social Poetry."

29. Golynko, "Applied Social Poetry."

30. Golynko, "Applied Social Poetry."

31. Golynko, "Applied Social Poetry."

32. Walt Hunter, *Forms of a World: Contemporary Poetry and the Making of Globalization* (New York: Fordham University Press, 2019), 11.

33. Golynko, "Socially Applied Poetry."

34. Golynko, "Socially Applied Poetry."

35. Platt, "Now Poet."

36. Nealand, "Dmitry Golynko's *As It Turned Out.*"

37. The notoriously offensive performance of Tatiana's letter from *Onegin* as a Buddhist chant is only one obvious example of Prigov's overidentification with taking literature sacredly. See also Aleksei Yurchak, *Everything Was Forever, Until It Was No More: The Last Soviet Generation* (Princeton, NJ: Princeton University Press, 2005).

38. Aleksei Parshchikov, "Neskol'ko slov o *Betonnykh golubkakh*," Vavilon.ru, 2006, http://www.vavilon.ru/texts/parshchikov2.html.

39. Hillel Schwartz, *The Culture of the Copy: Striking Likenesses, Unreasonable Facsimiles* (Princeton, NJ: Princeton University Press, 1996).

40. Dmitrii Golynko-Vol'fson, "Elementarnye veshchi," in *Betonnye golubki* (Moscow: novoe literaturnoe obozrenie, 2003).

41. Bak, "Sto poetov nachala stoletiia." See also Platt's description of the cycle as a "strange hybrid of personhood and philosophical abstraction of materiality" (Platt, "Now Poet").

42. Kukulin, "Ischeznoveniie spektaklia."

43. See Isabel Lane's insightful work on the fate of character after the Cold War's nuclear obsessions in "Narrative Fallout: The Russian and American Novel after the Bomb" (PhD diss., Yale University, 2019).

44. Viktor Pelevin, *Homo Zapiens* (New York: Viking, 2002), 82. See also Leila Guberina, "Postmodernism in Pelevin's *Generation P:* The New Society (ORANUS) and the New Man (*Homo Zapiens*)," *Knjizevna Smotra* 44 (2012): 85–92.

45. See also Oxana Timofeeva, "The End of the World: From Apocalypse to the End of History and Back," *e-flux* 56 (June 2014): http://www.e-flux.com/journal/the-end-of-the-world-from-apocalypse-to-the-end-of-history-and-back/.

46. Dmtrii Golynko-Vol'fson, "Demoktratiia i chudovishche: Neskol'ko tezisov o vizual'noi monstrologii," *Moscow Art Magazine,* 2005–2007, http://xz .gif.ru/numbers/77-78/democracy-and-monster/.

47. Golynko-Vol'fson, "Demoktratiia i chudovishche."

48. Golynko-Vol'fson, "Demoktratiia i chudovishche."

49. Golynko-Vol'fson, "Demoktratiia i chudovishche." "Żmijewski, known for his activist background and cooperation with the publication 'Criticism Is Politic,' in this work represents the political as a sign or sign predicting the emergence of an emancipatory political subject. Monstrous—that is, the demonstration of the implicit and unobvious—is already embedded in the very texture of the political, in the very nature of modern democracy, taken at the time of its crisis transition from representative, consensual and representative democracy to democracy absolute in the terminology of Antonio Negri, a democracy of disagreement and plurality."

50. Golynko-Vol'fson, "Demoktratiia i chudovishche."

51. Golynko-Vol'fson, "Demoktratiia i chudovishche."

52. Timofeeva, "The End of the World."

53. Nealand, "Dmitry Golynko's *As It Turned Out.*"

54. Eric Dickey, "Review: *As It Turned Out* by Dmitry Golynko," *Galatea Resurrects,* December 5, 2010, http://galatearesurrection15.blogspot.com/2010/12 /as-it-turned-out-by-dmitry-golynko.html.

55. Anne Boyer, "The Animal Model of Inescapable Shock," *New Inquiry,* https://thenewinquiry.com/the-animal-model-of-inescapable-shock/; reprinted on ARCADE, November 10, 2015, http://arcade.stanford.edu/content/animal -model-inescapable-shock, as well as in Boyer's collection *Garments against Women* (published by Ahsahta Press).

56. On the digital sphere and its uses, see Michael Gorham, Ingunn Lunde, and Martin Paulsen, *Digital Russia: The Language, Culture, and Politics of New Media Communication* (New York: Routledge, 2014).

57. Dmitry Golynko, "'New Thingness' and the Materiality of Trauma in Contemporary Art: A Brief Inquiry." As of yet unpublished; intended for a *Social Text* special issue edited by Marijeta Bozovic and Marta Figlerowicz.

58. Golynko, "'New Thingness.'"

59. Golynko, "'New Thingness.'"

60. Golynko, "'New Thingness.'"

61. Dmitry Golynko, "Keys to Yonder," trans. Kevin Platt, *Jacket2,* August 8, 2014, https://jacket2.org/poems/keys-yonder.

62. Platt, "Now Poet."

5. Poetry in the Age of Digital Reproduction

1. Portions of this chapter, which presents my research on Roman Osminkin's poetry, was first published as Marijeta Bozovic, "Performing Poetry and Protest

in the Age of Digital Reproduction," in *The Shrew Untamed: Cultural Forms of Political Protest in Russia*, ed. Birgit Beumers, Alexander Etkind, Olga Gurova, and Sanna Turema (Milton Park; New York: Routledge, 2017).

2. Tracy Jeanne Rosenthal, "Let's Take a Very Fucking Poetry Lesson: Art's Crush on Poetry," *X-tra Contemporary Art Quarterly* 18, no. 2 (2016): http://x -traonline.org/article/animated-reader/.

3. Rosenthal, "Let's Take."

4. Tom Healy, "Review: *The Animated Reader*," *Miami Rail*, Spring 2017, http://miamirail.org/reviews/the-animated-reader/.

5. Scott Indrisek, "S**t My Cats Read: Getting Poetic with Brian Droitcour," *BlouArtInfo,* March 5, 2015, http://www.blouinartinfo.com/news/story/1110973/st -my-cats-read-getting-poetic-with-brian-droitcour.

6. Osminkin has recently taken to using his patronymic Sergeyevich, always with performative irony, to encourage echoes with Aleksandr Sergeyevich Pushkin as well.

7. For further coverage of the scandal and its political stakes, see "Chto Delat Withdraws from Manifesta 10," https://chtodelat.org/b9-texts-2/chto-delat -withdraws-from-manifesta-10/; https://www.calvertjournal.com/articles/show /2193/russian-collective-chto-delat-withdraws-from-manifesta-10; and https://www.manifestajournal.org/issues/situation-never-leaves-our-waking -thoughts-long/different-shades-withdrawal-conversation.

8. Douglas Valentine, "The Russian Version of Politics and Poetry," *Counter-punch,* November 1, 2013, http://www.counterpunch.org/2013/11/01/the-russian -version-of-politics-and-poetry/.

9. Joan Brooks, introduction to *Not a Word about Politics!,* by Roman Osminkin (New York: Cicada Press, 2016), 14–15. See also http://www .cicadapress.net/: "Cicada Press is a New York City based publishing imprint founded in 2013 by Matthew Whitley and Anastasiya Osipova. Cicada is an artist run press, dedicated to poetic texts, art projects and works of non-fiction by artists and writers situated in the radical left."

10. Brooks, introduction to *Not a Word about Politics!,* 12.

11. Mark Lipovetsky, "Between Prigov and LEF: Roman Osminkin's Performa-tive Aesthetics," *Novoe literaturnoe obozrenie* 145 (2017). See also Jason Cieply, "The Anatomy of a Performance: On the Reception of Roman Osminkin's *Techno-Poetry,*" ASEEES annual convention, 2015.

12. I use the English translation from *Not a Word about Politics!,* excepting where the older YouTube recording differs, as indicated.

13. The 2016 edition expands the subheading to read: "A Poem about the Disappearance of the Figure of the Romantic Poet in the Period of Inauthentic Existence Web 2.0."

14. I am indebted to Megan Race for her insights on Pushkin and Nekrasov, in particular in her seminar work for "Russian Avant-Garde Poetry" in 2014.

15. See any Kraft edition back cover.

16. Roman Jakobson, "On a Generation That Squandered Its Poets," in *Verbal Art, Verbal Sign, Verbal Time,* ed. Krystyna Pomorska and Stephen Rudy (Minneapolis: University of Minnesota Press, 1985).

17. See also Groys's famous claim that the "total art of Stalinism" had its roots in the utopian dreams of the historical avant-garde. Boris Groys, *The Total Art of Stalinism: Avant-Garde, Aesthetic Dictatorship, and Beyond,* trans. Charles Rougle (London: Verso, 2011).

18. Slavoj Žižek, "Da capo senza Fine," in *Contingency, Hegemony, Universality: Contemporary Dialogues on the Left,* ed. Judith Butler, Ernesto Laclau, and Slavoj Žižek (London: Verso, 2000), 220.

19. Aleksei Yurchak, *Everything Was Forever, until It Was No More: The Last Soviet Generation* (Princeton, NJ: Princeton University Press, 2005).

20. See Franco Moretti, *Distant Reading* (London: Verso, 2013).

21. Medvedev, interview with author, Moscow, August 1, 2013, translated.

22. Quoted in Roman Osminkin, *Tovarishch Slovo* (St. Petersburg: Kraft, 2012), 58.

23. Lipovetsky, "Between Prigov and LEF." See also Jason Cieply, "The Poetics of Engagement: Revolutionary Affect and Collective Subjectivity in Roman Osminkin's Techno-Poetry" (paper presented at "Russian Politics beyond the Kremlin: New Concepts, Paradigms, and Sites," 2016).

24. Hal Foster, *The Anti-aesthetic: Essays on Postmodern Culture* (Port Townsend, WA: Bay Press, 1983).

25. Brian Massumi, *Semblance and Event: Activist Philosophy and the Occurrent Arts* (Cambridge, MA: MIT Press, 2011), 53.

26. The iconography of the 2011–2012 protests frequently highlights the presence and participation of children, especially little girls, occasionally in balaclavas or face masks when associated with Pussy Riot protests. Translations below, based on the recorded performance, are mine.

27. Brooks, introduction to *Not a Word about Politics!,* 17–18.

28. Malcom Gladwell, "Small Change: Why the Revolution Will Not Be Tweeted," *The New Yorker,* October 4, 2010, https://www.newyorker.com /magazine/2010/10/04/small-change-malcolm-gladwell.

29. Evgenii Morozov, "The Brave New World of Slacktivism," *Foreign Policy,* May 19, 2009, https://foreignpolicy.com/2009/05/19/the-brave-new-world-of -slacktivism//

30. Paolo Gerbaudo, *Tweets and the Streets: Social Media and Contemporary Activism* (London: Pluto, 2012), 8.

31. Zygmunt Bauman, *Liquid Modernity* (Cambridge, UK: Polity Press, 2000), 54. See Gerbaudo, *Tweets and the Streets,* 5–9, for a succinct overview of the leading voices of techno-pessimism of the 2010s. In 2016 that critique went viral, global, and took on paranoid neo–Cold War dimensions—as I explore in a new project cowritten with Benjamin Peters, tentatively titled *Imagining Russian Hackers.*

32. See Massumi, *Semblance and Event,* 16: the virtual "cannot be treated as a realm apart without being entirely denatured as a speculatively-pragmatically useful concept."

33. Gerbaudo, *Tweets and the Streets,* 13.

34. I follow Bolter and Grusin's use of the term in Jay D. Bolter and Richard Grusin, *Remediation: Understanding New Media* (Cambridge, MA: MIT Press, 2000).

35. Lev Manovich, "Understanding Meta-Media," *C-Theory.net,* October 27, 2005, accessed September 24, 2015, http://www.ctheory.net/articles.aspx?id =493, and Massumi, *Semblance and Event,* 81, respectively.

36. Aleksandr Skidan, "Poetry in the Age of Total Communication," published in Norwegian translation by Susanne Hege Bergan, in *Audiatur—Katalog for ny poesi* (2007). English translation by Thomas H. Campbell, accessed September 24, 2015, http://www.trans-lit.info/trans.htm.

37. Skidan, "Poetry in the Age of Total Communication."

38. Osminkin, *Tovarishch Slovo,* 6–7, translations mine (with the Cement Collective).

39. Kevin Platt, introduction to *Reported Speech* by Pavel Arseniev (New York: Cicada Press, 2018), 17.

40. Stephanie Sandler, *Russian Performances: Word, Object, Action* (Madison: University of Wisconsin Press, 2018), 115–116. Sandler writes of poets "covering" the work of others:

"The doubled performances, which make the poetry of another equal in status to one's own work, remind us of the ghosting of voices inherent in a poet's performance and of the ways that subjectivity and reperformance are always entangled. These readings let us study poetry as such in its current state in Russia: poetry as embraced by digital media and archived for repeated viewings; poetry as a connective tissue among practicing individuals who read each other's work and who dedicate poems to one another; poetry reading as the visible embodiment of a human being's work in creating poetry; and poetry as a curated activity, selected, sequenced, and framed by editors, translators, and other poets" (121).

41. Sandler, *Russian Performances,* 5.

42. Sandler, *Russian Performances,* 12–13.

43. Nathaniel Stern, *Interactive Art and Embodiment: The Implicit Body as Performance* (Canterbury, UK: Gylphi, 2013), 2.

44. Stern, *Interactive Art,* 63.

45. Stern, *Interactive Art,* 22.

46. Jean-Luc Nancy, *Being Singular Plural* (Stanford, CA: Stanford University Press, 2000); Nicolas Bourriaud, *Relational Aesthetics* (Dijon: Les Presses du reel Dijon, 1998), 46.

47. Bourriaud, *Relational Aesthetics,* 78.

48. Osminkin, *Tovarishch Slovo,* 31.

49. Richard Schechner, *Performance Studies: An Introduction* (London: Routledge, 2013), 158.

50. See Judith Butler, *Bodies That Matter: On the Discursive Limits of "Sex"* (London: Routledge, 1993).

51. See Hal Foster, *The Return of the Real: The Avant-garde at the End of the Century* (Cambridge, MA: MIT Press, 1996).

52. Sianne Ngai, "The Cuteness of the Avant-Garde," *Critical Inquiry* 31, no. 4 (2005): 838.

53. Ngai, "The Cuteness of the Avant-Garde," 97.

54. Ngai, "The Cuteness of the Avant-Garde," 59. See also: "There are historical reasons, in other words, for why an aesthetic organized around a small, helpless, or deformed object *that foregrounds the violence in its production as such* might seem more ideologically meaningful, and therefore more widely prevalent, in the culture of one nation than in that of another" (78). Ngai seems to have Japan and South Korea in mind primarily, but her observation proves extremely insightful for Russian cultural productions as well.

55. See the work of Fabrizio Fenghi, *It Will Be Terrifying and Fun: Nationalism and Protest in Post-Soviet Russia* (Madison: University of Wisconsin Press, 2020).

56. I am indebted to conversations with Marta Figlerowicz organized around a special issue of the journal *Social Text* that had been planned for publication in 2020.

57. Platt, introduction.

6. Art Must Be Communist

1. This chapter incorporates much of the text of an article I wrote on Chukhrov's work: Marijeta Bozovic, "The Voices of Keti Chukhrov: Radical Poetics after the Soviet Union," *Modern Language Quarterly* 80, no. 4 (1 December 2019): 453–478.

2. See, e.g., Keti Chukhrov, "The 'Afghan' Market: Kuzminki," trans. Thomas Campbell, *n+1* 26 (2016): nplusonemag.com/issue-26/new-russian-political-poets /the-afghan-market-kuzminki; see also "Communion," a collective translation in which I participated along with the author: Keti Chukhrov, "Communion," trans. Julia Bloch, Marijeta Bozovic, Ainsley Morse, Kevin Platt, Ariel Resnikoff, Stephanie Sandler, Bela Shayevich, and Alexandra Tatarsky, *Common Knowledge* 24, no. 1 (2018): 130–148.

3. Kevin Platt, Stephanie Sandler, and I took part in this roundtable interview with Chukhrov in 2015 at the University of Pennsylvania after working collectively on English-language translations of her work.

4. "Love Machines" is available online: Keti Chukhrov, "Love Machines," recorded performance, posted on September 30, 2015, www.youtube.com/watch ?v=MVDkt0NKvo0.

5. Osipova, "Haunted Realism."

6. Groys commissioned Chukhrov's "Communion" for the "Beyond the Globe" exhibition at the Ljubljana Triennial in 2016, and it too has also been staged and released as a video in a collaboration with Viktor Alimpiev, funded by the Rosa Luxemburg Foundation.

7. Keti Chukhrov, "Art Must Be Communist," *Chto Delat'*, 2010, https://vimeo .com/8723961.

8. Keti Chukhrov, "Genesis of the Event in Deleuze: From the Multiple to the General," in *Politics of the One: Concepts of the One and Many in Contemporary Thought*, ed. Artemy Magun (London: Bloomsbury Academic 2012), 51–61.

9. Chukhrov, "Genesis of the Event in Deleuze."

10. Sianne Ngai, "The Cuteness of the Avant Garde," *Critical Inquiry* 31, no. 4 (2005): 838.

11. See Harsha Ram's insightful discussion of the ways Georgian modernism diverges from Russian (St. Petersburg) categories and groups, such as symbolist, acmeist, avant-garde: "Andrej Belyj and Georgia: Georgian Modernism and the 'Peripheral' Reception of the Petersburg Text," *Russian Literature* 58, nos. 1–2 (2005): 243.

12. The translations given above are from the excellent version by Thomas Campbell; see Chukhrov, "The 'Afghan' Market: Kuzminki," recorded performance, posted on September 27, 2016, www.youtube.com/watch?v=Eln9 -n51LZs&feature=youtu.be; a video adaptation using this translation may be found online; see Keti Chukhrov, "The 'Afghan' Market: Kuzminki," trans. Thomas Campbell, *n+1* 26 (Fall 2016), nplusonemag.com/issue-26/new -russian-political-poets/the-afghan-market-kuzminki. I make a small modification in favor of a more literal translation for the title, "Afghan-Kuzminki."

13. Keti Chukhrov, "The 'Afghan' Market: Kuzminki." Recorded performance, posted on September 27, 2016, www.youtube.com/watch?v=Eln9 -n51LZs&feature=youtu.be.

14. Indeed, Chukhrov's actants are arguably in part inspired by Julia Kristeva's work on transformative shifts between oppositional subjects and objects in narrative.

15. See, e.g., Michael Idov, "The New Decembrists," *New York Magazine,* January 20, 2012, nymag.com/news/features/russian-revolutionaries-2012-1, or the article cluster, Alexei Penzin, ed., "The Russian Protests in Global Context," *South Atlantic Quarterly* (2014).

16. Paraphrased from a personal interview with Aleksandr Skidan in 2014. For more on the Chto Delat collective (the name is taken from the Russian phrase "what is to be done," title of both Nikolai Chernyshevsky's 1863 utopian novel and Lenin's 1901 political pamphlet), see their newspaper and website, available in English.

17. I borrow the term "political eros" from Chukhrov's *[Translit]* collaborators as well as work on classics and political philosophy. See, e.g., the English-language digest of *[Translit]* issue 14 (January 2014); see also Paul Ludwig, *Eros and Polis: Desire and Community in Greek Political Theory* (Cambridge: Cambridge University Press, 2002).

18. I have in mind Lars von Trier's 1996 film *Breaking the Waves* and the more recent two-part *Nymphomaniac* (2013); see Lori Marso, *Politics, Theory, and Film: Critical Encounters with Lars von Trier* (Cambridge: Cambridge University Press, 2016).

19. Jacques Rancière, "Politics, Identification, and Subjectivization," *October* 61 (1992): 62.

20. This is beautifully explored in Svetlana Baskova's 2012 film *For Marx . . .*, which reimagines Sergei Eisenstein's 1925 classic *Strike* for the twenty-first century.

21. Keti Chukhrov, "O pol'ze i vrede iskusstva dlia zhizni," *Chto delat'*, 2009, http://chtodelat .org / category / ar_4/nr_9/?lang=ru.

22. Danila Davydov, "Proem mezhdu sushchnostiami," *Novoe literaturnoe obozrenie* 107 (2011): magazines.russ.ru/nlo/2011/107/cha31.html.

23. Keti Chukhrov, "The Mobile Communist Theater," *[Translit]* 5 (2009): www.trans-lit.info/materialy/5/keti-chuhrov-peredvizhnoj-teatr-kommunista.

24. Peter Bürger, *Theory of the Avant-Garde,* trans. Michael Shaw (Minneapolis: University of Minnesota Press, 1984).

25. Keti Chukhrov, "Afghan-Kuzminki," recorded performance (posted on October 25, 2011), vimeo.com/31101019.

26. Chukhrov, "The Mobile Communist Theater."

27. Chukhrov, "The Mobile Communist Theater."

28. Keti Chukhrov, "Afghan-Kuzminki," recorded performance (posted on April 13, 2010), vimeo.com/10891733.

29. Keti Chukhrov, "Art after Primitive Accumulation; or, On the Putin-Medvedev Cultural Politics," *Afterall: A Journal of Art, Context and Enquiry* 26 (2011): 127–136.

30. Keti Chukhrov, "Afghan-Kuzminki," recorded performance (posted on September 26, 2011), vimeo.com/29630925; reviewed in Anna Landikhova, "Keti Chukhrov: 'Mne prisnilsia mir, v kotorom ne bylo sten'. Performans 'Afgan-Kuz'minki,'" *ArtUkraine*, June 20, 2012, artukraine.com.ua/a/keti-chuhrov-mne -prisnilsya-mir-v-kotorom-ne-bylo-sten—performans-afgan-kuzminki/# .WRM0Ksm1tE4.

31. Alina Gutkina, "Afgan-Kuzminki. Interv'iu," *Around Art,* November 3, 2011, aroundart.ru/2011/11/03/afgan-kuz-minki, my translation.

32. I read Chukhrov's work less as a rebuttal to critical work like that of Arjun Appadurai in *Modernity at Large: Cultural Dimensions of Globalization* (1996) than as taking such a position as her point of departure: Given the role aesthetic productions continue to play in the production and dissemination of violent nationalisms, how then to write in such a way as to imagine and encourage solidarity and emancipation?

33. I quote from the collective translation "Communion"; see Chukhrov, "Communion," trans. Julia Bloch, Marijeta Bozovic, Ainsley Morse, Kevin M. F. Platt, Ariel Resnikoff, Stephanie Sandler, Bela Shayevich, and Alexandra Tatarsky, *Common Knowledge* 24, no. 1 (2018): 130–148.

34. In a frequently screened video adaptation of the dramatic poem, Diamara is played by a Russian actress, Vera Kuznetsova. In other performances, Chukhrov herself has played all the roles.

35. Anne Carson, *Decreation: Poetry, Essays, Opera* (New York: Vintage, 2006).

36. Dan Disney, "Sublime Disembodiment? Self-as-Other in Anne Carson's *Decreation,*" *Orbis Litterarum* 67, no. 1 (2012): 37.

37. Chris Jennings, "The Erotic Poetics of Anne Carson," *University of Toronto Quarterly* 70, no. 4 (2001): 923–936; Patricia Yaeger, "Toward a Female Sublime," in *Gender and Theory: Dialogues on Feminist Criticism,* ed. Linda Kauffman (New York: Blackwell, 1989), 191.

38. Keti Chukhrov, "Nonsense as an Instrument of the Sublime," *Novoe literaturnoe obozrenie* 69 (2004): magazines.russ.ru/nlo/2004/69/s43-pr .html.

39. Keti Chukhrov, "O pol'ze i vrede iskusstva dlia zhizni," *Chto delat',* 2009, chtodelat.org/category/ar_4/nr_9/?lang=ru, my translation.

40. The piece was performed at the 2014 "Non-Academic Symposium" organized by Ekaterina Degot and David Riff in Cologne. See Chukhrov, recorded lecture about *Love Machines,* posted on YouTube on December 6, 2014, www.youtube.com/watch?v=eDEo14uOsYg.

41. Keti Chukhrov, recorded lecture about "Love Machines." The English quoted here is as in the original.

42. Oxana Timofeeva, "The End of the World: From Apocalypse to the End of History and Back," *e-flux* 56 (2014): www.e-flux.com/journal/56/60337/the-end -of-the-world-from-apocalypse-to-the-end-of-history-and-back, and "Manifesto for Zombie Communism," *Chto delat',* 2014, chtodelat.org/b9-texts-2 /timofeeva/oxana-timofeeva-manifesto-for-zombie-communism.

43. I agree, for example, with Martin Puchner's reading of the avant-garde manifesto as a performative and transnational form, but I hope I have given an

example here of the explicitly fraught stakes—and risks—taken by a post-Soviet avant-garde. See Martin Puchner, *Poetry of the Revolution: Marx, Manifestos, and the Avant-Gardes* (Princeton, NJ: Princeton University Press, 2005).

Coda

1. Marijeta Bozovic, Anjuli Raza Kolb, and Lindsay Turner, *"Life in Space—Galina Rymbu,"* *FullStop,* July 28, 2021, https://www.full-stop.net/2021/07/28 /reviews/marijeta-bozovic-anjuli-raza-kolb-and-lindsay-turn/life-in-space -galina-rymbu/.

2. Kirill Korchagin, "Poeticheskoe *my* ot avangarda 1920-kh godov do noveishei politicheskoi poezii," *Kritika i semiotika* 2 (2019).

3. Suyin Haynes, "How Russia's Feminists Are Changing What It Means to Protest," *Time,* December 21, 2020, https://time.com/5908168/russia-feminist -poets-protest/. Francesco Abel, "The Voice of Feminism. On F-Letter: New Russian Feminist Poetry," *The Los Angeles Review of Books,* December 6, 2020, https://www.lareviewofbooks.org/article/the-voice-of-feminism-on-f-letter-new -russian-feminist-poetry/.

4. See Eugene Ostashevsky, "Eugene Ostashevsky Introduces Three Poems by Galina Rymbu," *Music & Literature,* February 2, 2016, http://www.musicand literature.org/features/2016/1/31/eugene-ostashevsky-introduces-three-poems -by-galina-rymbu.

5. She clarifies, "a new type of 'criminalized worker' appeared, who would spend his days in the factory at a machine, and in the evening he would sell small bags of marijuana or go with some friends to break into people's dachas": Harriet Staff, "Love as Principal Powerlessness: An Interview with Russian Poet Galina Rymbu," Poetry Foundation, February 8, 2016, https://www.poetryfoundation .org/harriet/2016/02/love-as-principled-powerlessness-an-interview-with -russian-poet-galina-rymbu.

6. See Marijeta Bozovic, "For Marx: The New Left Russian Cinema," *Cinema: Journal of Philosophy and the Moving Image* 8 (2016): 108–130.

7. Elizabeth Frost, *The Feminist Avant-Garde in American Poetry* (Iowa City: University of Iowa Press, 2005), xiii.

8. Frost, *The Feminist Avant-Garde,* xiii.

9. Beth Holmgren, "Bug Inspectors and Beauty Queens," *Genders* 22 (1995): 25.

10. See "Three Poems by Galina Rymbu," trans. Joan Brooks, *Cosmonauts Avenue,* accessed August 20, 2019, https://cosmonautsavenue.com/three-poems -by-galina-rymbu/.

11. Ostashevsky, "Eugene Ostashevsky Introduces Three Poems."

12. Ostashevsky, "Eugene Ostashevsky Introduces Three Poems."

13. Joan Brooks and Galina Rymbu, "Love as Principled Powerlessness," Poetry Foundation, February 8, 2016, https://www.poetryfoundation.org/harriet/2016/02/love-as-principled-powerlessness-an-interview-with-russian-poet-galina-rymbu.

14. Brooks and Rymbu, "Love as Principled Powerlessness."

15. Brooks and Rymbu, "Love as Principled Powerlessness." See also Rymbu's critique of the focus on / distinction between monogamy and polyamory for a published debate in the journal *Stasis:*

This is evident meanwhile in both the relationships of the most vulnerable groups—the poor and the precariat (to some partial extent) and the proletariat (which formally continues to uphold monogamy), as well as among the middle class and even among the elite, who may permit themselves such a luxury in the form of polyamory or various other forms of open relationships. Monogamy is already a luxury the [poor and precariat] cannot permit themselves, as it is getting harder and harder to maintain the monogamous family and children in conditions of total poverty and social vulnerability. Open relationships are a luxury for the [elite], although it seems they are able to indulge themselves. Indeed, if we are talking about marriages (including both the polyamorous and monogamous kinds), then it is barely possible to adhere to any discourse of innocence and feelings, as relationships are not just about feelings, but also about shared domestic life, survival, and struggle: time and money." (Artemy Magun et al., "The Love of the Future: Openness / Totality," *Stasis* 4, no. 1 [2016]: 182–220)

16. Brooks and Rymbu, "Love as Principled Powerlessness."

17. Brooks and Rymbu, "Love as Principled Powerlessness."

18. Galina Rymbu, "This is my speech on utopia," in "Pointed Words: Political Poetry in the Global Present," Yale University, December 1, 2018. Translated by Rymbu and Yanis Sinayko and shared by permission of the author.

19. Rymbu, "This is my speech on utopia."

20. Rymbu, "This is my speech on utopia."

21. Rymbu, "This is my speech on utopia."

22. See the public program for the 2019 iteration of the Russian-English poetry translation event, "Your Language My Ear," https://web.sas.upenn.edu/yourlanguagemyear/public-program-2019/. All quotations from "Fragments from the Book of Decline" are given from the collaborative translation we began together in March 2019.

23. Galina Rymbu, "Depression and Melancholy Are Modes of Knowledge," interview with Marijeta Bozovic and Anastasiya Ospiova, here in my translation. Published in Russian on Colta.ru, October 11, 2019, https://www.colta.ru/articles/literature/22622-galina-rymbu-bolshoe-intervyu.

ACKNOWLEDGMENTS

*T*HIS BOOK WAS SPARKED in 2012 and has occupied more than a tumultuous decade. A veritable global village supported my research and writing during that time, across multiple university homes, languages, and continents. This is the work I wanted to write, but didn't yet have words for, when I went to graduate school for a PhD in Slavic literary studies.

I thank the seven protagonists of this book for helping me find those words a decade later. The poet-activists of *[Translit]* and the artist-philosophers of Chto Delat (Ilya Budraitskis, Aleksei Penzin, Oxana Timofeeva, Artemy Magun, Maria Chekhonadskikh, Dmitry Vilensky, Olga Egorova, Nina Gasteva, Nikolay Oleynikov, as well as Natalia "Gluklya" Pershina-Yakimanskaya), with unbelievable patience and politically telling generosity, shared their words, performances, and politics with me over the better part of that decade. I can attest to at least one life their work has changed. I wish I could celebrate the publication of this book with its cast of characters together, not scattered by war and struggling to survive the global present. I wish Golynko were still with us: I can only thank him here, now, and articulate a few months too late that I consider him the defining Russian-language poet and intellectual of his generation.

Golynko—Mitya—was one of the most brilliant, original, sensitive, and generous people I have known. Still insufficiently appreciated for the wild originality and unflinching insight of his poetry, he synthesized two generations of whiplash change and poked with his fingers (in the 2000s, earlier, every year) at the spreading circulatory systems of everyday evil, everywhere. A once-in-a-generation talent, he didn't believe in poetic talent. But he read seemingly everything in every language and put it all together into a coherent if damning understanding of contemporary human culture, simultaneously hilarious and horrifying. His comparatively clear essays and lectures will reverberate in unexpected places and forms, as will the casual ideas and gems he would toss out in text and conversation (all cultural study is monstrology; the zombie proletariat is on the rise). Perhaps part of the unusual clarity of his vision came from the fact that he belonged to two worlds, two eras: Mitya was an erudite autodidact of the late Soviet type—a dodo—yet young enough to have viscerally understood the bloody new era from inception.

The least parochial person I have known, Mitya was equally at home in his be-loved / clichéd home city of ghosts as, for example, at Yale—where he spoke often and inspired many—or Berlin, Iowa, or really anywhere he could find a few people to talk to about ideas. Looking back now, I am struck by the remarkable and un-derstated generosity he showed me and infinitely many others. He found so much time to talk, to invite and include, to host and guest, to analyze and explain things. A born teacher, he simply made a habit of opening new worlds to his students, friends, collaborators, translators, and interesting passersby. I wish I had asked him more questions. I wish I had told him how much of an impact he had made on the development of my intellectual life. But I am so grateful to have had any time and friendship at all. Светлая память.

I had comrades too in the discovery of the new Russian poetic avant-garde: it has been electrifying to interpret, translate, and debate this work—again, for a decade—alongside Kevin Platt, Joan Brooks, Eugene Ostashevsky, Ainsely Morse, Mark Lipovetsky, Anastasiya Osipova, Jason Cieply, Maksim Hanukai, Jonathan Flatley, Jodi Dean, Joanna Warsza, Dragan Kujundžić, Jacob Edmond, Stephanie Sandler, David Hock, Bradley Gorski, Roman Utkin, Fabrizio Fenghi, Ingrid Nor-dgaard; not to mention Liana Battsaligova, Masha Vlasova, Adam Leeds, Katie Holt, Thomas Campbell, and so many others. The best ideas in this book emerged out of dialogue with extraordinary people of all ages. Lines between mentors and students, artists and critics fade further as I think of the collaborative translations (not least via PennSound), shared intellectual programming, and frequent ex-changes of images and text on the topic of the new Russian left, of Russophone poetry, of avant-garde revivals, of utopias after utopias.

I owe so much to the unwavering support, inspiration, and sharp critical eyes of Molly Brunson, Bella Grigoryan, John MacKay, Katerina Clark, Katie Trumpener, Marta Figlerowicz, Walt Hunter, Rossen Djagalov, Harsha Ram, Anjuli Raza Kolb, Lindsay Turner, Jonathan Eburne, Gabriel Rockhill, Mina Magda, and Masha Hris-tova in particular; before that, Jennifer Stobb, Anne Beggs, Matthew Miller, Bill Martin and April Sweeney in my years at Colgate University; and more recent media reframings by John and Benjamin Peters, Francesco Casetti, Alice Kaplan, and curator-librarians Kevin Repp and Anna Arays. I will thank every time men-tors whose love of their work proved infectious: Valentina Izirlieva, Irina Reyfman, Boris Gasparov, Stephanie Sandler, the late Svetlana Boym, and the even more re-cently late Dubravka Ugrešić. Working on this book, moreover, gave me the chance to meet legends as well as ghosts: longtime heroes of mine like Fredric Jameson,

Etienne Balibar, Charles Bernstein, and Nina Živančević. Each time I felt the focus sharpen: both for this specific project and for my understanding of the political and aesthetic potential of academic work more generally.

I am so grateful as well to the institutions that supported me from 2012 to the present, including grants and subsidies but also brilliant editors and profoundly generous anonymous readers. This project was made possible by Yale University's Hilles Publication Subvention award; multiple Kempf and Griswold awards from the MacMillan Institute; Humanities / Humanity program grants from the Whitney Humanities Center; Colgate University's Major Grant for research; and Columbia University's Harriman Institute series, via the indefatigable Ron Meyer. The manuscript was reborn through the editing efforts of Paula Dragosh, Desi Allevato, and above all, my editor Emily Silk at Harvard University Press. I had no idea what a truly great editor could add to a project before meeting Emily.

I owe all else to my family: to Tim, who had unflagging, relentless faith in me and in the greater vision behind this project—even when it cost him, repeatedly; to my sister Dolores, who has made a habit of rescue and redirection. And this book is dedicated to my children, Dolores (Res) Bozovic Newhouse and Alexander (Sasha) Bozovic Newhouse. May you live up to your revolutionary names.

INDEX

Note: Pages in *italics* refer to illustrative matter.

absurdism, 23, 50, 179, 194

Acker, Kathy, 239

Adorno, Theodor, 1, 10; "The Cuteness of the Avant-Garde," 14

"Afghan-Kuzminki" (Chukhrov), 211–216, 219, 220

Afinogenov, Greg, 34

Agamben, Giorgio, 65

Aguirre, the Wrath of God (Herzog), 133

American L=A=N=G=U=A=G=E school, 9, 22, 26, 66, 79, 86, 88

Andrei Bely prize for poetry, 22, 25, 33, 64, 69, 107, 142, 246, 259n17

Andrews, Bruce, 66

androids, 208

"The Animal Model of Inescapable Shock" (Boyer), 168–169

The Animated Reader (New Museum), 173–174

"*Apartment Art as Domestic Resistance*" (Warsza), 174

Apollinaire, Guillaume, 101, 120

"Applied Social Poetry" (Golynko), 147–154

Arab Spring, ix

Arkady Kots (band), ix, 30–31, 36, 43, 51. *See also* Medvedev, Kirill

Arnheim, Rudolf, 130

Arseniev, Pavel, 6, *7*, 28–29, *91*; *Colorless Green Ideas Furiously Sleep*, 80; digital reproduction and, 58; emigration of, xi; paper utopias of, 91; "Performative Knowledge," 84–85;

"A Poem of Solidarity and Alienation," 80–83; on poetry and the market, 85–91; pragmatism of, 80–85; *Reported Speech*, 64, 68; "Russia Day," 92–97; *[Translit]* and, 64–80

"Art after Primitive Accumulation" (Chukhrov), 218

artistic readings, x–xii

assassination attempt, 202

"At the Top of My Lungs" (Mayakovsky), 83

Austin, J. L., 85

Avangard (publication), 74

avant-garde, overview, 6–7, 15–23, 255n47. *See also* avant-garde poetry, defined

The Avant-Garde (Sell), 6–7

avant-garde poetry, defined, 6–7. *See also* avant-garde post, defined; Russian avant-garde poetry

avant-garde post, defined, 24

A-ya (publication), 74

Badiou, Alain, x, 8, 12–13, 18, 106

Bak, Dmitrii, 142

Bakhtin, Mikhail, 101, 105, 116, 217, 271n19

Balibar, Etienne, 12, 13

"Bandiera Rossa" (song), x

Barthes, Roland, 8

Baudrillard, Jean, 8

Bauman, Zygmunt, 191

Beckett, Samuel, 211

Belgrade bombing, x, 2
Bella, Rebecca, 153–154
Bely, Andrei, 142, 147. *See also* Andrei Bely
  prize for poetry
Benjamin, Walter, 125, 128
Bertolucci, Bernardo, 132
"The Big Glass" (Skidan), 116–122
Blasing, Molly, 64
Bloch, Ernst, 11, 43
BOMB Magazine (publication), 32
Boston Review (publication), 32
Bourdieu, Pierre, 8
Bourriaud, Nicolas, 198
Bowles, Paul, 118
Boyer, Anne, 37, 168–169
Brener, Alexander, 23, 51–52
Brodsky, Joseph, 47–48, 50, 98, 120, 154
Brooks, Joan, 176, 231, 235, 236
Bukowski, Charles, 25, 38–41, 42
Bulatov, Erik, 23
Bulgakov, Mikhail, 127–128
Bulson, Erik, 71
Burden, Chris, 17
Bürger, Peter, 16, 18
Bykov, Dmitry, 202
Bykov, Iurii, 56

Cardew, Cornelius, 8
Carson, Anne, 227
catastrophe capitalism, 37, 164, 241
catastrophic communism, 164
Celan, Paul, 120
Cement translation collective, ix
Charles Bukowski: Poet on the Edge exhibit, 39
Chicago Review (publication), 32
Chirikova, Evgeniia, 53
Chomsky, Noam, 68, 80, 158
Chto Delat? (publication), 12, 74, 84–85,
  228
Chto Delat collective, ix, 13, 35, 64, 67, 92,
  102–103. See also *names of specific artists*
Chubarov, Igor, 23
Chukhrov, Keti, 6, 27, *219*; "Afghan-Kuzminki,"
  211–216, 219, 220; "Art after Primitive
  Accumulation," 218; on art and communism,
  190, 220–228; background of, 205–206;
  "Communion," 220–227; *Just People*, 211,
  220; "Love Machines," 205, 207–208; "The
  Mobile Communist Theater," 217–218;
  "Nonsense as an Instrument of the Sublime,"
  228; "Not Even Dead," 228–230; poetic
  experiments of, overview, 206–211; political
  eros of, 211–219; Russian life of, xi; "Viktoriia,"
  219
Churchill, Suzanne, 71
Cicada Press, 176, 279n9
Citizen Subject (publication), 13
Colorless Green Ideas Furiously Sleep (Arseniev),
  80
Colta.ru, 75, 98
commodification of art and poetry, 85–91,
  122–123, 195, 210
Common Knowledge (publication), 205
Commonwealth (Negri), 18
"Communion" (Chukhrov), 220–227
"Communiqué" (Medvedev), 34
Communist Hypothesis (Badiou), 12–13, 18
Communist Party of the Russian Federation
  (CPRF), 3
Comrade Word (Osminkin), 186, 195–196
Conceptualism, 22, 50, 149, 177, 182–183, 189
Concrete (Golynko), 145
Contamination (Skidan), 99, 137–138, 139
copyright, 35
Crary, Jonathan, 76, 77
Crimea, x, 92, 262n67, 269n80
Crowley, Stephen, 3
Cumming, Chris, 32, 50
cuteness, 177, 202–204, 254n36
"The Cuteness of the Avant-Garde" (Adorno),
  14

Davis, Mike, 43
Davydov, Danila, 211, 217
Dean, Jodi, 11, 13, 43
Debord, Guy, 8, 130
Decembrists, ix
Decreation (Carson), 227
Deleuze, Gilles, 12, 13, 14, 209–210
"Democracy and the Monster" (Golynko),
  162–165
Democratic Socialists of America (DSA), 37
De rerum natura (Lucretius), 156
Derrida, Jacques, 205
Dickey, Eric, 166–167
digital poetry, 58, 75–80, 190–195
disaster capitalism, 37, 164, 241
Disney, Dan, 227
Divine Comedy (Dante), 120
Dobrenko, Evgeny, 23

Dragomoshchenko, Arkadii, 9, 22, 66, 100–101, 141, 154, 257n79, 270n5
Dragomoshchenko Poetry Prize, 235, 271n10
"the dream is over, Lesbia, now it's time for sorrow" (Rymbu), 233, 236–239
Droitcour, Brian, 174

economic inequality, 3
Edmond, Jacob, 100, 141
Edwards, Brent Hayes, 71
e-flux (journal and gallery), 164, 205, *207*
"Elementary Things" (Golynko), 155–161
emancipatory graphomania, 154–161
emancipatory politics, 273n55
"The End of the Cease-Fire" (Medvedev), 33, 57
Evgenii Onegin (Pushkin), 183, *184*

Facebook, 74–78, 137, 174, 191, 192–194, 244
Fanailova, Elena, 100, 174–176
"The Faun and the Few" (Golynko), 165–169
feminist art and theory, 10, 27, 62, 102, 177, 201, 227–228, 232–236, 253n22. *See also* gender; Pussy Riot; Rymbu, Galina
The Feminist Avant-Garde in American Poetry (Frost), 235
Filipov, Semen, 207
Foreign Literature (publication), 41
formal materiality, as phrase, 268n75
Foster, Hal, 17, 18, 185, 254n40, 275n3
Foucault, Michel, 8
F-pis'mo, or *F-Writing* (journal and collective), 232, 233
"Fragments from the Book of Decline" (Rymbu), 242–243
Frankfurt School, 8
Free Marxist Press, 6, 35–36, 43, 253n17
Frost, Elizabeth, 235
Frost, Robert, 68
Futurism, 21–22, 63, 240–244, 272n21

Garments Against Women (Boyer), 37
Gatina, Dina, 87–88
gay rights activism, x, xi
gender, 166, 201, 202–204, 226. *See also* feminist art and theory
Generation P (Pelevin), 2, 161
Gerbaudo, Paolo, 191–192
Gessen, Keith, 8, 32, 54
Gladwell, Malcolm, 191

Golynko, Dmitry, 6, 26; "Applied Social Poetry," 147–154; background of, 140–141; *Concrete,* 145; death of, xi; "Democracy and the Monster," 162–165; "Elementary Things," 155–161; emancipatory graphomania and, 154–161; "The Faun and the Few," 165–169; *Homo scribens,* 145; "Keys to Yonder," 171–172; Kukulin on, 141–142; "Lots of Different Things," 142–145, 153; monstrology by, 162–169; "New Thingness' and the Materiality of Trauma in Contemporary Art," 170; poetics of, overview, 141–147; post-revolutionary poetics of, 170–172; Skidan and, 115–116, 135; socially applied poetry by, 147–154; "Untimely Notes on the Status of Literary Work," 146–147; "Whip It Out," 151–153
Gorky Literary Institute, 234
Gray, Spaulding, 201
Gronas, Mikhail, 45
Groys, Boris, 17, 22, 205, 208
Guardian (publication), 32
A Guide to N (Skidan), 136
Gurianova, Nina, 21
Gutenberg Galaxy (McLuhan), 130

Hanisch, Carol, 201
Hardy, Antonio, 18
Hartman, Saidiya, 151
Healy, Tom, 173–174
Hejinian, Lyn, 66, 88, 100, 104, 141
Herzog, Werner, 133
Homo scribens (Golynko), 145
hope, 164–165, 212, 231
hunger, 2–3
Hunter, Walt, 151

The Idea of the Avant-Garde and What It Means Today (Léger), 19
"I Love" (Mayakovsky), 83
Independent (publication), 32
Interactive Art and Embodiment (Stern), 198
Invasion (Medvedev), 44
"I recently ran into the poet Lvovsky . . ." (Medvedev), 44–45
"it happens you meet an underage girl . . ." (Osminkin), 199–201
It's No Good (Medvedev), 31
Iugov, Sergei, 177–178

Jacobin (publication), 75
Jakobson, Roman, 88, 116, 173, 181
James, Henry, 235
Jameson, Frederic, 11, 135
Jennings, Chris, 227
"Jesus Saves Pussy Riot" (song), 186–190
Jewishness, 121
Just People (Chukhrov), 211, 220

Kabakov, Ilya, 22
Kamensky, Vasily, 132
Kandelaki, Tina, 213
Kazhdan, Iakov, 78
kenosis, 227
"Keys to Yonder" (Golynko), 171–172
Kharms, Daniil, 21
Khlebnikov, Velimir, 20, 21
"Kino Eye" (Skidan), 131
Kirill Medvedev: Texts Published without the Author's Consent (NLO), 35
Kolb, Anjuli Fatima Raza, 231
König, Kasper, 92
Korchagin, Kirill, 62, 231
Kraft poetry chapbook series, 36, 64, 65, 80, 158, 179, 186, 230
Kruchenykh, Aleksei, 20, 138
kruzhok, 6–8
Krytyka polityczna (publication), 12, 74, 266n41
Kukulin, Ilya, 30, 45, 141, 156
Kulik, Oleg, 23
Kuzmin, Dmitry, 75, 117, 145

Laboratory of Poetic Actionism, 87–88, *89*, 196
Laclau, Ernesto, 13
Landikhova, Anna, 89
Last Tango in Paris (Bertolucci), 132
Latsis, Asya, 128
Lau, David, 63
LEF (publication), 74
Léger, Marc, 19
Lermontov, Mikhail, 101, 178, 179
"Let's Take a Very Fucking Poetry Lesson" collection, 173
LGBTQ+ activism, x, xi, 52, 61
LGBTQ+ poetry, 10
Life in Space (anthology), 231
Limonov, Eduard, 203, 204
Lipovetsky, Mark, 184
The Literary Map of Russia, 75–76
LitKarta, 190

Lomasko, Victoria, 238
London Review of Books (publication), 32
Los Angeles Review of Books (publication), 32, 233
"Lots of Different Things" (Golynko), 142–145, 153
"Love Machines" (Chukhrov), 205, 207–208
Lucretius, 156
Lvovsky, Stanislav, 44, 47
lyric forms, 1–2, 107, 242. *See also* Russian avant-garde poetry
lyric object, defined, 151

Macbeth (Shakespeare), 118
Magun, Artemy, 13
Mailer, Norman, 39
Manifesta Biennial, 91–92, 174
manifesto poetry, 86, 120
Mann, Paul, 16–17, 225
Manovich, Lev, 192
March on City Hall (Medvedev), 25, 33, 55, 57
Marx, Karl, 119
Marxism: of Chto Delat, 102; global, 8, 9, 12; progressive, 260n30, 262n68; during Putin's rise, 212; as term, 6; in *[Translit]*, 65; Western theory and Russian avant-garde, 57. *See also names of specific poets*
Mason, Paul, 77
Massumi, Brian, 185, 192
Mateev, Ilya, 33
Mayakovsky, Vladimir, 20, 49–51, 67, 83–84, 86–87, 89, 180, 197
McGrane, Sally, 92
McHale, Brian, 45–46
McKean, Benjamin, 13
McKible, Adam, 71
McLuhan, Marshall, 130
McQueen, Cilla, 141
Medvedev, Feliks, 47
Medvedev, Kirill, 6, 24–25; arrests of, x–xi, 30, 37, 263n76; Brener and, 51–52; Bukowski and, 25, 38–41; "Communiqué," 34; disavowal of literary institutions by, 35–38; *Invasion*, 44; "I recently ran into the poet Lvovsky . . . ," 44–45; *It's No Good*, 31; on literary criticism, 8; *March on City Hall*, 25, 33, 55, 57; on militant aesthetics and political violence, 52–57, 253n18; "My Fascism," 35; "On the way to defend the forest . . . ," 52–53; on Prigov, 183; publishing company by, 35–36,

43; translation work by, 25, 30, 31, 36,
38–44; *[Translit]* and, 33, 34; on war and
rebuilding, 247–249; working class works
by, 57–62. *See also* Arkady Kots (band)
"The Megaphone as a Tool of Production"
(Skidan), 98–99
memory, mediation of, 131
Meyerhold, Vsevolod, 218
militant aesthetics, 52–57
The Mirror (Tarkovsky), 131
mirrors, 120, 131
"The Mobile Communist Theater" (Chukhrov),
217–218
Monastyrsky, Andrei, 23, 67, 89
monstrology, 162–169
Morozov, Evgenii, 191
Moscow Art Journal (publication), 162
Moscow Conceptualism. *See* Conceptualism
Moscow School of New Literature, 64
Mouffe, Chantal, 13
Murphet, Julian, 135
"My Fascism" (Medvedev), 35

n+1 (publication), ix, 31, 32, 75, 205
Nabokov, Vladimir, 272n41
Nancy, Jean-Luc, 198
the *Nation* (publication), 32
National Bolshevism, 204
nationalism, 2, 37
Nealand, Eireene, 141, 166
Negri, Michael, 18
Nekrasov, Vsevolod, 51, 89
New Inquiry (publication), 32
New Left Review (publication), 8, 32
"New Literary Map of Russia," 86
New Literary Review (publication), 35, 98, 145,
178
New Museum, 173
"'New Thingness' and the Materiality of Trauma
in Contemporary Art" (Golynko), 170
New Yorker (publication), 32
New York Times (publication), 32, 92
Ngai, Sianne, 14, 27, 113, 177, 202–203, 210
"Nonsense as an Instrument of the Sublime"
(Chukhrov), 228
Norton Anthology of American Literature,
39
Not a Word about Politics! collection, 176
"Not Even Dead" (Chukhrov), 228–230
Nozh (publication), 28–29

OBERIU (publication), 21–22, 104, 211
Occupy Abai, 33, 191, 198
Occupy Wall Street, ix, 32, 170
Oleinikov, Nikolai, 36
OMON, 53, 54
"On a Generation That Squandered Its Poets"
(Jakobson), 181
"On Method" (Osminkin), 183–184
"On the way to defend the forest . . ." (Medvedev),
52–53
OpenSpace.ru, 75
Osipova, Anastasiya, 208, 242
Osminkin, Roman, 6, *7*, 26–27, *186, 199*;
Comrade Word, 186, 195–196; on cuteness
and gender, 202–204; digital reproduction
and, 58, 190–195; emigration of, xi; "it
happens you meet an underage girl . . . ,"
199–201; "Jesus Saves Pussy Riot," 186–190;
literary criticism on, 173–174; "On Method,"
183–184; performance poetics of, 176–182;
poetic embodiment by, 195–202; "Poetic
manifesto of the movement 'Occupy Abai,'"
198; political performance by, 182–190;
"Why do you poets . . . ," 177–182. *See also*
Technopoetry
Osmolovsky, Anatoly, 23
Ostashevsky, Eugene, 234, 237, 242

Paloff, Benjamin, 122
paper utopias, 91–97
Paris Review (publication), 32
Parshchikov, Aleksei, 155
Partosh, Zoltan, 47
Pasolini, Pier Paolo, 36, 43, 44, 55, 58
Pelevin, Viktor, 2, 161
Penzin, Alexei, 13
Perestroika Timeline, *4–5*
performance art, 182–183. *See also* Osminkin,
Roman
performance of Russian poetry, 176–177
"Performative Knowledge" (Arseniev), 84–85
photography, 128
Pivovarov, Viktor, 23
placelessness, 235
Platt, Kevin, 67, 142, 153, 244
"A Poem of Solidarity and Alienation" (Arseniev),
80–83
poetic embodiment, 195–202
"Poetic manifesto of the movement 'Occupy
Abai'" (Osminkin), 198

poetics of refusal, 9, 37
"Poetry in the Age of Total Communication" (Skidan), 85–86, 135–136
"Pointed Words" conference, 240
political eros, 211–219, 284n17
political poetry tradition, 37–38, 176–177, 239–240
political violence, 52–57
The Politics of Aesthetics (Rancière), 11
Poltoratsky, Daniil, x
Poriadok slov, 139
Post-Conceptualism, 257n84
postmodernism: Arseniev on, 82; avant-garde, 184–185; Golynko and, 142; Medvedev on, 51; post-, 164, 166; reactionary, 13, 56, 209, 221; response to modernist lyricism and, 45–46
poststructuralism, 17, 69, 100, 117, 122, 209
powerlessness, 210
pragmatism, 80–85
Prigov, Dmitry, 9, 22–23, 140, 154–155, 182–185, 277n37
Prilepin, Zakhar, 56
The Principle of Hope (Bloch), 11
privatization, 3
"Protocol on Negative Poetics" (Skidan), 107, 113
Pushkin, Alexander, 101, 138, 141, 168, 178–179, 183, 184, 190
Pussy Riot, ix, 30–31, 50, 51, 186–189, 205, 234, 280n26. *See also* feminist art and theory

Rancière, Jacques, 11, 12, 13–14, 65, 170, 216, 242
Rearticulation (publication), 162
"Red Shifting" (Skidan), 123–129, 131–136
Reported Speech (Arseniev), 64, 68
"The Resistance of/to Poetry" (Skidan), 123
Return of the Real (Foster), 18
Ridley, John, 41–42
Rockhill, Gabriel, 11
Rodnik (publication), 100–101
Rosenthal, Tracy Jeanne, 173
Rubinshtein, Lev, 23
"Russia Day" (Arseniev), 92–97
Russian avant-garde poetry: defined, 6–7; reemergent, 1–10, 63–65. See also *names of specific writers*
Russian Performances: Word, Object, Action, 197
Russian Revolution (1905), 1

Russian Socialist Movement, 6, 35, 252n11
Rymbu, Galina, 6, 27, *233*; arrest of, x–xi; coda on, 24, 27–28, 231–244; "the dream is over, Lesbia, now it's time for sorrow," 233, 236–239; "Fragments from the Book of Decline," 242–243; fragments from the future by, 240–244; on gender and sexuality, 201; on state socialism and hunger, 2–3. *See also* feminist art and theory

Sandler, Stephanie, 100, 114, 197, 242, 281n40
Sartre, Jean-Paul, 8
Schechner, Richard, 201
"Scholia" (Skidan), 108–114
Second World, x, 2, 12, 18, 68, 201, 236
Sedakova, Olga, 120
Sell, Mike, 6–7, 16–18, 71
Semblance and Event (Massumi), 185
Serge, Victor, 43
"Sergey Tretyakov between Literary Positivism and the Pragmatic Turn" (Arseniev), 84
Shalina, Margarita, 126
Shamir, Israel, 9
Shargunov, Sergei, 56
Shoot (Burden), 17
"A Short Tango" (Skidan), 131–133
Sinayko, Yanis, 240
Situationist International, 8
Skidan, Aleksandr, 6, 22, 25–26, *115*; background of, 98; "The Big Glass," 116–122; Chto Delat and, 102–103; on commodity of art, 122–123, 195; *Contamination,* 99, 137–138, 139; "The End of the Cease-Fire," 57; *A Guide to N,* 136; "Kino Eye," 131, 133–135; leftist poetry of, overview, 98–102; on Medvedev, 30, 38, 45; "The Megaphone as a Tool of Production," 98–99; "Poetry in the Age of Total Communication," 85–86, 135–136; "Protocol on Negative Poetics," 107, 113; "Red Shifting," 123–129, 131–136; "The Resistance of/to Poetry," 123; Russian life of, xi; on Russia's invasion of Ukraine, 244–247; "Scholia," 108–114; "A Short Tango," 131–133; *The Sum of Poetics,* 103–104; on trans-formation, 103–106; translation work by, 114–115, 122; *The Works and Days of Daniil Ivanovich,* 99, 136–137
Slap in the Face of Public Taste, 179
Slavic studies, as discipline, 253n25
Sleepers (television show), 56

"Slightly Edited" (Arseniev), 68
slow construction of culture, 59–60
socially applied poetry, 147–154
social media, 26, 58, 74–78, 192–194. See also *names of specific platforms*
The Society of Spectacle (Debord), 130
socioeconomic class, 2–3
Solaris (film), 179
"Songs for the Working Class" (Arkady Kots), 61
Sorokin, Vladimir, 23, 42
Specters of Communism exhibition, 205, 207
Specters of Marx (Derrida), 205
state socialism, 2–3
Statis (publication), 287n15
Stern, Nathaniel, 198
Stratton, Lucas, 104
subjectivization, 12, 14–15, 57, 150, 190, 195, 210, 212, 242
"Sublime Disembodiment?" (Disney), 227
summer of idealism (2012), ix
The Sum of Poetics (Skidan), 103–104
Surround Audience triennial, 173
Syntaksis (publication), 74

Tango with Cows (Kamensky), 132
Tarantino, Quentin, 53–54, 262n63
Tarkovsky, Andrei, 131, 179
techno-optimism, 77, 89, 191
Technopoetry, ix. *See also* Osminkin, Roman
Tekhnopoeziia, 185
theater-of-witness performances, ix
theodicy, 112
The Theory-Death of the Avant-Garde (Mann), 16
Theory of the Avant-Garde (Bürger), 16
time, 241
Time magazine, 233
Timofeeva, Oxana, 13, 164–165, 229
Total Art of Stalinism (Groys), 208
Traditsia.ru, 190
trans-formation, 103–106
"Trans-formation: The Poetic Machines of Alexander Vvedensky" (Chto Delat), 104
translation: Medvedev and, 25, 30, 31, 36, 38–44; Skidan and, 114–122
"A Translator's Annotations" (Arseniev), 78–79

[Translit] (publication), ix, 6, 22, 62, 70–80, 265n24. See also *names of specific writers and works*
transnationalism, 235
Tretyakov, Sergey, 84
Truppa Rupor, 207
Tsvetaeva, Marina, 215–216, 218
Turner, Lindsay, 231
Tweets and the Streets (Gerbaudo), 191
24 / 7: Late Capitalism and the Ends of Sleep (Crary), 76
two Russias model, 33

Ugly Duckling Presse, 31, 32, 231
Ukraine, 244–247
Understanding Media (McLuhan), 130
United States–Russian relations, x
"Untimely Notes on the Status of Literary Work" (Golynko), 146–147
utopia, 241–242

Vaingurt, Julia, 21
Vavilon.ru, 75–76, 190
Veprova, Anastasia, 203
"Verses to an Orphan" (Tsvetaeva), 215–216
Vey, Dora, 64
video poetry, 78
Vidokle, Anton, 205
"Viktoriia" (Chukhrov), 219
Visual Thinking (Arnheim), 130
Vivaldi, Giuliano, 68
Vvedensky, Aleksandr, 21, 104–106, 211

"The Walls" (song), 30, 186
Warsza, Joanna, 174
weak narrativity, as concept, 45–46
"Weak Narrativity" (McHale), 45–46
weapons and military aesthetics, 53–54
web poetry, 58, 75–80
"the West," as construction, 252n12
"Whip It Out" (Golynko), 151–153
Whitman, Walt, 50
"Why do you poets . . ." (Osminkin), 177–182
Wittgenstein, Ludwig, 78–79
Wollstonecraft, Mary, 12
The Works and Days of Daniil Ivanovich (Skidan), 99, 136–137
WTO (World Trade Organization) protests, 2

Yaeger, Patricia, 227
Yankelevich, Matvei, 136–137
"Your hand" (Celan), 120
Yugoslavia, x
Yurchak, Alexei, 151

Zabolotsky, Nikolai, 21
Zapatista resistance movement, 8

zaum, 19–20
Zavialov, Sergei, 64, 97
Zhitenev, Aleksandr, 99
Zhuravlev, Oleg, 36
Žižek, Slavoj, 8, 12, 183
Żmijewski, Artur, 66, 148
zombie proletariat, 162–169
"Zone" (Apollinaire), 120